GAMBLING AND GAMBLING DEVICES

John Philip Quinn

PUBLICATION NO. 48: PATTERSON SMITH REPRINT SERIES IN
CRIMINOLOGY, LAW ENFORCEMENT, AND SOCIAL PROBLEMS

GAMBLING

AND GAMBLING DEVICES

Being a complete systematic educational
exposition designed to instruct the youth of
the world to avoid all forms of gambling.

By JOHN PHILIP QUINN

Montclair, New Jersey
PATTERSON SMITH
1969

Originally published 1912
Reprinted 1969 by
Patterson Smith Publishing Corporation
Montclair, New Jersey

SBN 87585-048-0

Library of Congress Catalog Card Number: 69-14942

To

The Young Men of the World

I respectfully dedicate
this book.

THE AUTHOR.

PREFACE.

Of all the vices which have enslaved mankind, none can reckon among its victims so many as gambling. Not even the baneful habit of drink has blighted so many lives or desolated so many homes. Its fascination is insidious and terrible, and its power is all the more to be dreaded in that it appeals to a latent instinct in nearly every human breast. In view of these considerations it appears strange that English literature contains but one authentic work specially devoted to this subject, namely, " Fools of Fortune," which was published by the author of this present volume, in 1890.

For a quarter of a century the author witnessed and practiced every variety of gambling known to the profession. The next quarter of a century he has devoted to exposing the frauds of the gambler. Starting out in the lecture field, he realized his efforts would be futile unless he could show the public in a practical form the evil attached to gambling, to accomplish which he took machinery captured from the gamblers and thereby succeeded in saving thousands of young men from gambling.

This present volume is intended to not only show up the gambling profession in its true form, but to expose the implements used to capture the unwary. It is intended to educate the legislators of our country so that they may intelligently enact laws for the suppression of this monster vice, and to make them so that there will be no loop-hole large enough to allow a four-horse wagon to drive in and out again; for the benefit of the law officers so that they may know exactly what a gambling implement is; for the ministers of the Gospel who know that gambling exists, but cannot speak intelligently on the subject because it is foreign to them; for the public school teachers and leaders in moral reform so that they can demonstrate in a practical manner to their pupils and hearers the viciousness and rascality of the gambler, and the danger that besets the youth of to-day; for the parent that he may be able to warn the son of the dangers ahead; and lastly, for the young man himself.

No graver responsibility can be conceived than that which rests upon the shoulders of the parent to whom is intrusted the training of a young man. Upon the manner in which is fulfilled this sacred trust, depends not only the economic and moral value

i

of the future citizen, but also the welfare, for time and eternity, of a priceless human soul. The gaming resort opens wide its doors, the entrance to which means ruin, of both body and soul. Of what vital importance is it, therefore, that around the youth of the Republic every safeguard should be thrown, and that they should be shielded from temptation by exposing its fatuous character. " Forewarned is forearmed."

The author desires to return heartfelt thanks to those who have aided him in his task. He acknowledges his indebtedness to many clergymen and others who have given him encouragement, especially to Dr. Lyman Abbott who suggested that a work of this kind be presented in a cheaper form than " Fools of Fortune," and that it should be in the hands of all the young men of America.

JOHN PHILIP QUINN.

Canton, O., 1912.

CONTENTS.

CONTENTS.

A BRIEF SKETCH OF THE AUTHOR.

Early education, family training, and circumstances often apparently accidental, are potent factors in the formation and moulding of character. Yet not infrequently an event of seemingly little consequence may overturn the best considered plans for a successful career and alter the entire tenor of a man's life. The invisible power "that shapes our ends," to-day, lifts one born in a humble station to a pinnacle of fame and power, while to-morrow, it casts down from its exalted position the man intoxicated by the fumes of the incense of popular adulation.

However upright may have been my intentions at the outset of life, they were early turned aside through the influence of my surroundings and of a seemingly inborn propensity for gambling. After a long and eventful experience, I have turned to a better life, and for the past twenty-six years have tried to atone for the wrong I committed during the twenty-five years I wasted as a gambler. My past has not been without interest to those with whom I have been in contact. It is here reviewed very briefly with the earnest hope that it may prove a warning to many, who are now bent upon a similar journey.

If the record of my experiences shall prove an example to deter even a few of those who are sporting upon the outer waters of that whirlpool whose vortex is destruction; if its recital shall serve to open the eyes of but one of that vast host who are staking fortune, friendship, family affection, honor, even life itself, in the vain pursuit of an illusive phantom, this sketch will not have been written in vain.

I was born on the 19th day of March, 1846, three miles east of Roanoke, in Randolph County, Missouri. My father was a prosperous farmer and stock raiser. He was held in high esteem in the community, which he represented in the State Legislature during 1861-3. My mother was a " gentlewoman " in what has been, to me, the best sense of that often-abused term. Her generous self-sacrifice, and her all but unlimited capacity to forgive, none can know so well as the wayward son, who numbers among his most bitter regrets to-day the recollection of the years of anxiety and grief which he brought upon

1

that mother's head and of the numberless pangs which he caused that mother's heart.

As a boy I was mischievous and wayward; a ringleader in all "scrapes," and the terror of the orderly. Indeed, my reputation as an evil doer was so well established, and my name so thoroughly synonomous with every species of boyish deviltry, that I was often compelled to bear the blame of escapades which I had not conceived, and in which I bore no part.

Foot-racing, horse-racing, and card-playing were the pastimes of the county. We had card parties in our home and we began to play for fun. Then we got to playing for stakes of pennies, then for nickels, then for dimes, and finally for dollars. Then I began to look for broader fields of action, for the stakes were not large enough for me. There were six boys in our family, and the result of our playing was that five of them became professional gamblers.

My first venture from home occurred when I was fourteen years of age. I picked up a halter strop, one end being attached to my father's horse. I rode from my home to Glasgow, Mo. I sold the horse for seventy-five dollars. While at the Tremont Hotel in Atchison, Kansas, a stranger walked up to me and said, " Good morning, young man. Are you a stranger here? " I told him I was. " Have you had your breakfast? " he asked?

" No, sir," I answered.

" Well," he replied, " before taking breakfast, come out with me for a little while. I have a friend coming in on the train."

I went out with him. We met his friend, and it was only a few minutes before they relieved me of my seventy-five dollars at three-card monte—the three-card trick—which at that time was new to me. This friend turned out to be his confederate.

Being broke, I thought of what my father had often said to my mother when she worried about her children when they were away—" Don't worry, for the chickens always come home to roost! " I should remember that phrase if I lived to be a million years old, and there is more truth in it than poetry.

Knowing my situation, being robbed of all my money, away from home, and amongst strangers, a feeling like unto that which possessed the Prodigal Son came upon me, and I felt it was time to be up and doing. I went to the railway station, called for the ticket agent and told him I wanted a pass to get home. He told me that he could not give me a pass, and that I should see the superintendent of the road. I asked where I could find him. He rang a little hand-bell—there was

"Brother, promise me you will never gamble any more."

no electricity then—and a young man came who was ordered to take me to the superintendent's room. I said, "Good morning, sir. I want you to give me a pass to go home."

"Give you a pass!" he exclaimed, "What for?"

"I have been robbed of all my money," I replied.

The superintendent was a kind man. He looked at me in a fatherly way, and said, "How did you lose your money?"

"I have been gambling," I answered.

"What do you do when you are at home?" he questioned.

"I am a farmer, sir," I said.

He looked at me very earnestly, and then said: "Young man, if I came to your farm and asked you to hitch up your team, and take me to the neighboring town, would you do it?"

"If I was hitched up," I said, "and you were going my way, I'd let you ride."

That answer caught him. He picked up the little bell on the table and rang it. A young man came in, and the superintendent ordered him to take me out to the assistant and write me out a pass to take me to Moberly, my home.

When I arrived home the colored slave-girl—for my father was a slave owner in those days—opened the door and asked "Where have you been?" Then I went into my mother's room, and as I stepped behind the door I saw my little sister lying on her death bed. She beckoned with her little hand for me to come to her. She said, "Brother, promise me that you will never gamble any more." I did promise her, and felt at that time, and later, at her grave, that I would keep that promise. But the fascination for gambling was so strong, and my determination to take advantage of my opportunity, was so powerful, that I soon drifted into the gambler's life.

I left home and went to St. Louis, where I followed the gambling profession for fifteen years, and grew familiar with almost every secret known to the profession. I became such an inveterate gambler that I would gamble on anything, including wearing apparel, jewelry, and even saloons. Nothing was too big or too small.

While living at one time in St. Louis, I became involved in two or three transactions which brought me into some unpleasant notoriety. One was in connection with the sale of a saloon, known as the "White Elephant," on Sixth street, near Chestnut. I had an interest in this place, jointly, with a man named Henry W. Huthsing. Huthsing sold out the business to one Fred Beckerer, of East St. Louis, for $1,900. Payment was made in nineteen $100 four per cent. U. S. bonds, and my partner, finding that the premiums and accrued interest amounted to $375 gave Beckerer his check for that sum, greatly to the latter's surprise. Becoming dissatisfied with his bargain, the purchaser set up the claim that the bottles and barrels in the place were chiefly filled with water, a statement which was utterly untrue. He brought suit against us and caused our arrest. Our experience before trial was not of a character seri-

ously to impress us with respect either for the administration
of justice or for the integrity of some of the legal luminaries of
the St. Louis bar. We gave bonds in $1,000 each, signed by
Henry W. Godfrey, an old-time gambler and well known in
the courts of that city. We retained as counsel ex-judge William
Jones and C. R. Taylor, paying them retainers of $50 and $100
respectively. When the case was first called, Jones demanded
$50 additional, having ascertained that Taylor had received $100.
The demand was accompanied with a threat of withdrawing

Leaving Home.

from the defense and allying himself with the prosecution, and
we complied with his request. The case was continued, and soon
afterward we gave Godfrey $300 upon his representation that
the prosecuting attorney, R. S. McDonald, had agreed to dismiss
the suit. What became of the money I cannot tell, but Godfrey
repeatedly told us that he had given McDonald $250, and we
supposed that the matter was settled. Several months later we
were surprised to learn that the case was about to be called
again. Huthsing was obliged to give Jones his note for $100 to
appear and defend. The day before that set for the trial Jones
wrote to Mrs. Huthsing that the note must be paid at once or

he would refuse to appear. The money was not paid and we were accordingly deprived of the valuable services of the " Hon." (?) Judge Jones. I gave another attorney, Col. Nat Claibourn, $10 to move for a continuance, which was granted, and subsequently retained ex-Governor Charles P. Johnson, as our attorney. The case was called on January 16th, 1887, and at the request of my counsel, I was granted a separate trial. At the suggestion of Gov. Johnson, the evidence was submitted without argument to the jury, who re-entered the court room in exactly nineteen minutes with a verdict of acquittal. The case against Huthsing was dismissed. Thus the " White Elephant " was disposed of and the cheerful prophecy of the St. Louis *Globe-Democrat* came to naught; that paper had said before the trial, " the way things look, it appears that softly the cuckoo is calling for Quinn to come up the road."

I dealt faro-bank for a number of years at 614 Pine street, St. Louis, where I was one of the partners in a gambling house. A railway conductor came there and won fifty dollars every time he played for seven or eight times. One day I said to my partner, " I am going to clip the conductor's wings to-night." I told my regular players that there would be no game that evening, as I was tired and going to a circus. That night I fixed my crooked box, and had my confederates around the table to make it appear that the game was square. We waited some time, but the conductor did not come. Then I rose from my seat to go home, saying, " Boys, I guess our conductor is not coming." Just at that moment we heard his footsteps coming up the stairs. Each man hustled to his place as the conductor came into the room, so the game looked natural and square as when he had won the money. I beat him out of $3,100 before he left the room. His brother-in-law, another conductor, came to St. Louis after him. We discovered he had a good fat roll of money with him, and we gave him the same game we had given his brother-in-law for $3,000.

Besides faro, we also had roulette in our house. A man by the name of Miller, a collector for a wholesale house, came in one night and lost $2,000, money belonging to his employer. The merchant had Miller arrested by Matt. W. Pinkerton, one of our great detectives in Chicago, and Mr. Pinkerton, being a great friend of mine, sent for me to go to his office. I went. Then he sent for the merchant, and we prevailed upon him to allow us to demonstrate to him the impossibility of a man beating the wheel Miller had played against. The merchant, who did not know I was one of the men who had taken the money from Miller, refused for a time to accept any proposition whatever, but finally consented to see the wheel manipulated. He said, " Make me win ten times on the red." I did so. " Now," he said, " make me win ten times on the black." I did. Then he asked for Miller, who was brought in. He took Miller's hand and said, " I have accumulated a million dollars in my life, and I freely acknowledge I would have lost my money against this wheel. Therefore, I forgive you, and I want you to come back to-morrow morning and resume your old position in my office. I do this because I have a family myself, and love them, and know that you love yours."

If I had not proved to him that Miller could not have won, he would have prosecuted him and have had him sent to the penitentiary.

One incident, in connection with a poker game, may be of interest to the reader.

There was a brakeman on a railway who received only fifty-five dollars a month. One evening he came to my place and I won his fifty-five dollars. As I went downstairs he followed me and said, " I am in a bad way. I have lost all my money, and I have nothing in my house for my wife and two children to eat. Won't you lend me fifteen dollars till my next pay day?" I told him I would not lend, but would give the money to him on one condition—if he would promise me never to play cards again. He said he did not like to promise that, as he had lost so much and wanted to try and win it back. I told him I would talk plainly to him, and I said, " You are a working man, and any man who works for his money cannot afford to gamble, for while you are at your work earning your money, the gambler is practising methods of deception and fraud how to steal your money from you. Now," I continued, " you are as fine a sucker as I ever saw in my life. I'd rather have you gamble with me than find the money in the road, for if I found it there, somebody would be sure to claim it." Eventually he said he would promise not to gamble any more, and I gave him the money, which he wanted to pay back out of his next month's salary. I told him I did not want it, but I did want him to quit gambling and take care of his family.

Before I left him I said, " Young man, your first duty is to your wife and children. If you have any notion of gambling again, whatever money you have to spare from your wages, place it in an envelope and stick it, with your compliments, under the door of the house where you do your gambling. By doing this you will save your time." Then I told him never to come back to my house, as I was looking for bigger game in the shape of rich men, not for men who had to work for their money.

Ten years later I had been converted, and was lecturing in Columbus, Indiana. After my discourse, a man came up to me with his wife and four children, one of them a baby in arms. He shook hands with me, and I was delighted when he told me he was the man from whom I had robbed the fifty-five dollars and had given back the fifteen.

He told me he wanted me to go and dine with him, and I went to his little cottage. He said, " Brother Quinn "—for he called me brother—" you cured me of gambling by the way you talked to me the day you gave me the fifteen dollars. From that time to now I have never gambled for as much as one single penny." Then he told me that, as the result of his steady life, the cottage in which he lived belonged to him, and was already paid for in full. My heart was filled with joy, when he and his wife, with tears in their eyes, told me of their gratitude for what I had done for him.

Although I followed the gambling profession for so many years, my conscience was never at rest very long together. Several times I tried to break away from it but with no avail, and even went into other lines of business to try and rid myself of the habit which had eaten into my very nature until it seemed to be a necessary part of my life.

During my career as a professional gambler, I operated in many cities in the West, St. Louis, Kansas City and Chicago being the principal ones, also in Philadelphia.

At one time in Chicago I went into the commission business and became a member of the firm of Stockton, Young & Co., who referred by permission to Wm. Young & Co., then the leading commission house of that city. I found operating " on change " different from running a " squeeze spindle," which I had practised at fairs and carnivals, etc., but the " squeezing " was effectually accomplished in both cases. In the spring of 1882 the composition and title of the firm was changed; Ben

Demint was admitted to membership, and the firm became Stockton, Quinn & Co.

While a member of the firm, I was causelessly arrested for defrauding a Mrs. Morgan out of $700. By way of defense I produced her receipt, and was thereupon honorably discharged.

In addition to all the other forms of gambling, I also went in for the gold brick swindle. A business man of a certain town gave us information that one of the bankers was a close-fisted,

"He had them tested with acid."

miserly fellow, who, he believed, would buy some gold bricks. For this information the business man was to, and did, receive ten per cent. of what we made. We played for the banker, took him into the woods, where we told him an Indian named Charlie, was in possession of the alleged gold bricks. The banker paid over, for four bricks, one hundred notes of a hundred dollars each, making ten thousand dollars in all. He was such an easy mark we told him that Charlie, the Indian, had four more bricks he could have at the same price. He at once took out his book and wrote his check for the other four, to be cashed on delivery. Then I went back to town and met the business man, who received his ten per cent. of the first $10,000, and I told him I was going to present the check for that amount at the bank. He was scared almost to death, and begged me not to go to the bank, as he felt sure the banker would suspect the trick we had played on him, would have us arrested, and he would be brought into the matter for the $1,000 he had received. The spurious brass bricks which he bought for gold the banker had placed in the vaults of the bank. They remained there for six weeks, after which he had them tested with acid. On seeing the result of this performance, he realized the fraud that had been practised upon him, but came to the conclusion, in this case, that " silence was golden."

For twenty-five years I played the crooked game, looking for the best of it, like all other gamblers. From my experience, I say unreservedly to everyone, when you find that a man is a professional gambler give him a wide berth, for it is impossible for him to make it a success and for him to be honest at the same time.

My conversion came about in this way. I was on my way from St. Louis to Chicago with two friends, and we stopped at Terra Haute, Indiana, to get an affidavit, so that an old soldier could get his pension from the government. There we found that a man had been robbed of $3,000 at bunko, another confidence game which was played very largely at that time with much success. We, being suspicious characters and strangers, were arrested. The man who had been robbed had offered $500 for the arrest of the man who had taken his money. Two detectives went to him and told him they had three suspicious characters locked up, and if he would identify them he would get his $3,000. On this he said we looked like the men and the detectives got the reward. We were tried, convicted, and sentenced to three years' hard labor. When the jury pronounced the verdict of " guilty," the judge asked each of us what we had to say. I said, " Judge, as you pass sentence on me so the Almighty will pass sentence on you in the near future, for you know we are not guilty of this crime."

In less than three months that judge was dead.

When the sheriff took us to the prison, he told the warden we were not guilty of the crime. One of our senators, who had acted as our attorney, came to the prison shortly after and told us he could get us out in ten days if we would pay him $10,000. I asked the warden if I could speak freely to the senator, and when he said "certainly!" I spoke to the senator and said, "Senator, you know we are not guilty of this crime, and you are working in league with the prosecuting attorney to rob us of our money. I would see you as far in hell as a pigeon could fly in a million years before I would give you a dollar." That settled our fate.

I had been in prison about four or five months when I received a letter from my wife telling me that our son, our only

Dealing Faro.

child, was dead, and the last words he spoke were, "I want my papa to come home!" A few months later I received a farewell letter from my wife, saying she wanted to have nothing more to do with me. I fell on my knees at nine o'clock that night, and when I came to myself the clocks were striking midnight. I rose up and said to myself, "Is this all that is left?" The next day when I went out with the other prisoners, the foreman of the prison told me that I need not work that day with them, but that I was to clean out some benches. In doing this I found an old well-worn Bible. As I looked at it, I saw an inscription on the fly-leaf. It read as follows: "From your broken-hearted wife."

I took the Bible away with me, and in reading it I came to the passage in which Paul and Silas prayed at midnight, and the prisoners heard them, and the doors of the prisons were opened and Paul and Silas were liberated. I said to myself, "Is this the same God that I am reading about that Paul and

Silas prayed to?" If so, He answered their prayer, and, learning from this old Book that He has no respect of persons, He will answer my prayer. I said, " Lord, you know I never committed this crime, and I want the guilty people caught."

In three days from that time my prayer was answered. The guilty parties were caught in Detroit, Michigan, and taken back to Brownstown, Indiana, where the crime had been committed, whereupon Governor Grey pardoned us three innocent men. One of them, feeling he was a disgrace to the daughter he loved so much, hanged himself in his barn. The other was affected with nervous prostration and never recovered; while I have consecrated my time and talent to the service of God and to the saving of young men from a gambler's life.

In my long hours of solitude I found leisure for reflection, and looking backward I reverently and sincerely return thanks to a merciful Providence that thus rescued me from plunging yet deeper into the maelstrom of folly and vice. The prison cell and the convict's dress accomplished what all other warnings had failed to effect—my reformation. I saw that it was to the accursed vice of gambling that I owed the loss of reputation, of home, wife, child and liberty. Bitterly did I lament my per· sistence in the sinful practice, and from the bottom of my soul I absolutely abjured it forever.

My pardon was signed on November 9th, 1888, and two days later I walked from the prison a free man. Mr. George Eastman, my foreman, was kind to me. He placed his hand upon my head while praying, and said: " Poor boy, come and go home with me." How bitterly I wept when his hand was laid upon me. The touch meant a great deal to one so lonely. It has been said that it is weakness to cry. There is a sacredness in tears. " Jesus wept." Did He not weep at the grave of Lazarus, and again, over the city of Jerusalem? He could sorrow with others; but He could also weep over His children on account of their sin, when they would not weep for themselves. Some people's sin brings them no sense of shame until they are found out. Tears speak more eloquently than ten thousand tongues; they are the messengers of overwhelming grief, of deep contrition, of unspeakable love.

When I stood upon my feet and this man took me by the hand it seemed my heart would burst. O yes, there is an awful pleasure in tears, and if I thought there were none on earth to shed a tear for me I should be loth to live, and if I thought no one would weep over my grave I could never die in peace.

After enjoying the kind hospitality of my new friend for about a week, a feeling of loneliness came over me and I felt I must go to St. Louis without further delay, to gaze once more at the home where I had last lived with my wife and baby, now departed from me. The lines which I penned in my prison cell, upon hearing the death of my child and the desertion of my wife, reverted back to my memory with a greater force than ever. The lines are as follows:

> Why do I sit alone in this cell
>   And weep o'er this three years' time,
> When God Himself knows full well
>   I am innocent of this crime?
>
> Wife, come and see me just once more,
>   For my brain is almost wild;
> And tell me through the old iron door
>   The story of our dead child.
>
> I have lost enough; My brain's most wild,
>   Oh God! why do you spare my life?
> I have lost my liberty, my home, my child,
>   But, last of all, have lost my wife.
>
> Oh, what would I give, what would I do,
>   If I could but go home once more
> And see our baby's little muddy shoe
>   Lying upon our bedroom floor.
>
> But it is not so strange to me now
>   Since our boy lies beneath the sod,
> For its instrumental friends, I vow,
>   In leading his papa home to God.

Now that my home was gone, and I was left alone in the world, I went to Chicago with two objects uppermost in my mind. One was to prepare and deliver a lecture, in which I might demonstrate my innocence of the crime for which I had been convicted; the other was to publish a work on gambling, through which I might, by exposing the cheats and frauds of the professional gamester, deter others from entering upon the path " whose gates take hold on hell." My first lecture was delivered in the auditorium of the First M. E. Church, at Chicago, on the evening of Monday, May 20th, 1889, and in the following year my book, entitled " Fools of Fortune," containing 640 pages, was published, and had a large sale.

From the time of my first lecture in Chicago, I received numbers of calls from all over the country, to lecture, and to fight against the gambling dens and other social evils. A Wall street banker engaged me to go to Saratoga for one lecture. It resulted in my remaining there about three weeks and closing the gambling houses, with the assistance of Matt. W. Pinkerton. For the first time in thirty-three years their doors were locked. Many threats were made to run us out of town, and our posters were torn down. Mitchell, the mayor, was running John Morisay's old club house, the largest gambling house in the place, if not in the county.

At Minneapolis, Minn., I commenced a crusade against gambling and other forms of vice. I fired the first gun in the Congregational Church, and in my discourse made the statement that someone in the city was receiving a corrupt consideration, for failing to enforce the law. The next morning the mayor sent for me to come to his office. He asked me to retract what I had said the night before in my lecture. I said "Sir, I will never do it." I fell down on my knees in his office and commenced to pray for him. As the words of prayer rose from my lips to heaven he trembled and became very uncomfortable. I knew the situation that existed in the city, and had been informed that everything the devil had done in other cities to help his cause was done in Minneapolis. I thereupon challenged the mayor to a public debate for the next evening to take place at the Y. M. C. A.

When the time for opening the meeting had arrived, the hall was filled to its utmost capacity. I spoke from the passage of Scripture found in Ecc. viii., 11. During the course of my speech, I said, "I am glad to-night to have the opportunity to draw back the curtain which obscures the life of the gambler, and of those who are his friends, and exhibit to you as never before the shame, misery and degradation which was my portion, as is the portion of every other professional gambler, but from which I have happily escaped through Divine mercy and Providence. For the twenty-five years that I spent in the devil's service as a professional gambler, I wish to impress upon the minds of this audience that I never opened a gambling house anywhere without having to pay a stipulated sum of money per month for police protection. I have here in my hand an affidavit saying that there are twenty-seven houses of prostitution running in your city, the madam of each house paying $50 per month, and the inmate of each house paying $10 per month; also that seventeen gambling houses are in operation, each paying $50 per week to the executive of your city. Now there is one of two alternatives, or both. Either some one has promised protection to the gamblers or prostitutes, provided they elect a certain man mayor, or some one who now stands close to the administration is receiving a corrupt consideration for failing to enforce the law. A city with a leader whose fertile brain teems with imagery and whose vivid imagination can clothe the most matter-of-fact subject with an interest which renders it captivating, to say there is no gambling and no houses

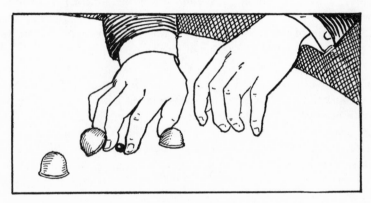

Three-Shell Game.

of prostitution running in your city,—what a farce! What a commentary upon your Christianity in a civilized community where a syndicate of gambling savages, who are strangers to humanity, strangers to honesty, and strangers to God, should attract such little attention from the ghastly mockery, called law."

Turning round to the mayor, who was on the platform, and pointing my finger at him, I said, " Sir, you are the man responsible for the conditions existing here. You have it within your power to stop it, or to endorse it." Then turning to the audience, I made an appeal to the mothers to take a firm grip of the situation and stand on the side of truth and honor. I brought the truth home to them in such a manner that they would not easily forget it. I said, " Mothers, under the present administration, your daughters can become madams of houses of prostitution by paying $50 per month, or they can become inmates of a bawdy house by paying $10 per month, or your husbands and sons can run a gambling joint by paying $50 per week, in return for which they will receive police protection." Many in the audience wept as well as myself, and those who were present to hiss me, after knowing the truth of conditions, applauded me, while the mayor himself was so broken up that while he was still upon the platform he wept in a most pitiable manner.

I once heard of a poor boy who went to the mill. The miller said " John, what do you know? " " Well," answered John, " I know the miller has fat hogs." " What is it you don't know," asked the miller. " I don't know whose corn fats them," was the answer. And I say to the reader, do you believe that the officials of any city will allow the gamblers and prostitutes to pay tribute without taking out toll?

I have lectured to many Y. M. C. Associations, churches, etc., and while at Erie, Pa., in the Catholic auditorium. In New York city I rented several business places where I gave demonstrations with crooked gambling machinery, some of which had been captured in raids. In Philadelphia, Cleveland, Chicago, and many other cities, I have repeatedly given my demonstrations, which have been productive of much good in saving young men from the evils of gaming, and many thousands have signed the anti-gambling pledge.

In 1907 I went to England to carry on a crusade there, and was accompanied by Messrs. E. N. Hills and George D. Lane. I stayed there three years lacking ten days.

My first lecture was given at the great hall in the Cannon street hotel, under the auspices of the Lord Mayor of London. The Hon. J. G. Jenkins, representing the Australian government, presided. The meeting was composed of some of the best business men of the city of London, noted clergymen of various denominations, and others who were more or less interested in moral and social reform.

Soon after this I labored under the auspices of the Free Church Council of England, representing 17,000 churches of various denominations. Also for the National Open-Air Meeting Association, speaking for them on the various race-courses. We used to address large crowds of people during the day, and then hold meetings in the churches at night. I have seen many converted at these meetings.

It was also my pleasure to address a convention of teachers at Bournemouth, over which the late Duke of Devonshire presided. The teachers were much impressed with the practical demonstrations that I gave, and suggested that it would be a good thing for me to visit all the colleges and schools throughout the country, thus giving the boys and young men an opportunity of being warned of the evils of gambling, by practical demonstrations. I will venture to say that my demonstration will do more good to save young men from gambling than a thousand sermons on the subject.

Another interesting event while in London was a visit to the Savage Club, of which the late King Edward was a member. My demonstration of cards and dice was an eye-opener to the gentlemen present.

After lecturing and demonstrating in many of the churches and halls throughout England, it was felt advisable by some of the leading clergymen that I secure engagements at the theatres in order to reach a class of people that could not be reached by any other means. Accordingly I secured a ten weeks' engagement to give my demonstration twice a day, at Maskelyne and Devant's, Oxford Circus, London, the most high-toned place of entertainment in the world. No parent need be ashamed to be seen taking their children there. Of course I know there are critics who would condemn me for working on the stage, but I believe it is my duty to be in the place where I can do the most good. The leading members of the nobility came there to see my demonstrations, some of whom came upon the stage to act as a committee to assure the audience of the correctness of the cards called and the numbers of the dice thrown, etc. The Archbishop of Canterbury came three times to see my work. The "Christian Age," one of England's leading religious periodicals commented on my work as follows: "The other day a minister of the gospel who went to Messrs. Maskelyne and Devant's 'Hall of Mystery' to see the remarkable performance of Mr. John P. Quinn, told Mr. Quinn that he really hadn't known sufficient about gambling to be able to preach intelligently upon the subject; but now he would be able to preach a sermon in which he could show his people how the professional gambler invariably gets the better of his victim. I imagine many other ministers will be using Mr. Quinn as an illustration in their addresses, especially those delivered to young men. I looked in at St. George's Hall the other night and saw how neatly this white-haired, spectacled gentleman with the benevolent aspect tricked those who thought they were winners of five-pound notes. No one on earth seems to have the faintest idea how Mr. Quinn arranges matters so that, no matter what game of chance is played, he wins, but he does it, and I cannot imagine a bigger fool than the man who sees such a demonstration and yet goes on allowing himself to be duped in the card-room, or on the race-course. . . . It is quite an unusual thing for any place of amusement to be recommended in these columns, but I think Mr. Quinn is in the right place on the stage at St. George's Hall. Often the young men whom he addresses at our churches have few temptations in this particular direction. Before the fall of the curtain the ex-gambler, now devoting the remainder of his life to warning his fellow-men against that which has brought ruin to thousands, says a few sharp words to the audience, reminding them that in playing with the sharper it is absolutely impossible.to beat him, though of course he loses occasionally in order not to excite suspicion. The anti-gambling movement has a fine missionary in Mr. Quinn, and strong supporters of the movement like Canon Horsley have, I hear, gone on to the stage and taken a keen interest in his performances. It is quite a novelty. While I watched Mr. Quinn I thought of the miserable scenes I have seen on the race-course, of tricksters I have seen put up for trial in the police court, of half-witted creatures I have seen trying to win in a Belgian gambling resort, and of the untold number of young men who are fooled and robbed on the railways and on steamships. And I wished there was a Quinn on the stage of every theatre and music hall in London."

Gambling houses do not flourish in England as they do in the United States of America. Card playing is the favorite pastime of " society," and high stakes are indulged in at many of the clubs. The working man confines his little bets chiefly to his favorite horse. Many of the daily papers publish betting tips, but the " London Daily News " has proved beyond a doubt that it is possible for a daily paper to exist without inserting the betting tips and news of the races.

In September, 1910, I returned to my own country once more by way of Montreal, accompanied by Mr. W. C. Ashby, a Methodist evangelist, and we are still working together.

We gave our demonstrations in several theatres in Montreal, Quebec, Buffalo, Cleveland, Detroit, Pittsburgh, etc. While at Pittsburgh in 1911, we were asked if we had ever been to Canton, Ohio, as it was claimed that a hotbed of gamblers existed there. I had no further intention of making an open fight on the gamblers, but to merely educate the public by means of practical demonstrations, " not to bet on the other man's game."

We went to Canton in July, 1911, and opened up our campaign there by giving demonstrations at the Y. M. C. A., and the following week, as the result of our work, a number of ministers caused two raids to be made at Myers Lake. The county sheriff, Adam Oberlin, a fine Christian gentleman, was called in to make the raids. A large number of slot machines were put out of business, besides spindles and a striker.

A few days later we put up a tent and for five weeks held services and demonstrations. These were well attended, and sometimes we were compelled to give three or four demonstrations in an evening to accommodate the people.

On September 21st of that year, four citizens met and decided to fight gambling and other forms of vice existing in Canton. We were engaged to assist them in the work. The city officials said that they did not know of any gambling going on in Canton, yet we obtained the evidence of five gambling houses in existence within a block of the city hall. It really is marvellous how gambling houses will flourish so near to the eyes of the law. To open the eyes of the officers of the law to the conditions existing so close to them, one afternoon Sheriff Oberlin raided two of the largest gambling houses in Court street, which has been notorious for its gambling for the past twenty years. Three wagon loads of gambling paraphernalia were taken, and after the cases were disposed of, a nice little bonfire was made.

Impeachment papers against Mayor Turnbull were presented to Governor Harmon, asking him to remove the mayor from office. Among the charges were:

" Said mayor has been guilty of misconduct in office in that he has appointed to and retained in office as chief of police of said city one H. W. Smith, well knowing said Smith to be grossly

immoral and that said Smith habitually and knowingly permitted and protected the violation of laws of the state and
ordinances of said city, and particularly those relating to gambling, houses of ill-fame, cock-fighting, and the regulation of the
liquor traffic, and Smith himself aiding and abetting such violations by his personal presence and patronage, and permitting

Does this look natural?

extensive gambling resorts to operate openly and notoriously
within two hundred feet of his office and elsewhere in said city.

" Said mayor has been guilty of misconduct in office in that
upon the occasion of a raid by the sheriff of Stark county upon
gambling houses within the block adjacent to the city hall and
police office, in October, 1911, he instructed the chief of police,
if called upon by said sheriff for assistance, to refuse such assistance, directing said chief to tell the sheriff to go to hell.

" Said mayor has been guilty of gross neglect of duty in
that he knowingly permitted gambling rooms to be operated openly
and publicly in all parts of said city and has made no attempt to
prevent the same, although frequently by citizens apprized
thereof and admonished with regard thereto, that he has know-

ingly permitted saloons to be kept open and intoxicating liquors to be sold upon Sundays and election days throughout said city and has made no attempt to prevent or check the same, although frequent complaints and specific violations of law in this regard have been made to him by citizens of said city. That he has knowingly permitted houses of prostitution and assignation to be kept and conducted in open and notorious violation of law and has permitted lewd women to frequent the streets of said city and openly solicit men to engage in illicit intercourse with them; that he has knowingly permitted well known and notorious criminals to conduct saloons and houses of ill-fame and to harbor therein habitual gamblers, prostitutes and criminals of all classes, and citizens who have sought to lay before him knowledge and complaints concerning the violation of laws and his non-enforcement of laws in said city."

The impeachment papers were signed by Rev. E. B. Townsend, pastor of the Calvary Presbyterian Church, and Rev. Le Roy DeHays, pastor of the First Church of God. Governor Harmon never took any further steps in the matter.

I addressed a mass meeting in the United Brethren Church on the crusade one Sunday evening, when it was estimated that over 3,500 persons were present, and it was found necessary to hold an over-flow meeting in the Baptist Church, close by.

The following Thursday we showed pictures on the curtain which we obtained of the houses of prostitution, gambling houses, and saloons that were open on Sunday. A meeting for men only was held in the U. B. Church, and two meetings for women only, in the Baptist Church, the same evening. The city had never been so stirred in all its history as when the truth of the vice conditions were put plainly before the people.

Soon after this we were called to Oil City, Pa., where we labored under the direction of Rev. E. B. Welsh, Rev. W. Mitchell and Mr. Black, secretary of the Y. M. C. A.

We stayed at Oil City about four months for the purpose of gathering information on gambling houses, white slavery and liquor violations. The committee required the information for the purpose of knowing just what was going on in the town, and not necessarily for prosecution. At one gambling house we discovered that whisky was frequently sold and men got drunk there on Sundays. There were plenty of house players to be

found in the various houses, and it was no uncommon thing
for men to lose two weeks' wages at one sitting.

The Oil City committee sent us to Franklin, Pa., for a week,
during which time we obtained evidence on poolrooms and
saloons. In most of the poolrooms young boys could be found
playing pea pool for money. At one gambling house, over the
five and ten cent store, a club of business men met for the purpose of gambling. There was no rake-off at this game, but each
player had to purchase five dollars' worth of checks on week
days, from which fifty cents were deducted for his seat; on Sundays each player had to purchase ten dollars' worth of checks,
from which one dollar was deducted. The game was a twenty-
five cent ante and a dollar limit. In this game were to be found
many of the prominent business men of the city, and court
house officials.

Another house was running in which one of the prominent
doctors of the town was a leading member. To obtain access to
the gambling room one had to pass through four different doors.

Another game was running over the public library, kept by
the Knox brothers. From inside information we received it was
alleged that crooked work was carried on in this establishment. I
know personally of one man who lost over $1,000 and another
$400 at this place. Warrants were issued by county detective
Brown for the two brothers, but on hearing this they decided
Franklin was no longer a fit place for them.

While giving testimony in the license court at Franklin, the
saloon lawyers did all they could to damage my evidence and
reputation by bringing up my past, and referring to the time
when I was in the penitentiary (which case has already been
stated), and tried to prove that I was not pardoned, but only
paroled. They sent telegrams all over the country to try and
work up something against me, but without success. All
through the last twenty-six years this case has been constantly
brought up against me, and I have had to struggle hard against
it. Even ministers of the gospel have been ready to believe
the slarders that the opposition have repeatedly brought against
me. I am thankful to say that while man may misjudge me,
that God is on my side and He understands all things.

The Rev. E. B. Welsh wrote to several gentlemen who

were interested in the case at the time, and received one in reply from ex-Governor Charles P. Johnson, of Missouri.

The following article is from the Franklin *Evening News,* Saturday, April 6th, 1912:

Rev. E. B. Welsh, pastor of the First Presbyterian church, Oil City, who is one of those named by Quinn as having brought him to Venango county, has issued the following statement:

The Oil City Ministers' Association took action some months ago committing that body to an effort to protect the youth and homes of our community by securing better moral conditions. A committee was appointed with authority to secure a detective and investigate alleged violations of law. This committee after careful inquiry, selected and engaged two men highly recommended by a similar committee in Canton, O., by whom they had been employed for work of the same sort. These men, Messrs. Quinn and Ashby, are not professional detectives, but have been working together in a fight against vice, writing, speaking, demonstrating gambling methods and occasionally doing such investigation as that for which they were called to Oil City.

They came here at the end of last November and have given a large part of their time from that date until March 30th to work required, with results satisfactory to the committee. During the recent license court hearings a determined effort was made to discredit Mr. Quinn, and good people have doubtless been influenced by the insinuations brought forward. Therefore, the Ministers' Associations, at a meeting held April 1, directed the writer, as chairman of the committee, to make this statement through the press:

" Mr. Quinn was engaged after careful inquiry, and considerable information about his past. We have confidence in those who commended him, and our confidence in him has been, as is now, complete. In Oil City he has done only what a man would be expected to do in the course of such work, and nothing for which we need apologize. We believe him to be a Christian gentleman, engaged from conviction of duty in a work which few men would have courage to undertake. Mr. Quinn's enemies made an attack on the ground of facts which he himself told, about his prison life. He made no defense of his earlier career. He was a gambler, was a law breaker, and several times was arrested, but the imprisonment in question was for a crime of which he was not guilty, and he was released. Mr. Quinn was converted while in prison, and has since devoted his life to fighting the vices which had so nearly ruined him. His work has been commended by prominent reformers like Rev. Dr. Charles H. Parkhurst, by Y. M. C. A. secretaries, such as C. W. Dietrich and George H. Mahy, by the clergy of the Roman Catholic church; for instance, the Rev. Father P. M. Cauley, of Erie, by the Ministers' Association of Erie, and other cities; by Matt. W. Pinkerton, the Chicago detective, etc. The following letter was a reply to inquiries recently addressed by the chairman of the committee to ex-Governor Johnson, of Missouri:

St. Louis, March 28, 1912.

Rev. E. B. Welsh:

Dear Sir: I take pleasure in endorsing Mr. John P. Quinn as an honest and worthy citizen, who has for years fought a good fight for the suppression of vice, especially the vice of gambling. He does not deny that at one period of his life he was addicted to the practice, but he reformed and did so in sincerity and truth. So far as his prison life is concerned, he was the victim of one of the most unfortunate cases of mistaken identity that I ever knew. Traveling in Indiana in 1887, he was arrested and charged in company with others, by a farmer, of swindling him in a trade of some kind, the nature of which I cannot now recall. However, they were hurried to trial and convicted without any intelligent defense. Mr. Quinn, whom I had known in St. Louis, sent for me and I went to Indiana to see him, and thereupon I undertook to investigate his case. I not only established the fact that Mr. Quinn and his companions were not the parties that the farmer supposed, but I succeeded in having the real parties to the swindling hunted down, arrested. brought to trial and convicted, the farmer himself admitting that he was mistaken. Of course, when this was effected, Governor Gray very promptly pardoned Mr. Quinn and his companions. I think from that time on Mr. Quinn has devoted his time to doing good, as far as lay in his power to do so. This experience was a bitter one, but instead of making him a hater of mankind, it made him more sympathetic and humane. I write this in response to your inquiry and in justice to Mr. Quinn. I am,

Very truly yours,

(Signed.)   CHAS. P. JOHNSON.

We believe the majority of Oil City people stand with our association in its ideals of moral betterment, and that they will endorse the work and the workers, when the facts are once fairly set before them. We wish to speak in praise of the good work already done by our present police force in suppressing those evils against which our efforts are directed.

(Signed.)   E. B. WELSH.

Returning to Canton to resume our fight there, we discovered that during our absence over one hundred slot machines had been placed in saloons and cigar stores and were in operation. We obtained evidence on these with the help of Kenneth and Donald Miller, of Navarre, two brothers who had recently been converted. Over ninety arrests were made and other gambling houses raided. Two of these houses were raided twice

within a short time. The illustration here shown is that of the
Derby saloon on East Eighth street, over which was a notorious
poker joint. The building at the time was owned by Forest
Whitmer, and one " Butch " Wagner was charged with running
the gambling house.

The other gambling house mentioned was over the Arcade
saloon on East Tuscarawas street. The building said to be
owned by the Home Brewing Co. It is claimed that the income
of this gambling joint was about $1,500 a day. Race boards,

roulette, telegraph instruments, etc., were found there. Those
arrested in connection with the place were Edward A. Polman,
Tom Burke, J. F. Farn, Charles Salnave, Harry Cummings and
F. Garret. They were bound over to Probate Court by Justice
Rinehart, but Judge Bow decided that the Probate Court had no
jurisdiction in the matter. At the time of going to press we were
given to understand that the decision would be appealed to the
higher courts.

We obtained much evidence on various forms of vice which
was never acted upon by the vice crusade committee.

We concluded our work at Canton on September 10th and
11th, 1912, when we delivered two illustrated lectures in the
First United Brethren Church. We showed about eighty pictures of houses where there were violations of the law, and

named many of the property owners. After these lectures were given several of the houses mentioned had "to rent" signs in the windows.

I am now in my 67th year. Whether I shall ever be called upon by God to take part in any other great crusade I cannot say, but I am content to leave all to His Divine guidance. The remainder of my life I hope to spend in the service of the Master, and thus I hope to be found when the great and final call shall come.

John Philip Quinn

THE THREE STAGES OF A GAMBLER'S LIFE.

The foregoing illustration presents, in a form calculated to strike the eye and impress the mind, a view of the gradations in the downward career of a gambler.

Starting out, with high hopes of pleasure to be derived and wealth to be gained through a life devoted to the ruin of his fellowmen, he boldly enters upon the way whose end is death and whose steps "take hold on hell." Costly is his attire and elastic his step as he at first ventures upon the road whose path is a quagmire and whose downward course is beset with thorns.

As he advances, he finds the declivity growing deeper; his feet are sore and his raiment torn. Too late he perceives his error, and realizes that it is far easier to descend than to climb the torturous, slippery path. The illusion is dispelled; the glamour has gone out in darkness. No longer the jovial, roystering, "hail-fellow-well-met," he has become the midnight prowler, dependent for his very subsistence, upon the scanty earnings which he derives from the percentage doled out to him

27

by more prosperous members of the same villainous craft for betraying the confidence of his friends and luring the unwary to their destruction. He realizes his situation, only to curse it; he would retrace his steps if he knew how, but his chosen sin holds him with a grasp as close as the coil of the deadly anaconda.

In the figure of the forlorn tramp, a destitute, penniless wanderer, a pariah and an outcast, we see him approaching his wretched end. The pitiless storm that beats in his face is but the sighing of the summer wind as compared with that which rages in his breast. The wind that howls in his ears seem to chant the requiem of home, happiness, hope, honor,—all that men hold dear. And yet he must go on; on, into the blinding sleet; on into the unknown future; on, until he reaches the Potter's field; on until he stands before the bar of God.

Certainly it can be no mistake to call such an one a "fool of fortune," a fool enslaved by his own degraded instincts and besotted passions, a fool who, in the words of Scripture, " has said in his heart there is no God." But professional blacklegs are not the only " fools of fortune." The young man, just entering upon the path of life; the middle aged man of family, who squanders at the gaming table the money which should go to buy luxuries, comforts, perhaps even necessaries for those dependent upon him; the old man, who, about to sink into the grave, finds it impossible to overcome the fascination of the vice which has reduced him from affluence to penury—these, one and all, are fools. The savings of a lifetime, dissipated in an hour, the cherished hopes of years blighted by the turn of a card—these are every day occurrences in the hells where one class of fools worship " Fortune," and another class delude themselves by the belief that it is possible for money dishonestly acquired to bring with it anything but a curse.

It is with the hope that those who have not already entered upon this course may be deterred from entering upon it and that those who may have already tasted the false pleasures of an unhealthy excitement may be induced to pause before it is too late, that the author has made his frank confession of his own follies and his revelation of the secret arts of the gambler's devil-born arts.

POKER.

The game of poker is undoubtedly one of the "peculiar institutions of the United States and, like baseball, may be called a 'National game.'" It finds an abiding place alike among the pineries of the frozen Kennebec and the orange groves of Florida, in the gilded *salons* of Manhattan Island, the backwoods of Arkansas, and the mining camps of California. It numbers among its devotees men of letters and of the proletariat, the millionaire and the shoe-black, the railway magnate and the tramp. It recognizes no distinction of age, color, or previous condition of servitude. It draws not the line of sex, and is equally at home in the fashionable club house and the gambler's den, the private parlor and the cheap lodging house. Men who avowedly abhor it, play it behind closed doors and drawn curtains, and ladies of culture and high social position are among its most devoted and most skillful patrons. To describe its fascination is as difficult as to account for it, yet the undisputable fact remains that of the vast army of men connected with mercantile pursuits in the United States, comparatively few can be found who have not some knowledge of the game; and were the whole truth disclosed, no insignificant number might reveal a tale of losses of no little magnitude.

Gentlemen, who would not, for worlds, enter a gaming hell, and who are apt to pride themselves upon their ignorance of faro, play poker at their clubs and by their own firesides, without either compunction of conscience or pretense of concealment. Intelligent, thoughtful men, eulogize the game as far removed from vulgarity, as calling into exercise some of the highest faculties of the human mind, and as resulting in healthy, moral effects.

This enthusiastic laudation of the game is all very well, but the naked facts remain, that whatever argument may be advanced against any form of gambling, may be urged with equal force against poker; and that this game sanctioned as it practically is, by the countenance of the reputable men who never set foot within a gambling house, has done more to weaken the moral sense of the country at large as to the general question

29

of gambling than any other single agency.   Its growing popular-
ity and increasing prevalence constitute a menace by no means
to be ignored to the prosperity, the morals, even the perpetuity
of the people.   A nation of gamblers is a nation whose course
is already turned towards the setting sun.

In playing a fair game of poker, the deal is of no special
value and anybody may begin.

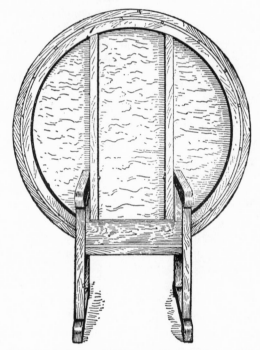

Arm Chair Poker Table, supplied with **Invisible**
Attachment for Holding-Out.

The dealer, beginning with the person at his left, throws
around five cards to each player, giving one card at a time.

The dealer shuffles and makes up the pack himself, or it
may be done by the player at his left, and the player at his right
must cut.

To begin the pool, the player next to the dealer on his left,
must put up money, which is called an " ante," and then in suc-
cession, each player, passing around to the left, must after looking at his hand, determine if he goes in or not; and each player

deciding to play for the pool must put in twice the amount of the ante. Those who decline to play throw up their cards, face downward on the table, and per consequence in front of the next dealer.

When all who wish to play have gone in, the person putting up the ante can either give up all interest in the pool, thus forfeiting the ante which has been put up, or else can play like the others who have gone in, by " making good," that is, putting up, in addition to the ante as much more as will make him equal in the stake to the rest.

The players must throw away their discarded cards before taking up or looking at those which they draw.

In poker, as fairly played, every player is for himself and against all others, and to that end will not let any of his cards be seen, nor betray the value of his hand by drawing or playing out of his turn, or by change of countenance, or any other sign. It is a great object to mystify your adversaries up to the " call," when hands have to be shown. To this end it is permitted to " chaff," or talk nonsense, with a view of misleading your adversaries as to the value of your hand, but this must be without unreasonably delaying the game.

When the drawing is all complete, the betting goes around in order, like the drawing, to the left. The ante man is the first to bet unless he has declined to play, and in that case the first bet is made by the player nearest to the dealer on his left. But the player entitled to bet first may withhold his wager until the others have bet round to him, which is called " holding the age," and this being considered an advantage, is very frequently done.

Each bettor in turn must put into the pool a sum equal at least to the first bet made; but each may in turn increase the bet, or "raise" it, as it comes to him; in which case the bets proceeding round in order must be made by each player in his turn, equal to the highest amount put in by any one; the party who fails being required to go out of the play, forfeiting his interest in the pool.

When a player puts in only as much as has been put in by each player who preceded him, that is called "setting the bet."

When a player puts in that much, and raises it, that is called seeing the bet and " going better."

When the bet goes around to the last bettor, or player, who

remains in, if he does not wish to see and go better, he simply sees and "calls," and then all playing must show their hands, and the highest hand wins the pool.

When any one declines to see the bet, or the increase of bet, which has been made, he " lays down " his hand; that is, throws it up with the cards face downwards on the table. If all the other players throw down their hands, the one who remains in to the last wins, and takes the pool without showing his hand.

To " bluff " is to take the risk of betting high enough on a poor hand or a worthless one, to make all the other players lay down their hands without seeing or calling you.

When a hand is complete so that the holder of it can play without drawing to better it, that is called a " pat " hand. A bold player will sometimes decline to draw any cards, and pretend to have a " pat " hand, and play it as such when he has none.

A skillful player will watch and observe when each player draws, the expression of his face, the circumstances and manner of betting, and judge, or try to judge, of the value of each hand opposed to him accordingly.

No one is bound to answer the question, how many cards he drew, except the dealer; and the dealer is not bound to tell after the betting has begun.

Poker Checks.

One of the most vital adjuncts to poker games as played in the many " club rooms " scattered throughout the United States is technically termed the " take-off." It is an amount taken by the proprietors out of the pots as a percentage due the " house " on every hand " called," and shown down; a pair of aces and another pair, and you must " go to the hole " with a check. The "hole" is a slot cut in the table, leading to a locked drawer underneath, and all checks deposited therein are the property of the keeper of the place. At other resorts the house takes off for each pair of jacks or any better hand shown on the call, while at others the percentage is exacted for any two pairs shown. It will be readily seen, by any intelligent reader, that it is only a question of time when all the player's chips will go into the "hole." The exaction of the "take-off" is justified on the score of incidental expenses, lights, etc., but a compound interest note, on which interest is computed quarterly, will not take away your money more surely or more rapidly than this innocent looking "hole."

In "stud-poker" the dealer attends to the "take-off." He is supposed to take one check for every pair in sight, and for every "call," but owing to a manual dexterity acquired through long practice he is enabled considerably to exceed the stipulated limit, and it is but a short time before all the money played against the game is in the table drawer.

There are many methods in vogue for cheating at poker, the explanation of the principal ones being as follows:

Strippers. Prepared cards are either "strippers" or "briefs." In preparing "strippers" the professional selects from the pack two hands, which may be either "fulls," "flushes," or "fours." The sides of the remaining cards are then prepared so that they shall be a little narrower than the hands selected. The cards withdrawn for stripping are then cut slightly convex on the sides, somewhat after the manner of strippers prepared for faro.

The number of cards taken out varies according to the character of the hand to be made up. If the sharper wishes to deal flushes he will require ten cards of the same suit. If full hands are desired he picks out two sets of three of a certain denomination together with four smaller cards of a kind. The object of this selection is to give variety to the hands to be dealt. The manner of conducting this scheme of fraud is substantially as follows: As the gambler shuffles it is not difficult for him to feel along the sides of the pack with the fingers of the right hand; he then draws out the wider cards, which he places upon the top of the pack. When he has succeeded in getting the wide cards on top he next divides the pack, then taking each portion by the outer ends, he places the two halves evenly together and then, with comparative ease, but instead shall alternate over and under each other throughout the whole deck.

The reader who will carefully study the foregoing explanation will see that the cards will run off "four-handed;" that is that they will fall to the hands of the opposite players.

Briefs. The "brief," which is a card used not only in poker, but also in various other games, is a card nicely trimmed on the sides to such a width that it can be readily distinguished by the dealer's touch.

The advantage of using such a card is that it enables the party knowing of its existence to cut at the point where it lies. Sometimes the "brief" is placed on the top of the prepared hand and the confederate of the dealer uncovers the pre-arranged cards by making precisely the correct cut.

Stocking. By far the most common description of frauds employed by professional gamblers in playing poker, however, is that of "stocking" the cards. Four varieties of "stocks" are employed by the fraternity, commonly known as the top stock, the bottom stock, the jog stock and the palm stock.

The Top Stock. Of all these, perhaps the one most ordinarily employed—possibly because the one most easily accomplished—is the top stock. In preparing the pack for the perpetration of this fraud, the dealer selects a pair and places between the two cards as many others as there are players at the table, less one. Thus, if there are four persons playing he inserts three cards between the two constituting a pair; if five, he places four; and so on, as the number of players is greater or less. His next step is to place above the pair thus arranged, the same number of cards which he has placed between them, the result being that when he deals, the two cards which he desires must necessarily fall to his own hand. If the sharper can manage to get hold of the three cards of the hands which are thrown up he may sometimes find it practicable to arrange "threes of a kind" in this way as well as a pair.

The Bottom Stock. In executing the bottom stock the tactics employed are substantially the same as in the top stock, by that the pair are placed on the bottom of the pack instead of on the top. The dealer takes great care in shuffling in that he does not disturb the lower part of the pack. The point at which the deck is cut makes considerable difference in the success of this maneuver. If, after cutting, it is found that all of the pack, except the cut, is necessary to supply the players with the requisite number of cards, then the pair will fall to the hand which has the last card, for the reason that the player who receives the bottom card must necessarily have received the other; but if the dealer sees that the bottom card is not destined to fall to himself, when he reaches the last two cards he "shifts" them, that is, reverses the order of dealing so that the party who should receive the top one receives the lower, while that uppermost falls to the next player. It may be readily perceived that by this trick the dealer has separated the pair, one falling to one hand, and the other to the player seated immediately upon the dealer's left.

The Jog Stock. The jog stock is a device which it is absolutely impossible to execute without the aid of a confederate, yet it is regarded by professionals as one of the most effectual means of defrauding an honest player. As in the case of the top and the bottom stocks, a pair is arranged by the dealer, who places upon it a sufficient number of cards to make the pair fall to his own hand. He next shuffles the pack once or twice in such a manner as to keep the arranged cards on the top, after which he slides a portion of the deck over the pair, leaving a narrow break or jog along the side, thus separating the hand which he has put up from the remainder of the pack. His confederate, it should be remembered, always sits on his right, then takes that part of the deck which rests upon the top of the stocked hand, with the thumb and finger of his right hand grasping them by the ends. Then with the thumb and middle finger of his left hand he seizes, in the same manner, the pre-arranged cards underneath; he draws out the latter and places them on top of the others, leaving them in precisely the same position as they were before his confederate offered them to him to cut.

An expert sharper, after winning once through these means, on his next deal so arranges the pack that the pair shall fall to his partner, with whom he bets, and to whom he apparently loses money. After this the cards are permitted to run naturally

for one or two hands, when the second scoundrel repeats the
same tactics.

The Palm Stock. No little dexterity is required to manipulate the palm stock. I have seen professionals attempt its execution and come to no small grief through its being detected in
consequence of their clumsiness. In order to execute this
maneuver effectually, the party intending to employ it must be
on the left of the dealer. He obtains possession of a high pair-—
perhaps kings or aces—and while he is holding one in each hand
in such a way that neither can be perceived, he asks that he be
allowed, after the shuffling and cutting, to cut the deck again.
Permission having been granted, he seizes the pack in his right
hand, places one of the cards which he has withheld in his right
hand on top of the pack, and as he cuts he leaves as many cards
on the table as may be necessary to intervene the pair in order
that they may be "put up." Then as he grasps these cards with
his left hand he places the other card of the pair on the top and
throws them on the top of the pack. It is not difficult to see that
the result of this maneuvre is to place the two cards which he
has " palmed " in such a position that they will inevitably fall
to himself. Of course it is not possible to practice this trick
frequently without exciting suspicion, but I have, myself, by
employing it judiciously, managed to win no inconsiderable
sums. As a rule, after executing the " palm stock," the black-
leg " goes a blind," and the trick is rarely attempted unless
there is a large ante.

False Shuffle. Another favorite practice among the black
legs is the " false shuffle." Almost all sharpers have their own
individual methods of shuffling; but perhaps the one which is
most approved is that known among the profession as " the
intricate shuffle." It is executed substantially as follows: The
cards are " ripped," that is, the deck is divided into two halves,
which are pushed entirely through each other, after which they
are drawn out at the ends, and the half which was previously
on top is replaced in the same position. Some professionals
shuffle only the lower half of the pack, not disturbing the top,
but concealing the upper cards by means of keeping three or
four fingers over the end of the pack which is towards their
antagonist. Sometimes a very quick shuffle is employed which
does not disarrange the cards on the top, and after this the pack

is given a double false cut, by means of which the cards originally uppermost are retained in the same position. The device,
which, if rapidly executed, appears to the unsophisticated player
a perfectly fair shuffle, only a practical acquaintance with the
operation of the trick enables the verdant amateur to detect
this trick when executed adroitly.

False Cuts. Besides false shuffles, professionals also have
resort to false cuts. Of these, there are but two varieties in
common use, known respectively as the "over hand" and
"double" cut. In the former about one-third of the pack is
taken with the right hand, while one-half the remainder is concealed in the left. The party cutting brings the left hand towards him, that portion of the deck which is left on the table is
then covered by the dropping of the cards held in the right hand,
the hand still being kept over them, while those in the left hand
are thrown over and beyond the others; the maneuvre is completed by placing the cards in the right hand on the top.

In the execution of the "double" cut, the middle of the
pack is drawn out at the end with the thumb and middle finger,
after they are brought to the top of the deck, the cards originally
uppermost are caught by the lower part of the thumb and three
fingers, drawn out at the end and once more placed on the top.
In either case the pack is left in precisely the same position as it
was before the seeming cut had been made. The object is the
same as in the case of both false shuffles and false cuts; that is,
to leave the pre-arranged pack in precisely the condition in
which the dealer wished it to be.

Double Discard. Yet another device of the professional
poker player is known as the "double discard." The black-leg
does not discard until after he has made a draft. He separates
the cards which he wishes to discard from the four which he
nominally proposes to retain, holding the former in his left hand
and the latter in his right, ready for a fraudulent discard, in
case he sees fit. Calling for four cards, he drops those which
he has in his right hand immediately in front of him. Next,
he lifts the draft with his left hand, the odd card of course
coming on top; if now he finds in the draft one or more cards
which he perceives will, with the aid of the four cards lying in
front of him on the table, improve his chances, he retains that,
and again discards the four cards. He then drops the one

which he has retained, upon the four originally rejected, raises the hand, and of course is prepared to wager, with an approximate certainty of success.

HOLDING OUT.

Of all the practices of a dishonest gambler at poker, "holding out" is perhaps the most frequently resorted to. It consists

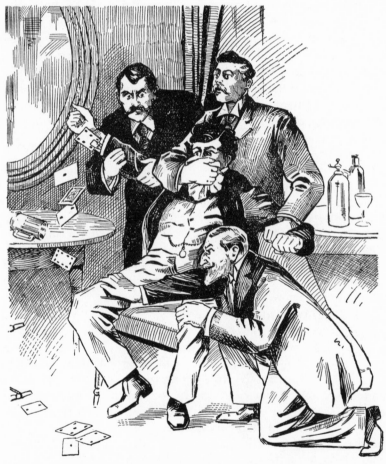

of abstracting one or more cards from the pack, which are secreted either about the person of the player, or beneath the table. The object of course is that the sharper may have desirable cards ready to produce when a favorable opportunity offers. The illustration shows a man detected with a sleeve hold out. If the person to be deceived is especially verdant the cards withdrawn from the pack are sometimes concealed behind the collar, or under the joint of the knee or may be laid upon a handkerchief in the lap.

Professionals differ considerably in the methods used, and I will now describe some of those in vogue.

The Bug. This instrument is a very simple device and is often made by the gambler himself. " B " represents a piece of watch spring which is fastened to the table by means of an awl " A " in such a way that the point may curl over. The awl is pressed into the under side  of the table. The watch spring snaps up against the bottom. Some high card is secreted in the spring which holds it firmly in place. When the party receives one or more cards of the same denomination he has secreted, he takes the concealed card from its place and replaces it with an inferior card taken from his hand. It will be seen that he thus obtains two or more high cards of the same denomination.

The Sleeve Hold Out. This apparatus consists of a leather band (lettered A in the illustration) fastened around the right arm, beneath the coat sleeve, near the elbow, to which is at-

tached a spring pressure upon which works a rod which connects with a plate (lettered B in the cut). The method of using this device is shown in the illustration. The cards which are " held out " are placed beneath the plate B, which holds them in position. When the player wishes to draw from his sleeve, he presses his arm against his body, thus setting in operation the spring which works the rod and throws forward the concealed cards from behind the plate, as shown in the cut.

The Vest Hold Out. Some gamblers prefer this contrivance to any other, for the reason that it permits the holding out of an entire hand if the player so desires. The accompanying illustration shows the method in which it is worked. " A " indicates the location of that part of the mechanism which holds the abstracted cards; " B " is a piece of catgut attached to that part of the apparatus concealed beneath the vest, and running underneath the clothing to the heel, where it is fastened either to the shoe or the clothing. The cards selected to be " held out " are placed inside the clamp underneath the vest. When the player stretches out the leg along which runs the catgut, the plate inside the vest comes forward and the cards may be easily withdrawn; when the heel is drawn back beneath the chair the tension on the catgut is increased, and the clamp recedes behind the vest.

The Table Hold Out. This differs from others in that it is permanently attached to the table, instead of being carried about by the player himself. A card may be seen protruding above the surface of the table, directly where the cloth covering joins the wooden border. This card is forced up through a concealed slit at the will of the gambler, by means

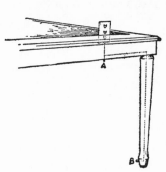

of a hidden mechanism. The dotted line running from the slit to the foot of the table's leg represents a wire which operates a spring whereby the card is forced upward, or lowered, through the slit, at the option of the manipulator. " A " is a point at which is inserted a small knob, or button, pressure upon which works the spring. By pressing with his foot at " B," the player accomplishes the same result. This forces the cards up, and the sharper takes them in his hand, at the same time discarding an equal number of cards from his hand into the slit.

The Mystery Card Table. This table is considered excellent for magic and sleight-of-hand work. The table is made so that the operator, when sitting down by it, in a natural position, with his hands lying on the table, can cause cards to come into or leave his hands at will, without anyone seeing the operation. This is done by pressing the knee against a little squeeze under the table, which causes a false, well concealed opening in the .op of

the table to open up. With the same operation a little receiver comes up and the operator merely drops the cards into the receiver, which he wishes to make disappear. Should he wish the cards to reappear or come into his hand again, he merely presses the squeeze, as before.

SHINERS.

Of all the devices for defrauding at poker, the " shiner " is perhaps the most simple and the most effective. They are of various forms. At first a circular piece of silver highly polished and convex in form, about the size of a five-cent piece, was used. The player employing it places it on the table in front of him, using the utmost pains to conceal it from observation. The advantage resulting from its employment is the power of reflecting whatever is held above it at any angle, thus enabling the dealer who used it to read the face of each card as it was taken, face downwards, from the pack. Of late years, however, the makers of these implements have greatly improved the process of manufacture.

Poker Check Mirror. A very fine glass is set in five poker chips, and can be played at any distance from the deck, up to 20 inches. Reflector can be placed in any kind of checks, of any color desired. It is claimed that this mirror stack mixed in with the other stacks is a big success in getting the money.

Triangle Reducing Glass. This is made to set between two stacks of poker checks. It is made of very

fine glass, and can be played from four to twenty inches from edge of table, set with friction hinges so glass can be lowered or raised as required; is very light and compact, can be closed up like a book and concealed in an instant.

Pipe Reflector. This is a genuine French briar pipe, with a reflector made of the finest imported Swiss flint glass, so ar-

ranged that the glass can be put in or out at a second's time, and the player can continue to smoke.

The above illustrations are sufficient to show the many ways of securing knowledge of what the other fellow holds.

STUD POKER.

Another variety of poker in great favor among the gambling fraternity is called " stud poker," a stud poker table now considered a necessary adjunct to every first class gambling house. The necessary outfit for the game consists of checks, cards and a table large enough to seat ten or twelve persons. Regular dealers are employed and usually four or five "pluggers" (by which term are designated men who play for the house and with money belonging to the proprietors). The game is very simple, and any one acquainted with the game of draw poker can play, and lose his money as easily and rapidly as he could possibly desire. The game may be illustrated as follows: Suppose four persons, whom we will designate as A, B, C and D, sit down to play. In some games, in fact usually, each player puts up one check as an ante. This having been done, the dealer deals the first card, face downward, to each player, beginning with the one who sits on his (the dealer's) left; another card is then dealt around with the face exposed, as must also be the other three cards in case a hand of five is dealt. Let us suppose

Stud Poker Table.

that A's exposed card is an ace, B's a queen, C's a nine spot and D's a ten. He can wager any amount he chooses, and the others can throw away their cards or "stay in," by putting up an equal stake to that of A's. If B, C and D should throw down their cards, the checks in the "pot" belong to A, and the dealer shuffling, begins another deal. Should either B, C or D "see" A's bet or "raise" him, the dealer, deals off another card, face upward, when the player who has the highest cards in sight, has another opportunity to "pass" or bet, while the others have the choice of throwing away their cards or "seeing" the bet, and so on until five cards are dealt, when the players must guess at each other's buried card, or "hole card," as it is technically called.

Sometimes at stud poker an instrument known as "the buck" is used. This is employed where all the players do not "ante." Any article may be used for this purpose. Sometimes an ivory chip with a string running through it; sometimes a circular piece of leather, its material and form are unimportant. It passes in rotation, one to another, the player in front of whom it is placed being required to "ante" a chip and receiving the first card dealt. The game then proceeds as already described. The chances for "crooked work" are legion. In a word nearly every fraudulent device in draw poker may be utilized in stud poker.

FARO.

The origin of the game of faro, like that of most games of cards, is obscure. There is a tradition that it emanated from the shore of the Nile, and that its antiquity is as venerable as that

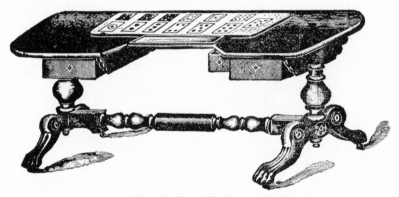

Faro Table with Layout.

of the pyramids. Perhaps this rather fanciful theory has grown in favor from the fact that its name is sometimes spelled "pharo," the name of the founder of the great Egyptian dynasty, whose head is said, in ancient times, to have been depicted upon one of the cards. Be this as it may, it is certain that centuries ago it was popular among the gamesters of France and other countries of Europe, whence it crossed the channel to the British Isles and later was brought across the Atlantic to America. In the United States, it is a game *par excellence* at every gambling establishment, being at once the most absorbingly fascinating to players and the most profitable to the bank. Across the green cloth which separates the former from the latter, fortunes are hourly lost and won. The monotonous, droning call of the dealer, falling upon the ears of the players, whose interest is breathless in its intensity, has proved to thousands the knell of doom to wealth, honor, integrity, and happiness. With its allurement of excitement and its tempting bait of gain, it woos its votaries to shipwreck equally certain and no less terrible than that which befell the mariner of old, whose charmed senses drank in the intoxicating music of the siren's song. Faro has been happily likened to the tiger, which, crafty, treacherous, cruel and relentless, hides under cover waiting, with impatient eagerness, for the moment when it may bury its velvet covered claws within the vitals of its unsuspecting victim and slake its fiery, unquenchable thirst with his life's blood.

As preparatory to a discussion of the first branch of the subject, it may be remarked that faro is pre-eminently a game of chance. Even when played with absolute fairness, success or failure, fortune or misfortune, depend—not upon the skill of the player, but upon the caprice of blind chance. It is true that mathematical science has attempted to reduce this chance to some sort of law, and has formulated a theory as to the inherent probability or improbability of certain events happening or failing to happen, and there are devotees of faro who play upon what they believe—with a faith which approaches the sublime—to be an infallible " system." But the doctrine of chance is, after all, but an approximation to accuracy, and the only certainty about any system, however cunningly devised, is the certainty that at the supreme moment it will prove a delusion and a snare.

But, to return to the method of playing: Any number of persons may participate in the game, which requires a full pack of fifty-two cards. The dealer acts as " banker," and may, at his discretion, limit the sums to be played for, according to the amount of his capital. At public games, this functionary, assisted by one or more persons known as " lookers-out," whose duty it is to watch the table, the players and the bets, with a view to seeing that the bank's winnings are promptly gathered in, and that the interests of " the house " are properly guarded. In order to facilitate the making of bets, players purchase checks, usually made of ivory or bone or composition, though sometimes of paste-board, from the banker, who redeems them at the option of the holder. Their value is denoted either by their color, or

figures stamped upon them. The limit, which the banker sets,
may be of two kinds, known as the *plain* and the *running* limit.
The *plain limit* is usually twice as much for double, treble or
quadruple cards as for single cards. That is to say, if a player
may bet $50 on either or all of the latter, he may bet $100 on all
or any of the double. The *running limit* is any sum named and
its multiple of four. To illustrate : The running limit may be 50
and 200 ; in that case, the player may bet $50, and if he wins,
may suffer the original stake and its increase (which would
amount to $100) to be where it is or move it to another place,
where he may win another $100, thus giving him with his first

Folding Board with Faro Layout.

stake $200, which is the limit. This is known as parleeing a bet,
and if the first bet is five, the second will be ten, the third
twenty, and the fourth forty, and so on. Almost all bankers will
allow a player to " parlee," as the percentage is largely in favor
of the bank.

The ace, deuce, queen and king are called the big square ;
the deuce, tray, queen and jack the second square, and so on ;
the six, seven and eight are called the pot. The players select
their cards upon which they wish to bet, and lay upon them
their checks.

Before any bets are made the dealer shuffles and cuts the
cards and places them face upward in a metal box, containing an
aperture at the top, sufficiently large to allow the full faces of
the cards to be seen. Near the top of one end of this receptacle
is a horizontal slit, wide enough to admit the passage of a single
card, and at the bottom are four springs, which, pressing upward,
automatically force the pack toward the top of the box,

thus keeping one card always opposite the slit. The top card, called the " soda," having been seen, is not used for betting, and is laid aside. The card immediately below is the banker's card, and it wins for him all stakes placed upon it in the " layout," provided it has not been " coppered," as explained below. The next is the player's card and wins for him in the same manner. Each pair of cards taken from the box and exposed constitute what is denominated a " turn." It may happen, however, that the player may wish to bet that a certain card may lose. In that case he places a copper (which is provided for the purpose) upon the top of his stake. This is called " coppering," because originally old fashioned copper cents were employed for this purpose.

Faro Copper.

Whenever two cards of the same denomination appear in the same " turn," the dealer takes half the money found upon such card. This is called a " split," and is, in effect, a percentage taken by the bank. If a player wins his bet and allows both stake and winnings to remain on the same card for another " turn," he is said to play a paroli or parlee. At the end of a " turn " a pause is made, to permit the paying of bets already determined and the making of new ones. And the same routine is followed until the pack is exhausted, when a fresh deal is made and the process repeated.

When there is but one turn left in the box, the player may " call the last turn;" that is, guess the order in which the cards will appear. If he guess correctly, he receives either two or four times the value of his stake, according to the advantage which he enjoys through the character of the turn. If the three cards are three denominations they may come out in any one of the six different ways; if, on the other hand, two of the three cards are of the same denomination, only three arrangements are possible. Hence, in the former case, if he guesses correctly, the banker pays him four times the amount of his wager; in the latter (which is technically called a " cat hop ") he wins double its value.

When the dealing box was first introduced, nearly a century ago, it was claimed in its behalf that it insured absolute protection against fraud on the part of either dealer or players.

Practically, as years have passed and new features have been engrafted upon it, it has become the most effective agency for unlimited fraud that the most nefarious dealer could desire.

In order to have a thorough comprehension of the following description of the " fake " box now in use, it may be well that the reader understand the object sought to be gained through them. The rules of the game require that but one card shall be dealt at a time. To a dealer determined to win, it is of the utmost importance to know, before the card issues from the box, what that card is going to be. To give him this advantage he uses a box so constructed that he can control its operations at will. It will thus be seen that his cards and his box supplement each other. To know the cards would avail him nothing unless he might use those which he needed; to be able to deal fraudulently would be of no possible advantage, unless he knew precisely which card to deal. Taken together, they form a combination so strong as to be impregnable to the dupe who fancies that he and his crafty opponent meet on a fair field in the open, even if not honorable, combat.

The accompanying cut shows the mechanism of the " screw box," which is used by gamblers for dealing crooked faro, and which is also a special favorite in dealing " red and black."

The front side of this box, " A," is provided with three thin perpendicular plates, of which two are stationary, but all of which seem to be solidly joined together. Between the stationary plates " B " and " D," whose inner surfaces are so highly polished as to reduce friction to a minimum, slides another and invisible plate, marked " C," and which is adjustable and highly sensitive to the secret manipulation of the practiced dealer. This

center piece " C," when properly placed and at rest, presents an
upper edge a trifle above the two stationary plates, leaving an
aperture so narrow that the dealer can take but one card from
the box at a time.

" F " is a screw which operates a secret lever, " E C," between the two plates " B " and " D." This lever hangs on a
pivot and by slightly pressing the screw with the thumb the adjustable plate " C " quickly responds, and drops until its edge is
even with those of the stationary plates " B " and " D," thereby
enabling the dealer to take two cards from the box at one time
without observation.

Upon removing the thumb pressure from the screw " F,"
the adjustable plate " C " rises to its original position.

There is a flat metal piece in the inside of the box at the
bottom which, when pushed forward, instantly and securely
locks the box, preventing the discovery of its mechanism,

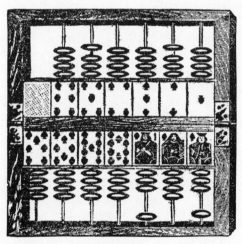

Faro Case Keeper

should any of the players request permission to examine it.
Such permission is always cheerfully and usually courteously
given.

Finally, inside of the box, as in all others, is a thin plate
the size of the cards, which is placed in a level or horizontal
position, upon which the cards rest, and which is supported by
four steel springs that force the cards up to the top of the box
so that they may always be ready for dealing.

A record of the game is kept by means of an implement known as a "case-keeper," which is usually placed in care of an employe of the establishment. This device is a miniature layout, with four buttons attached to each wire as shown in the illustration. These buttons run on wires, one of which extends from the end of each card. When the deal begins, all the buttons are shoved up close to the cards; as soon as a "turn" is made, the two buttons opposite the cards dealt are shoved to the opposite ends of their respective wires. This enables any one around the table to see, at a glance, how many cards of each denomination remain in the dealer's box. When all four cards of any one denomination have been dealt, that is said to be "*dead.*" When three cards of any one denomination have been dealt, the one remaining in the box is called the "*case,*" or "*single card.*"

It may sometimes happen that the tally of a player will not agree with that of the case keeper, owing to the fact that the dealer has withdrawn two cards where he should have taken one. In such a case, a trick known as the "put back" is employed. A confederate of the dealer attracts the attention of the players while the extra card or cards taken from the box are adroitly returned to it by the dealer. Of course, there must be a perfect understanding between the latter and the case keeper, so that when two cards are dealt at once a signal may be given showing the denomination of the second card.

In case a player making a bet finds that he has been misled by the incorrectness of the record kept by the cue keeper, the invariable rule is that the bet must be determined by the cards remaining in the dealing box, a regulation which is, to say the least, not at all to the disadvantage of the bank.

But the cheating is not all on one side, and a device called a hair "copper" is sometimes employed by players to guard against such a possible loss on a certain description of bets. This hair "copper" consists of a piece of shoemaker's wax, the color of the check, a horse hair, and a string of rubber attached to a band around the wrist, secreted in the sleeve. The wax adheres to the copper at one end of the horse hair, which is invisible, the other end being fastened to the rubber string which is extended in the hand to the tops of the fingers. Placing this "copper" on a bet, if the turn comes in favor of the dealer the player quickly and without observation loosens the rubber which jerks the "copper" into his sleeve, causing the dealer to pay the bet he may have fairly won.

One of the methods used by the players for cheating, is to perforate all the cards of a certain description, perhaps of either dark suit, from the two to the ten, with an instrument known as the "card punch," of which the accompanying illustration will enable the reader to form a fair conception.

It is made of the finest steel, and is employed to puncture cards at the center. A "deck" thus prepared is substituted for that which the banker intends to place in the box. Sometimes, however, in this "diamond cut diamond" game, an entrance is effected to the dealer's room and the "punch" is employed on his own cards. The substitution of the prepared pack for that of the banker is the fundamental point to be attained, and occasionally resort is had to desperate expedients. A fight is raised, and in the mêlée which ensues the dealer's box is thrown upon the floor and the substitution quickly accomplished.

The holes made by the punch are so small that the player is often beaten by it. Whenever a white surface is seen through this small hole, the player is perfectly certain that the card underneath is the deuce, four, six, seven, eight or ten, and may accordingly back these cards to win for himself with absolute certainty. If a colored surface is discerned, he is equally certain that the next card will be of another denomination.

Besides the methods of cheating already described, which relate more particularly to the preparation of the cards and the construction and operation of the dealing box, there are other methods well known to professionals, which may be employed with comparative immunity and great success against the unsuspecting.

"Faked" dealing boxes are not always the "thing of beauty" and perennial source of joy which their manipulators would like to see them. They occasionally "get out of order." A little of the sand which has been used in the preparation of the cards, works its way between the plates, and even an expert "brace" dealer finds it more or less difficult so to use the device that its employment cannot be detected. At Laredo, Texas, some years ago, a "professional," who was a dealer in a famous house in a Western city, encountered a difficulty of this sort. He " pulled " two cards, but so clumsily that the " sucker " observed it. " What's the matter with your box?" the player asked. " O, it's a little old, and don't work just right," was the answer. " Well, see here," said the Texan, " that was an almighty short deal, somehow. Reckon I'm going to lose money any way; but hadn't you better go a little slower and make one of them long deals? I'd like to take a little more time." The game progressed and the stranger rose from the table a loser to the amount of three hundred dollars. " Look here," he remarked to the dealer, " I reckon you'd better give me back the money you've cheated me out of." The gambler. with an air of the utmost nonchalance, replied that he would be blanked if he gave back any of it. " Well," remarked the countryman, as he drew down his slouch hat over his eyes and left the room, " I'll be back in a few minutes." No sooner had he gone than one of the employes of the establishment took the proprietor aside and advised him either to return the money or close the place at once, if he did not want the victim to return and shoot him " on sight." The proprietor was a capital " brace " dealer, but physical courage was not his chief characteristic. He lost no time in acting on his subordinate's suggestion. Hastily raising the window he called out to the victim—whose rapidly vanishing form was still in sight—" I say, you! Come back here a minute; I want to see you." The " sucker " came back; the gambler greeted him cordially. " You old idiot," said he, " can't you take a little joke? Of course I knew that you were 'capping' (i. e., acting as 'capper') for the game. Here's your money old man." He handed him a roll of currency, which the stranger pocketed with a grim smile of satisfaction. But subsequent events proved that the proprietor " had builded better than he knew." Sitting around the room were other men who had lost money and seen a fellow sufferer receive back his losses, it did not take long for the crowd to extinguish the lights, and in the darkness the unlucky dealer was " held up " for every dollar that he had with him.

ROUGE ET NOIR; OR, RED AND BLACK.

As played in this country, this game differs materially from the mode of playing in vogue on the continent of Europe. Here the method of play is vastly simplified, but it has degenerated into a mere scheme of robbery. The players are utterly at the mercy of the manipulators of the machine.

The game is always played with the adjunct of a layout. The outer line, as shown in the illustration, represents the outer edge of the table, which is covered with a green cloth. The middle line serves no special purpose, but adds one more striking feature to the device. The inner line serves to mark off that portion of the table on which are depicted the representation of

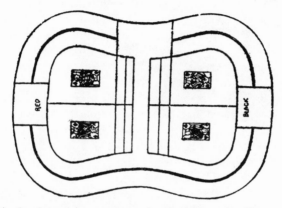

the four jacks found in every pack of cards. At the two ends of the table and on the top are blank spaces. Those at the ends are colored—the one red, and the other black. The space on the top is for the placing of wagers.

Any number of persons may play.

Bets are made in either one of the four ways—on the red; on the black; on either jack, or on any one of the four jacks. In the two cases first mentioned the bettor places his wager on the color which he selects. If he wishes to bet on any particular jack (that of hearts, clubs, diamonds or spades), he lays his money on that one which he chooses. If he prefers to bet that some jack (without indicating which) will win, he lays his venture upon the blank space at the top of the table as shown in the diagram.

If he bets on the winning color, the bank pays him an amount equal to the sum staked, which latter, of course, he receives back. If he selects a particular jack and the one on which he has placed his wager happens to win, his stake is returned to him, together with an increment of ten times the amount. If he places his wager on the blank space at the top he is understood to have bet that some one of the four jacks will win, and if his hazard prove successful, his gains are measured by a sum twice that of his original bet.

The bets having all been made and placed, the play commences. The banker places a full pack (fifty-two cards) in a dealing box, similar to those used in playing " faro," which have been already described, but with this variation: In " faro " the cards are inserted and dealt face uppermost, the opening being

large enough to afford a clear view of the card; in rouge et noir they are inserted and dealt face downward, and the aperture in the box is only large enough to permit the dealer to run them off readily with the index and second fingers of the left hand.

The first two cards, after being withdrawn from the box, are laid upon the table, face downward, and the third is turned over. This constitutes a " run," and the gains or losses of the players are determined by the color (and sometimes the denomination) of the third card. If it happens to be the red the bank pays all bets placed on the space at the end of the table marked " red," and gathers in all other wagers placed upon the table. If it chance to be a jack, and any player has placed his money on the representation of that particular jack upon the layout, the fortunate individual wins ten times the amount which he ventured. If a player has bet upon " jacks," without naming any particular one—placing his money in the space at the top of the table—and a jack of any suit is turned up, he is given, as his winnings, double the amount of his wager.

Even when fairly played, the chances in favor of the bank are large enough to satisfy any banker whose greed for gain is not abnormal. But as in all other games, the rapacious sharks who operate it are not satisfied with even the most extraordinary percentage of chances. What they seek is absolute certainty, and in the game of rouge et noir, as conducted in even so-called " square " houses, they have contrived to secure it.

" Faked " boxes, similar in construction to those used in " faro," are employed, and the cards are sanded as in that game.

The red and black cards are placed alternately, so that when the players call the color of the next card, the dealer knows just what it is, and is thus in a position to manipulate the cards to his own advantage. For the success of his operations, it is

necessary that the cards be kept in perfect condition, and for this purpose he uses card presses, as shown in the illustration. The manipulation of the pack in the box is practiced in the same way as has been already explained under "faro." If the dealer considers it necessary to change the color before exposing the card to the view of the players, he just touches the spring of the "faked" box, which enables him to draw two cards instead of one through the aperture, thus reversing the run of the colors.

DIANA GAME.

The accompanying diagram represents the Diana Game, which consists of a handsome layout, and one dealing box as

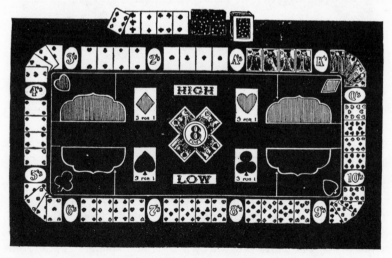

is used in faro and rouge et noir, the difference being that the diana box is made to hold two decks of cards instead of one.

The cards are well shuffled and placed in the box face down-ward; the dealer then draws out two cards, leaving them as they came from the box, then turns the third card face up, say deuce of spades, this means that low wins, the black wins, both paying even money. That the spade suit wins paying three to one, that the deuces win, paying eight for one. Whenever the dealer turns " jack " he takes all bets excepting those made on the jacks, which also pays eight for one, the jacks being the dealer's per cent. Player may also bet on any card he may wish to, and in the event of his winning he receives thirty-two for one.

The chances for cheating in this game are the same as in faro and rouge et noir.

THREE CARD MONTE.

This is an ancient device of sharpers, and is commonly re-sorted to by gamblers and confidence men, who find their most successful field of operation upon railway trains, fair grounds, etc. The game is played with three cards, which are held by the operator, who is known in gamblers' slang as the " spieler,"

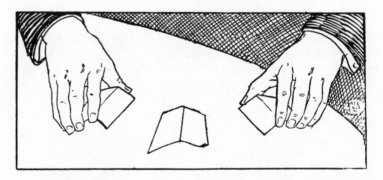

in his right hand, between the thumb and first two fingers, the backs towards the palm, and the cards themselves slightly bend-ing inward. To work the trick successfully, some sleight-of-hand is necessary, to acquire which considerable practice is necessary. The cards are thrown by the " spieler " upon some flat surface, faces downward. Before throwing them, he shows the bystanders the cards which he holds in his hand, and after they have been thrown he invites bets as to the location of some particular card.

To illustrate: he may hold in his hand two aces and a queen; these he shows; he then places them in his right hand, in the position above described, and throws them upon the flat surface, faces downward; he then asks some one to bet which is the queen. The queen may have been the middle of the three cards as they were held in his hand, but it by no means follows that it will be the middle of the three cards as they lie upon the table.

To work the game successfully one or two confederates are necessary. One of them will sometimes come forward and bend one of the corners of the queen so that he will know it again after the cards have been through the "spieler's" hands. Of course he wins. This induces the bystanders to bet with certainty, and when the "spieler" again picks up the cards to throw them the victims stake their wagers. The operator, however, with his little finger dexterously flattens out the corner which his accomplice had bent up and bends up the corner of an entirely different card. When the cards are next thrown, the victims select the one with the bent corner, and are deeply chagrined to discover that it is not the one they believed it to be.

Probably, the king of the monte men was a man known in sporting circles as "Canada Bill." He was recognized as a general "all round confidence operator," and so distrustful were those who knew him of appearances which he put forth that on the occasion of his funeral, as the coffin was being lowered into the grave, one of his friends offered to bet $1,000 to $500 that "Bill was not in the box." The offer found no takers, for the reason, as one of his acquaintances said, "that he had known Bill to squeeze through tighter holes than that." It was reported some years before his death that he had offered one of the Trunk Lines of Railroad a premium of $25,000 per annum to be allowed to practice confidence games upon its trains without molestation, a condition of the offer being that he would not attempt to victimize any class of passengers except preachers.

It is to the credit of many of the railroads that they have issued orders forbidding gambling on any part of their property, also forbidding their employes to practice gambling, either on or off duty.

TIPPING THE HAND.

2   1   3

The accompanying illustration affords a view of two " skin " gamblers engaged in victimizing a " sucker " by means of a trick familiarly known among the fraternity as " tipping " or " signing the hand." Large sums of money have been won through this means, not only from verdant dupes, but even from professionals who prided themselves upon their astuteness. In order to work it successfully, marked cards are indispensible, and at least one of the confederates, who act in unison, must be an expert at the use of " paper," as marked or " advantage " cards are called among the gamblers.

The cut shows the method in which the trick is carried on. Player number 3 represents the " sucker;" player number 2 the swindler who has induced him to play on the promise of " tipping " the " hand " of number 1, who is in reality the partner of number 2, although, of course, this latter fact is unknown to number 3. The method of playing this nefarious confidence game may be best shown by an illustration. Number 2 always faithfully signals number 3 precisely what cards are in the hands of number 1. The latter being an expert marked card player, of course, knows with absolute certainty what cards are held by number 3. Let us suppose that number 1 holds a pair of sixes and number 3 a pair of fives. Number 2 signals to number 3 that number 1 has in his hands a low pair. Number 3 is naturally in the dark as to whether the pair in question is of a lower denomination than his own, and in the hope that it may prove to be makes his bet. Number 1 immediately "raises" him, and this is continued as long as the victim can be induced to wager, or until number 3 has "staked" his "pile." The hands being "shown down," of course number 1 takes the stakes.

ROULETTE.

Roulette, as will be seen in the illustration, is played upon a table in the form of an oblong square, covered with green cloth, at one end of which is a round cavity, around the sides of which, equidistant one from the other, are arranged several metal bands—usually of copper — which, commencing at the top, descend to the extremity of the machine. The cavity is movable, and in the center is a circular bottom containing thirty-nine holes to which the bands are attached, and upon which are painted alternately, in black and red, thirty-six numbers, running from 1 to 36, besides (0), a (00), and a picture of an eagle or the word itself printed thereon. In the middle of the cavity, are three or four metal prongs, centering at " D," which are used in imparting a rotary motion to the bottom. The revolution of the ball is checked by slender metal plates (indicated on the diagram by the letter " B ") about two inches in length and rising about one-quarter of an inch above the lower surface.

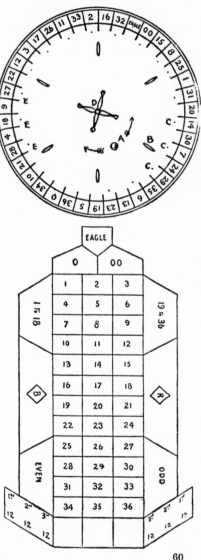

The remainder of the table is laid out as shown in the cut. The figures are arranged in three columns, and above them in two divisions nearest the roulette, are single and double 00 respectively. The figures are painted black or red, to agree with the corresponding color of the numbers on the wheel. At the head of each column there is a compartment for placing a stake which is made on the column. On each side of the foot of the columns of figures are three spaces, each of which contains the number twelve. These are known, respectively, as the 1st, 2nd, and 3rd twelves. Stakes placed on the first space are considered to be bets on the numbers 1 to 12; the second space is for bets on numbers 13 to 24; the third space for numbers 25 to 36, all inclusive.

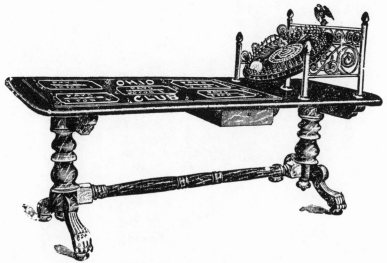

Bookmaker's Wheel.

The space on either side of the entire length of the columns is divided into three parts. The upper left hand division is for bets on numbers 1 to 18; the corresponding right hand division is for numbers 19 to 36. The large division in the middle of the left hand side, lettered " B " in the illustration, is for bets on the black; the similar one on the right, marked " B," is for wagers on the red.

The lower division on the left hand is for bets on even numbers; the division opposite on the right is for odd numbers.

There is a banker and several assistants; an unlimited number of persons may play.

One of the assistants sets the machine in motion, at

the same instant throwing an ivory ball into the cavity in the opposite direction to the movement which he has given to the movable bottom. The ball makes several revolutions with great rapidity until its momentum being exhausted, it falls into one of the thirty-nine holes formed by the copper bands. It is the hole into which the ball falls that determines the gain or loss of the numerous chances which this game affords to players.

If the reader will examine the cut showing the layout, he

Bookmaker's Wheel.

will perceive that there are numerous chances to be played for: Single and double (0); the "eagle;" black and red; the three columns; the first and last half of the numbers, respectively, consisting of 1 to 18, and 19 to 36 inclusive; the three 12's, which consist of 1 to 12, 13 to 24, and 25 to 36; odd and even; and lastly, the numbers, either single or in groups.

Stakes bet on black or red; the first or last half of the numbers; also on odd and even, are called single stakes. Stakes on either of the three 12's, or on either of the three columns, win double the amount. Stakes on any single number, or on either of the (0's), or the eagle, are paid thirty-five times their amount if they are successful.

Bets may be made on groups of not over six consecutive numbers, and win as many times the amount of the stakes as the grouping is contained in thirty-four, omitting all fractions; so that a bet on any four designated consecutive numbers would win eight times the amount of the stake, provided any one of these numbers comes out.

It has already been stated that the space occupied by thirty-six numbers are either red or black; and as the numbers are equally divided between the colors eighteen to each, a stake on either color is a single bet. The (0's) and the eagle are painted

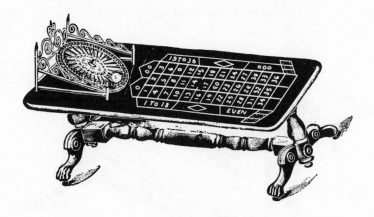

Upright Roulette Wheel.

green, and if a zero or eagle turns up, bets on either black or red are lost by the players.

The legitimate percentage of chances in favor of the bank in this game is enormous. Out of thirty-nine chances, the bank runs eighteen of losing and has twenty-one of winning, or three additional chances in its favor, which is equivalent to fully 5 1-2 per cent. in favor of the bank in all cases, even where a bet is placed upon either of the zeros or the eagle. In the latter case, the bet on either zero or on the eagle is paid 35 to 1, the same as on any single number.

Here the bank has thirty-five chances out of thirty-nine of winning, and only one of losing, or four more chances in its favor than the payments warrant, thus yielding the same 5 1-2 per cent.

It follows that the odds against the players in the various chances may be expressed as follows:

Upon a single number.......................37 to 1
Upon any twelve numbers..................13 to 6
Upon two numbers ....18 to 1
Upon three numbers ....11 2-3 to 1
Upon four numbers ....17 to 2
Upon six numbers ....16 to 3
Upon odd or even, red or black.............10 to 9

In the case of a bet on the first or last eighteen numbers, the odds are ten to nine, the same as on odd or even, or red or black.

When, however, a stake is laid on all the numbers, and the bank only pays the winner thirty-five times his stake, it clears four; thus, supposing thirty-nine dollars to be a stake, and that the ball is thrown twice in a minute, the gain of the bank, without incurring the slightest risk, would be eight dollars per minute, or $480 per hour. Although, in whatever way a player may bet, the chances are always in favor of the bank, still the latter's risk varies in proportion to the number of chances which are not filled up. To illustrate: if only ten numbers are filled, and the ball were to enter one of them, the bank would, in that case lose thirty-four dollars, and only win eight; whereas, when all the numbers are filled, it wins four without risking a cent.

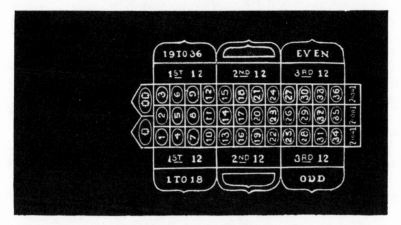

New York Style Roulette Layout.

From what has been said, as to the chances in favor of the bank, it would seem to be hardly necessary to use any addi-

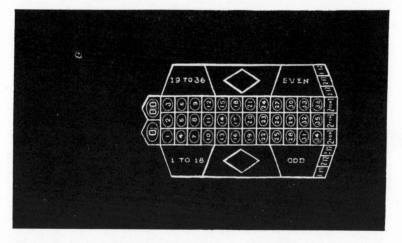

Western Style Roulette Layout.

tional means of swindling, inasmuch as the percentage in its favor is so large that the game is very seldom beaten, even if " played on the square." An old gambler once remarked in my presence, that the percentage of the game was forty per cent. worse than stealing. However, despite this fact, the gambler is not satisfied, and has succeeded in devising schemes, whereby he may win every bet made against him if he sees fit.

The first method of cheating which I will describe, is as follows: The roulette is manufactured for the purpose, the machinery being entirely concealed from view. The gambler who manages the game can cause the ball (A) to fall in a red or black number, as he may think proper. After throwing the ball he watches it closely, and if it should fall in the red, when he wished it to go into the black, while still revolving, its course can be quickly changed to the desired color. This is accomplished by means of a lever attached to the circular wheel, and connecting with one of the legs of the roulette. This leg has the same appearance as others, but is a trifle shorter, not quite touching the table on which the roulette rests. The gambler has only to touch this leg while the wheel is revolving, and in a second the ball is changed from one color to the other, as he may prefer. In fact, so quickly can the ball be changed, that it is difficult to detect the motion after one has been shown how it is managed, unless the wheel is turned slowly. This is one of the most ingenious contrivances in use.

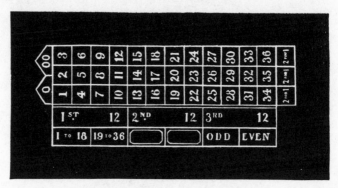

The Latest Improved Layout.

There is yet another kind of roulette, which is made in the following manner: One-half of the small pieces of metal which form the pockets for the ball are made a trifle longer than the others lettered on the diagram E, E, E. After the stakes have been placed, if the proprietor wishes the ball to fall into a red color, it is necessary for him merely to throw the ball around to the right hand, and if he wishes it to fall into the black, he casts the ball toward the left. The players may observe that he throws the ball in a different direction on different occasions, but no suspicion is aroused as the action appears to be so trivial.

Another fraudulent contrivance used in playing this game consists in the gambler having two centers to a wheel, apparently identical, one of which, however, is "square" and the other "faked." This device is known to the members of "the profession" as the "double center." The "square" wheel is used at first, and, at an opportune moment, the "fake" is substituted, after which the sharper has everything his own way. This wheel is operated on very much the same principle as the "needle wheel," for the construction of which the reader is referred to the page containing a description of that device. A system of levers radiating from the center of the apparatus is operated by a rod terminating at the edge of the table. By bringing to bear the requisite pressure, these levers cause fine needle points (lettered C, C, C, on the diagram) to rise through the cloth, one coming up in front of each alternate compartment

Miniature Roulette Wheel.

on the rim, thus obstructing the entry of the ball and causing its course to be so changed that it shall fall into one of the next adjacent divisions, as in the case of the "needle wheel" above referred to.

It is easily perceived that the players can have no possible chance when playing against such roulettes as these, and there is a large number of them in use all over the country.

Electricity is now the popular method of controlling the larger roulette wheels. The electricity is often attached by placing the battery down in the cellar, and running the wire through one of the legs. It in no way affects the outward appearance of the wheel, but, as previously explained, all controlled wheels give the house an enormous advantage over the "sucker." These electrical attachments can be purchased from $50 up.

It is very difficult to detect when a wheel is made crooked by means of the electrical apparatus. Should the reader ever happen to be in a place where a roulette wheel is running, and you have a good pocket compass in your possession, just take and hold it over the wheel when it is running; if the electricity is applied, you will see the needle of the compass swing around. Of course you must hold the compass in such a manner that no one suspects what you are doing.

Within the last few years enormous sums of money have been lost at the gambling houses where the electric wheel is in use. The large cities such as New York, Chicago, San Francisco, etc., have several of these appliances in their gambling houses.

At the notorious Rothstein gambling house in West 46th Street, New York, young Gates lost the sum of $40,000 in one session at roulette and faro, but principally at roulette. During all the various spasms of virtue that has overcome New York, this house has remained open, in spite of the rigid investigations that have been made. A man by the name of Shea was Rothstein's partner at this time. The night Gates visited this house, the two partners made the entertainment so cordial and interesting that before he was ready to depart, and long after the banks were open, he had left his check with Shea, for the sum of $40,000. The gamblers were loath to part with him, but the time comes when "the best of friends must part," even should the "best friend" be the hard cash.

The gamblers being a little suspicious lest their guest should find cause to complain of their hospitality, it was decided that Shea should accompany Gates to the bank where the check was cashed.

Unfortunately for Rothstein, Shea failed to return to the house on 46th Street, deciding it was unnecessary, as he had intended to keep the entire roll for his own personal use.

When Rothstein finally located his former partner, he demanded an explanation and an accounting.

The partners failing to agree caused the whole incident to come to light.

Miniature Book-maker's Roulette Wheel, with Layout.

There are a number of gamblers who feel they have a sort of a roving commission to prey upon the unwary public, at will. It being impossible for them to carry large machinery about with them, for more reasons than one, pocket editions have been ingeniously devised for their accommodation.

These outfits are not toys, but are perfect wheels and fac-similes to the larger wheels. They are used very largely on fair grounds, race tracks, steamers and hotels. The cigar stores and saloons are also introducing these machines, as they are easily handled, and can therefore be put out of sight "when necessary."

The device shown in the illustration on preceding page, can be run in many ways. It may run as roulette, red and black, also as a paddle wheel for raffles. It is claimed to be a great stimulator. Yes, it stimulates the "sucker" to throw away his week's wages upon it.

This wheel is made specially for men on the road. It cannot

The New Book-maker Wheel.

get out of order and has a strong per cent. in favor of the game keeper, and is said to always get a play. The glowing descriptions sent out by the manufacturers would try to lead one to believe that it is the only machine that is sure of getting a play. But then, of course, they say the same about all other machines. It all depends upon the machine a person may be particularly interested in.

It reminds me somewhat of a doctor, who always tried to please his patients. He never failed to ask the patient if he took intoxicating liquors. If the answer was in the affirmative, he would invariably tell them to regulate the quantity; but if the answer was in the negative, he would tell them it was all in their favor, and it would be well for them to let it alone.

The cut shows this wheel as a red and black wheel, also as

a chuck-a-luck wheel, being two distinct and different games in one, and can be run as either game or both.

It is sometimes made as a roulette wheel, or a crap wheel, or as a book-maker's wheel (five horses). Electrical control is also furnished if desired. In fact, the gambler can be accommodated in any way he desires.

This machine is made of aluminum, weighs only six ounces, and is three and a half inches in diameter. At first sight it would

Pocket Roulette Wheel ("Another New One").

appear to the uninitiated a nice little toy. It looks simple, but is not so simple as it looks. Unfortunately, the young boys are usually the victims of this machine. It is the introduction to some bigger game. They play their pocket money against this device, which, of course, they lose, and then wonder where it has all gone to. It is no uncommon thing to see boys who are just entering upon manhood, and who think they are a little too old to be tied to mother's apron strings, hanging around the cigar stands, looking for a little fun. They have contracted the habit of smoking, thinking it necessary to their rising manhood. The man behind the cigar stand will often find an opportunity to introduce such a device as mentioned above. Of course he does not keep it on exhibition on the counter, but introduces it in such a manner as to excite curiosity among the boys. He loses to the boys at first, and this being successful in stimulating their desire to win more, and having won their confidence, he then commences to win for himself. I want the boys of this country to remember that the other fellow is not there for fun, but to steal all he can. If he cannot get the cash by fair means, he will by foul means. I will ask the reader to kindly excuse a little digression here. Although I was a gambler for twenty-five years, much to my present shame and sorrow, I am thankful to say that I have never tasted a drop of intoxicating liquor, or used a piece of tobacco in my life.

This is another crooked device made to catch the unwary. The operator can win at will, absolutely sure. He can either

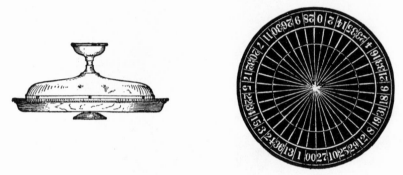

The New Game Round Table Roulette.

bank and win or play against the game and win. It can be made as a "represent joint," that is, a double-up system, which is the quickest way of getting the money.

As a roulette wheel it is played as follows:

1. Each player banks until the ball falls into 0 or 00 (which is the bank's percentage).

2. The bank then passes to the player to the right, and so on until all the players have had a bank.

3. If the one banking should be behind on his bank he has the privilege of continuing.

Rates: 1 number pays 35 for 1; 2 numbers pay 17 for 1; 3 numbers pay 11 for 1; 4 numbers pay 8 for 1; 6 numbers pay 5 for 1; 12 numbers pay 2 for 1.

The dial of the roulette watch is an exact representation of the regulation roulette wheel.

The Watch horse race game consists of eight horses represented on the dial, but there are no jockeys to pull the horses, unless it is the one who operates the game. He has thoroughly learned the art of " fixing " the race.

The Roulette Watch.   Horse Race Game.

These devices are very cunningly contrived, and although small, big money is sometimes put up on the play.

SOCIAL CARD PLAYING: THE KINDERGARTEN TO THE GAMBLING HELL.

Social card playing in the home has been the cause of much misery to hundreds of thousands of souls. The seemingly harmless bit of pasteboard has wrought the destruction and damnation of many precious souls and the ruination of many homes. It is the curse of many churches not only in America, but in almost every civilized country. Civilization does not always dispense with moral evils, but in many instances cultivates them

Charles G. Leland, of England, says: "It is humiliating to reflect that while the Mohammedan religion has successfully repressed gambling, Christianity has witnessed its worst excesses."

One of the greatest arguments used in "society" in favor of card playing is that it "kills time." What an excuse! This surely must be born of the low mind and the watered brain. To kill time—the most precious thing that God has given us—is to defeat the Divine purposes of God. It cannot be classed as recreation, neither can it be called a legitimate game of skill, for the element of chance is so great that success depends almost entirely upon the cards held in the hand. Time spent in this manner cannot be recalled. The regret of many good people is that they have not sufficient time to accomplish all the good their hearts desire, while on the other hand there are multitudes who have no direct purpose in life except it be to gratify their own selfish pleasures.

I have previously stated that out of six boys in my family five of them became professional gamblers. Card playing was freely indulged in. While children are young parents are responsible for their actions. The parent who trains his child in the right paths is greater than he who commands a great army. The home is the most sacred place of all. My father loved his children but never realized the danger in social card playing until it was too late. My mother, at all times, bitterly opposed card playing in our home, or anywhere. Had I never learned to play cards at home I might have lived an honorable life all the way through. Not one of our boys had a profession.

Social card playing soon loses its attractiveness unless some stake is played for. Boys will often be found sneaking off to some quiet spot where they can play penny-ante. It gives zest to the play. This inculcates the desire to obtain money easily and to get it away from the other fellow. If men want to play for stakes they will usually find their way to the poker room. Women will meet in their parlors and indulge freely in bridge-whist, euchre, etc., while their husbands are busily engaged in the battle of life seeking to earn the means of sustenance.

It is unfortunate that many church members indulge in social card playing for prizes. The stakes are sometimes so high that they even stagger professional gamblers. A few years ago the Legislature of the State of Nevada passed a law prohibiting gambling at bridge-whist and poker, under a penalty of six months' imprisonment.

While I was lecturing in Chicago some years ago, a case came under my notice wherein a wealthy widow, who was an active member of the ——— Church, began to play cards in a women's club where the stakes played for were usually pianos, watches, diamonds, etc. On one occasion it was suggested that poker be played instead of bridge-whist. The money was placed on the table and this woman lost $15,000 that same evening.

The pastor of the church employed Matt. W. Pinkerton to investigate. Mr. Pinkerton prevailed upon her to come to one of my lectures on social card playing. After the lecture she came to the platform and invited me to call upon her at her home. When we called upon her she told us that she was satisfied that she had been swindled out of her money, for every time she would hold a good hand it would be beaten. She said it was nice to shuffle cards and win money. "Yes," Mr. Pinkerton said, "but it is not so nice when you lose and become flushed with the excitement and pathetic with the misery of defeat. Then comes bottles of wine. The rest is easily told. Too often, alas, are losses at cards paid with honor." The tears flowed freely over her cheeks. I said to her, "Madam, in Wheeling, West Virginia, a lovely young woman formed the acquaintance of a commercial traveller, who was a gambler. They first met at a social card party. Becoming quite familiar with each other, they were to be seen frequently at whist drives, dances, theatres, and other

forms of amusement. Finally the gambler induced her to go to Chicago. After a few weeks she wrote to her sister to come on to Chicago. In a short time the sisters were walking the streets of Chicago in search of men with full pocket books, while poor old mother and father were at home broken hearted." Before leaving her house the widow signed the anti-gambling pledge, and she later resumed her active work in the church.

There are many women's clubs in existence to-day where the members each pay the small sum of ten cents weekly. This money is devoted to the purchase of prizes, and are played for each week. I have unimpeachable evidence that many of these

women are Sabbath school teachers, church workers, etc. I have before me, while writing this, the notice showing that a certain man (who is a trustee of a certain reform league) and his wife, with others, acted as host and hostess to a military euchre party, where prizes were distributed to the winners.

If we sow cards we shall reap gamblers.

The Rev. W. A. Sunday, the evangelist, has the following to say: "Men who have been spending their funds and lives to ferret these things out tell us that nine-tenths of the gamblers are taught in their homes by their mothers.

"The Chicago Civic Federation which was forced into existence at the close of the World's Fair because after the fair was over Chicago was the Mecca for gamblers, found that out of 3,200 gamblers nine-tenths had learned in their homes, and eight out of ten in the homes of professing Christian parents.

"I tell you it takes a woman with more than ordinary brass to stand up and defend these things.

"A man in Chicago in the Methodist church was going around the country visiting prisons and a woman came to him and said, 'You are going to Auburn penitentiary; will you take this and give it to my son?' She handed him a photograph with her name written on the bottom, with the words: 'With love, Mother.'

"When he reached the prison he saw the young man and handed him the picture and said, 'I saw your mother and she asked me to bring you this picture.' He looked at it and said, 'That is mother. There are wrinkles in her face, not there the last time I saw her.' 'Yes, your mother is aging fast.' The young man said, 'You take that picture back and give it to Mother, and tell her, —— her! I never want to see her. She taught me to play cards and I killed a man at a gambling table, and am serving fifteen years to pay for it. Now she has the audacity to send me her picture after she pushed me behind the prison bars.'

"You will say this is incredible, but it actually occurred.

"I say it may not injure you, but it is damning others.

"They are just as much degenerate black-leg gamblers as the gambler in the gambling hell. They ought to be put in the calaboose with the rest of the gamblers.

"I have just as much respect for the old gambler who will bet his last sou as for the women who will sit around in their homes and play cards for prizes.

"You have no right to find fault with the city officials when they don't suppress gambling when a thing so near akin to it is carried on right in your own home.

"I believe that society as it is constituted to-day is doing more to damn the spiritual life of the church than the grog shops.

"My friends, more people backslide on the social side than on anything else that I can think of.

"A seemingly estimable woman will tear and snort and pout an afternoon, what for? So she can take home a dinky cream pitcher or whisk broom.

"There is nothing so tame as to ask a fellow to play cards for the fun of it.

"It does not make any difference whether it is a penny-ante or a sky limit. So we have progressive euchre, and lots of church members have cards on their tables as often as food, and they are progressing to hell.

" In a town where I was preaching they had all the parties to get them off their hands before I came. They had a big affair and the prize was a $20 cut glass dish, and a woman worked and sweat, and lied and cheated, and took progressions which she didn't win and then she lost the dish by two points.

" She was sick in bed for two days. Now listen! Her boy, a nice bright fellow, came in one morning and kissed her and said, ' Here, ma, here is a $20 gold piece; take that and go down to the jeweler's and get a cut glass dish like that prize. I won this up at Richardson's last night.' She said, ' My boy! I take a $20 gold piece that you won at gambling to buy a cut glass dish?'

" He told her that it was just the same to buy a prize with the $20 won at gambling as to win the prize.

" She said to me afterwards, ' I was just as low down as that man Richardson was, whom I looked at with horror.'

" You are as low down as the gambler.

" But some woman says, ' Mr. Sunday, I am teaching my boy to play cards so that when he grows up he won't have to play cards.'

" I have heard that; but say, why don't you send your daughter to live in a brothel so that she won't want to be a prostitute when she grows up? You are a fool and a jackass to talk that way. Your argument won't hold water three minutes.

" I don't care who you are, there is only one thing to do, and that is to go and throw every card that you have into the furnace and get rid of the thing.

" But fortunately or unfortunately, we are made up of many families. If you are lax in the care of your children, you make it that much harder for me to take care of mine."

I am heartily in accord with what Mr. Sunday has to say on the evils of social card playing. It would be better if the ministers of the Gospel would take a bold stand on the right side of this question.

At the last General Conference of the Methodist Episcopal Church there were quite a number desirous of eliminating the paragraph from the general rules forbidding card playing among its members. When the vote was taken it was found that there was still a majority in favor of retaining it. Should this paragraph ever be eliminated, it will prove the biggest disgrace ever offered that section of the Christian church, and they must lose all legal claim to the name of " Methodist." It is none of the business of the church to make the teachings of Jesus Christ conform to the desires of the flesh, but to endeavor to win the world so that it will conform to the teachings of Jesus Christ.

At a recent social gathering in the parlors of one of the " élite," after the card games had been dispensed with, the hostess handed round a concoction known as grape-juice. When the ladies (?) left for their homes it was discovered that although they were all in a hilarious mood they had great difficulty in getting there. This occurrence was only one of many.

Rev. C. W. Recard, pastor, United Brethren Church, Canton, Ohio, in describing gambling as the " cancer crime of Canton," said, " Gambling is the bottomless pit among the slime holes and its mouth is open in Canton. The city is known among the good and wise to the ends of the earth as the home of Mc-Kinley. It is also known in a great circle of shysters whose fingers are always pointing to the purses of others. To these it is known as a safe retreat and a fat pasture. Gambling is the pit from which many other contagions spread and to stop it the place to begin is in the church. There is now a prevalent contagion among nominal Christian people for cards. I serve notice upon the members of the gentler sex that in the present crusade of the iconoclasts not only their wares but their reputations may go to smash. At a recent card party a woman who had won almost

REV. C. W. RECARD D.D.

a whole set of china lost the last piece through the cheating of another woman and became so angry that she remained awake all night thinking about it. To fill the slime pits and drive away the diggers we must go to work in the house of God."

Every leader in social and moral reform looks upon the card table as the starting place for the gambler's hell. Parlor games for money or prizes has proved the moral hell-place to thousands of precious souls. To this, weeping wives and broken-hearted mothers can bitterly testify. Let anyone, if they dare, who possesses just one spark of Christianity, before going into a game for a prize kneel down and say, " Blessed Jesus, my Saviour, who is able and willing to keep our hearts from all sin, gambling, drinking, licentiousness, covetousness, and defrauding or oppressing our neighbor, please give me the winning hand, for Christ's sake, Amen."

If fathers and mothers who are indulging their children in gambling at home, knew the wail of hopeless misery which has been sounded upon my ear during the last twenty-six years, this subject would appeal to them as being one of the most serious. If the names of all the young people who have been ruined by social card playing were written upon cards, thousands of packs would be signed across with the blood-stained autographs of doomed souls.

Professing Christians; God pity them who make of the painted paste-board a social snare in their homes to lure their precious boys to the fatal slaughter-house where they murder souls. Hell's utmost anguish surely has no deeper depths than that of the father and mother who see their sons degraded sodden gamesters, and remember that they taught them to handle the implements of their ruin in their own homes.

6

THE UPWARD WAY.

1. The illustration here shows the young man being raised in a pious home. The father is in the attitude of reading, seeking to obtain knowledge and improve the intellect, and so become useful members of society.

2. The Church has a place in the young man's life. He must be devout in his attitude toward God as well as being just in his attitude toward his fellowmen.

3. Healthy recreation is good for both mind and body. Physical fitness is necessary to success and happiness in life. Legitimate pleasure was never intended to be denied us by God.

4. The first work given man was to till the soil. Do not be too anxious to leave the pure air of the country to seek the foul atmosphere of the city. Honest toil is commendable to all. Do not try to live by your wits.

5. In the eventide of life if you have followed a straight course and not abused nature, you may have the good-will of your fellowmen and the satisfaction of peace with God. Your home will be a place of love and joy.

THE DOWNWARD WAY.

1. In this home social card playing takes a predominant place. It is the kindergarten for the gambling house and hell. It is the serpent that trails you all through life.

2. The young man having commenced dissipation at home, he goes further afield and seeks pleasure in the saloon. He plays cards for drinks, probably the first time he ever played for a stake.

3. From the saloon he is enticed into the gambling house. In connection with this he will soon take to other forms of vice, each more vicious than the last, until he becomes a complete physical wreck.

4. To regain his losses at the gaming table he will often resort to some form of crime against his fellowmen and—God. In prison he is left to "think upon his ways."

5. The time comes when he may again be thrown upon the world. Without home, love and joy, he seeks a livelihood at the back doors by taking odd jobs of sawing wood. He might have been a respectable member of society, but,—

GAMBLING AT WIESBADEN.

When gambling was in the ascendant at Wiesbaden, society there was in a very mixed and deplorable state. The fast were in full possession, almost, and respectable women dare not take a stroll in the grounds outside the Cure Hall. When gambling, with "hideous mein," stalked through this fair scene, the aged, broken down courtesans of Paris, Vienna and Berlin made Wiesbaden their autumn rendezvous.

In all the world cannot be found an inland watering place so charming as Baden. The climate is invigorating, from every point of view, exceedingly beautiful. Situated on the confines of the "Black Forest," in the beautiful valley Olebach, and surrounded by green and graceful hills, Baden resembles both Heidelberg and Freiburg, but is more lovely than either.

The gambling rooms at Baden usually had six roulette and rouge-et-noir (trente-et-quarante) tables running. The games opened daily at eleven o'clock in the morning, and ran continuously until eleven o'clock at night. The place was almost as public as the street. Everybody went in or out, played or refrained from playing, as he pleased. No attaché of the establishment was ever known to ask any one, even in the most indirect manner, to take part in the game.

The Directors paid a license of $75,000 a year and paid out as much more for the running expenses of the establishment, yet reaped immense profit. The season extended from May until October and was at its height from the middle of July until the first of September.

A traveller, visiting the Cure Hall, witnessed the following:

"Almost immediately on our entrance our attention was attracted to a young Englishman, fashionably dressed, but yet of such rakish and sinister aspect that I set him down at once as a black-leg who had figured at Epsom or Newmarket; a London roué, who, having lost character and means at home, now formed one of that base band of English sharpers who are to be found on the continent, and who initiate our young bloods into the mysteries of the gambling tables, or fleece them at private gaming parties. In eager excitement this person pressed through the crowd, and, bending over the table, repeatedly deposited a handful of silver florins, until nearly every yellow line or space had a stake place upon it. It seemed as if he had set his life upon the cast and was resolved to take the bank by storm. Within a few minutes, however, his entire cash was lost, and as the croupiers remorselessly gathered it in with their little rakes, he turned abruptly away.

"But whose are the small gloved hands and rounded arms which, just at my left, are suddenly thrust forward to obtain silver for the Napoleon d'or which she gives to the markers? I look around and see an elegantly dressed French lady standing at my side. She cautiously deposits one or two florins on the

Gambling Saloon at Wiesbaden.

board, and with subdued excitement watches the progress of the game. At length the silver pieces are all staked and lost. Now, with gloved hand, she unfastens the string of her purse and other gold is produced and changed, until all is gone, and she, too, suddenly disappears.

"The game has progressed but a few minutes when our countryman returns and proceeds as before, with the same result, and then disappears again. Now, here is also the French lady again, with her silk purse containing gold pieces, and playing with greater excitement than ever; but after some winnings, she, too, loses all.

"Yonder stands a tall, thin lady, who seeks the table on

which small sums can be played. See how anxiously she glances over the table, and how cautiously she deposits her little sum. Once or twice she wins, and her pale cheeks become flushed, and her eyes kindle; but in a short time it is all gone, and then, leaving the place, she retires to one of those garden chairs sitting apart from the rest of the people, her cheeks more wasted, her eyes duller, apparently broken-hearted, as if the thought of her confiding husband and little ones far away oppressed her spirit. But look again and you will see another lady with a younger lady by her side. It is her daughter, and she is ini-

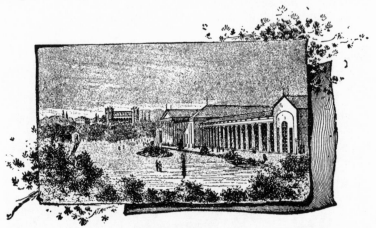

The Kursaal at Wiesbaden.

tiating her into the mysteries of gambling. Who would like to marry such a woman, thus trained into the mysteries of such a game as this?

"A man now enters the room. His dress and person are neglected, his face is unwashed, his long and curly hair falls wildly over his forehead, seamed and furrowed with deep wrinkles. A little girl is by his side. She, too, is miserably dressed, and his rank seems to be that of a peasant. He is an inveterate gambler and cannot do without his excitement. He takes a seat at the foot of the table, deposits a florin from time to time, and carefully examines a small marked card on which is marked the result of each revolution of the deal. For a time familiarity with the game seems to give him an advantage, and with a calm satisfaction he rakes in his winnings in a heap, on which the little girl bends her glistening eyes. And there he sits until the evening closes, when he departs, having passed an evening of feverish excitement and lost all. The face of that gambler and the little girl, who was always with him and who seemed as if she were the only one left of a ship-wrecked and ruined family, haunt me to this hour.

"At rouge-et-noir is a more select class than is generally found playing at roulette. English, French, Germans, Russians, and Poles, and the fire of mammon always burning on his altars and the doomed flies buzzing about them, some with already scorched-off wings; it is a scene of external gaiety with all that is internally hollow and deceiving.

"The lights are burning brightly overhead, the players nearly all seated, and a large number of people forming an outer circle.

"Here are two gentlemen who are bold players. They never stake silver. A pile of Napoleons lies at the side of each. One player is about sixty years of age, tall and robust; the other a little, dark-haired, black-eyed man, and both appear to be habitués of the place. Three gold pieces formed the first stake, and the player winning, the same was doubled. Five more Napoleons are won.

"At this moment one of the proprietors can be seen talking with some friends nonchalantly, and apparently uninterested in the game, in the background; but if you will watch him carefully, you can see that he ever and anon casts a searching glance toward the table, for this evening the game is going against the bank. But soon caution on the part of the player is gone, and golden visions beckon onward. One of the gentlemen leaves ten gold pieces on the cloth, another turn and all is gone.

"It is here that an Englishman played one night until he lost $940,000, and announced his determination to win back or to lose everything; but he was doomed to drink, and justly too, the cup of bitterness; he lost everything."

Mrs. Trollope has thus described two specimens of the gamestresses, who were wont to frequent the German watering places:

"There was one of this set," she says, "whom I watched day after day, during the whole period of our stay, with more interest than I believe was reasonable; for had I studied any other as attentively, I might have found less to lament.

"She was young, certainly not more than twenty-five, and

though not regularly nor brilliantly handsome, most singularly winning, both in person and demeanor. Her countenance was expressive of anxious thoughtfulness. She was constantly to be found at the rouge-et-noir table.

"Her husband, who had as unquestionably the air of a gentleman, as she had of a lady, though not always close to her, was never very distant. He did not play himself, and I fancied, as he hovered near her, that his countenance expressed anxiety. But he returned her sweet smile, with which she always met his eye, with an answering smile; and I saw not the slightest indication that he wished her to withdraw from the table.

"There was an expression in the upper part of her face that my blundering science would have construed into something very foreign to the propensity she showed; but there she sat— hour after hour, day after day, not allowing even the blessed Sabbath, that gives rest to all, to bring it to her;—there she sat, constantly throwing down half-franc pieces, and sometimes drawing them back again, till her young face grew rigid with weariness, and all the lustre of her eye faded into a glare of vexed inanity. Alas! alas! is that fair woman a mother?

"Another figure at the gaming table, which daily drew our attention, was a pale, anxious old woman, who seemed no longer to have strength to conceal her agitation under the air of callous indifference which all practiced players endeavor to assume. She trembled, till her shaking hand could hardly grasp the instrument with which she pushed, or withdrew her pieces; the dew of agony stood upon her wrinkled brow; yet, hour after hour, day after day, she too, sat in the enchanted chair. I never saw age and station in a position so utterly beyond the pale of respect. I was assured she was a person of rank; and my informant added, but I trust she was mistaken, that she was an Englishwoman."

WHEEL OF FORTUNE OR CHUCK-A-LUCK.

This is the name given to a gambling device which has been a favorite with the "fraternity" for many years, and which has never failed to prove a sure bait to trap the unwary and an unfailing source of rich income to its manipulators.

It is made with or without a "fake" attachment, its general appearance in either case being the same. The nature of the "fake" and its mode of operation will be explained on the following page; the construction of the wheel will be first described.

It is a handsome apparatus, standing about seven feet high. The wheel itself is usually about four feet in diameter, and rests upon a tripod three feet in height. Inside the rim of the wheel is a twelve-pointed star, between each two points of which are inscribed either five or six numbers, the figures being painted on the rim and running one to sixty or seventy-two, consecutively. The wheel and star revolve simultaneously around a common axis. At the top of the wheel is an arrow, pointing downward, which serves as an indicator.

Around the wheel is a wooden frame which is covered with cloths on which, when the seventy-two number wheel is used, are painted the numbers one to six, or on which are arranged paddles, each one of which is marked with either one or six numbers, the uses of which will be described later.

The wheel is used either as an adjunct to a scheme for the distribution of cheap prizes or as a means of making bets. The former plan is the one generally adopted at small fairs, when a "lay-out" of inexpensive queen's or glassware is spread upon the table, each article, or lot, bearing its own number. In this case, the manipulation of the wheel is sometimes conducted fairly, the legitimate odds in favor of the proprietor being sufficient to justify him in giving the dupes some sort of a chance.

Where the game is played for prizes, the common practice is to use the paddles above referred to, each inscribed with six numbers, the twelve paddles embracing the range from one to seventy-two. Each person wishing to take a chance pays for a paddle (usually five or ten cents), and when all possible have been sold, the wheel is set in motion. When it comes to rest, the indicator at the top points to a number, and the holder of the paddle bearing the corresponding number has it at his option either to take the prize or a sum in money.

The most profitable form of the wheel, however, is that which is sometimes designated as the "six number wheel" or the "big six," so called because the spaces between the points of the star are each numbered from one to six. When this device is operated, the frame is sometimes covered with oilcloths, each containing six squares, numbered from one to six. Sometimes six paddles, each bearing a separate number (running from one to six) are employed besides the cloths; and not infrequently a double set of paddles, similarly numbered,

In the latter case, the players place their stakes on some

one or more numbers upon the cloth. The paddles are used when the crowd is too great to be accommodated at the cloths. When the wagers have all been placed, the wheel is set in motion. Breathlessly the players await the result. When it ceases

Big Six.

to revolve, the indicator at the top points to some number. The player who has staked his money upon that number has it returned to him, increased by four.

As a matter of fact, however, when the wheel comes to rest it is usually discovered that no heavy player has been fortunate enough to make just that bet. The reason is simple. The reader who will carefully examine the accompanying cut will perceive the representation of a rod running through the upright support of the wheel and one of the legs of the tripod, thence turning to the right and terminating under a plank in the floor, directly below the operator's foot. By simply pressing on this mechanism, the latter checks the motion of the wheel by application of friction at the pivot, and brings it to a standstill at any point which he may desire.

The rod which you see in the illustration, is of the latest construction, and represents an electric attachment. This makes it possible to operate by other means than the foot. To show that it is considered to be of great value in getting the money, the reader may be interested to know that the price of this little piece of mechanism is $100.

Not always, however, is the proprietor of the wheel the only sharper on the ground. Unless he is very careful, he sometimes discovers, when it is too late, that he has been playing a game of " diamond cut diamond." His apparatus fails to work as he had expected, and when he realizes his percentage has not reached up to his expectations, he carefully examines his wheel, and learns that some more astute scoundrel than himself has plugged some point on the circumference with lead, bringing it to rest by the simple but sure operation of the law of gravitation.

Sometimes, instead of the numbers above referred to, there are used certain printed inscriptions, representing speculative articles dealt in on the floors of the stock and produce exchanges, such as pork, lard, corn, oats, rye, barley, seeds, and various kinds of corporation stocks. This form of the device is ordinarily known as the " Board of Trade Wheel," and is sometimes found to be very popular in rural districts.

The paddle wheel is very popular at carnivals, picnics, fairs, turkey raffles, saloons and church fairs. It is simple in construction, and small in price. Possibly the simplicity of the device makes it the more dangerous. At the fairs you will find girls handing out the paddles and urging women and children to buy a paddle for five cents. It is a shame that county and city officials should tolerate and allow these devices to run. If the duly elected officials have no respect for the laws which they have sworn to enforce, how can they expect to have law-abiding citizens in their communities? If a murder is committed there is a great outcry against such an outrageous crime, and efforts are generally made to capture the perpetrator of such an act.

But if we condemn the police officials for not acting and pushing the law against the gamblers, what shall we say against those churches that not only tolerate such a condition, but actually use these devices at their fairs? Chief of Police Smith,

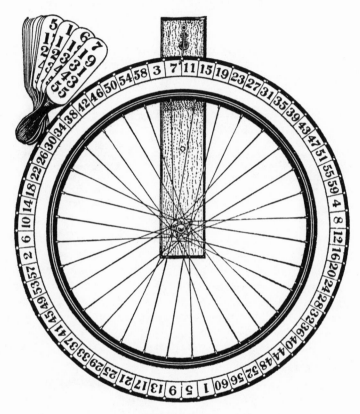

Paddle Wheel.

Canton, Ohio, once asked the question, " when have the churches stopped their gambling? " This is probably what he had reference to.

We are, unfortunately, living in an age when men are not guided so much by principle, as they are to get the best of their neighbor. It is useless to sing hymns and psalms where this form of gambling is allowed in the church, for it is a direct violation of the commandment " Thou shalt not steal;" and if we violate one of the commandments we are guilty of all.

MONTE CARLO POOL.

" The wise saloon man takes hold of good games and novelties as they come out and he is the one who gets the business."

The above is a quotation from the game-keeper's catalogue to induce saloon men and others to invest in this game. The description as given by them is better than any that could be substituted, and is as follows:

" The Monte Carlo outfit consists of one composition ball, white, one handsome enamel layout with three colors on it, red,

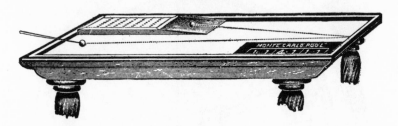

white and blue. One Monte Carlo Board; the board contains 38 holes—16 red, 16 white and 6 blue; even money being paid on the white or red and 4 to 1 on the blue, which makes this one of the strongest per cent. games ever invented. We have customers who win from $50 to $500 every Saturday night with one of these boards. The game is also run on the commission basis; each one of the holes are numbered from 1 to 38, the game-keeper selling numbered balls at ten cents each, then banks the cue ball against the end rail, which returns it up the incline of the board, and finally settles in one of the holes, the player having the numbered ball to match the number on the board, or the nearest to it, receives the purse, less the commissions deducted by the house for running the game; or, if you are not allowed to gamble, you can use it as a trade game, each player shooting six times and adding the sum total of the numbers of the holes he puts the ball in, the low man having to buy the drinks."

It will be perceived that either way the game is played it cannot be anything else but gambling.

THE STOCK EXCHANGE.

The idea of a commercial exchange germinated in the United States before the war of the American Revolution. Here, as in Europe, the basis of every mercantile exchange is a voluntary union of business men, who deem it for their mutual interest regularly to assemble in some convenient locality for the purpose of effecting the sale of commodities or securities, and of profiting by the fluctuations in market prices. Stock exchanges, produce exchanges, chambers of commerce and boards of trade are all essentially identical in character, the principal point of difference being the nature of the commodities bought and sold.

As an institution, the commercial exchange has been productive of some good, but much harm. If restricted in its scope to the legitimate purposes of commerce, it is unquestionably of the highest benefit to the business world. When its operations are diverted into illegitimate channels it becomes a source of incalculable injury to society. As a great market place, it plays an important part in modern civilization; as a gigantic agency for the promotion of gambling in the commodities of the world, it is a snare, a delusion and a curse.

Not all the gambling hells of the country combined afford facilities for gambling equal to those furnished by these organizations. The faro dealer places a limit upon the stakes wagered; upon the floor of 'Change one may bet without limit. Not everyone can obtain admittance to the gilded *salon* of the tiger; the commission merchant, or broker, who does business upon the Stock Exchange or Board of Trade accepts orders from all comers. The character of the transactions in which his principals engage is to him a matter of indifference, his interest being centered in their frequency and extent.

Members of these bodies may be classified on any one of several general principles. One system of classification has relation to the character of their operations; in other words, all members may be divided into two classes, the first comprising those who venture on their own account (popularly known as " speculators "), and the second embracing those who buy or sell only on the receipt of orders from outsiders (i. e., brokers). Un-

der another system, members may be classified as those who wish
to enhance the prices of commodities on the one hand, and those
who, on the other, seek to depress the market quotations. The
former are technically known as "bulls," and the latter as
"bears." These sobriquets are derived from the well known pro-
pensities of the two descriptions of animals, and one to hoist and
the other to pull down. The distinction between "longs" and
"shorts" is substantially of the same nature. A "long" is a
speculator who, believing that the price of a certain commodity
is destined to advance, buys freely in anticipation of a rise. It
follows that he is naturally, if not inherently, a "bull." On the
other hand, a "short," judging that the quotations are destined
to decline, sells wherever he can find a purchaser. He, naturally,
is a "bear." It must not be forgotten, however, that neither of
these parties for a moment actually expects either to receive or
deliver the articles which he buys or sells; and the reason for
this apparently inconsistent statement will be explained later.

With these few prefatory words of explanation, we will pur-
sue the course of the speculator, after which will be given a definition of the slang terms used.

And first, as to the speculator: He may fall within either
one of two categories—the professional or the occasional. Yet
even under the general caption of professional speculators, operators may be divided into two classes. One embraces men
whose large wealth enables them to contrive and engineer what
is popularly known as a "corner;" the other includes those who
follow in their wake, believing that they can discern their intentions, and laying the flattering delusion to their souls that they
can presage the course of prices. The professional speculator, as
being the "larger fish," should first claim our notice. He it is
who originates for any given commodity to a point far beyond
their legitimate value, with a view to enriching the few at the
expense of the many. Men of this stamp ordinarily associate
with themselves kindred spirits, whose natural bent is the same
as their own, and whose capital may prove of value in carrying
out their schemes. The combination having been formed, the
first objective point is the selection of some commodity or stock
to "corner." The choice having been made, the next step is,
quietly and unostentatiously to buy all of it that can be purchased. Let not the unsophisticated reader for a moment suppose, however, that the syndicate thus formed proposes to buy

the article in question at current rates. Far otherwise. Prices must be depressed, and there is an obvious way in which to effect this result. Every market in the world is supposed to be governed by the normal relations between supply and demand. It follows that free offerings of any commodity are likely to reduce its quotable value. What, then, are the tactics of the " operator?" Evidently to offer to sell freely. Under the influence of the precipitation of large lots, prices recede, and the speculator is shrewd enough to purchase " at the bottom of the market." Of course he does not expose his policy by buying such enormous quantities in his own name. He has recourse to firms doing a strictly commission business, of whom he employs a multiplicity, and who always refuse to disclose the name of their principal—not from any high sense of honor, but from motives of self-interest, for the simple reason that such exposure would result in a pre-emptory withdrawal of business. Having secured the desired quantity of stock or commodity selected, the clique proceeds to advance the price, not abruptly but gradually, selling a little here and buying a little there, the object being the mystification of the miscellaneous dealers. At last comes what is known as the " squeeze." The cabal having all, or at least the great preponderance, of the article where they can, if they choose, call for its immediate delivery, refuse to entertain any offers at less than the limit fixed. The consequence is, that the " shorts "—i. e., the men who have sold to the syndicate—are compelled to settle at the price to which the coalition has forced quotations. The method of operation can be best illustrated by a suppositious case. Let us suppose—simply by way of illustration—that a coterie of dealers in grain resolve to force up the price of wheat, although not to localize the illustration we might assume the formation of a " corner " on some one of the numerous stock exchanges with which the country is blessed (?) or cursed. But let us take the Chicago Board of Trade, with whose methods the author is most familiar: Let us suppose the article to be " cornered " is " July wheat," and that the combination has been formed in March. Resort is had to the tactics above explained. Wheat for July delivery is first depressed, then bought, and in the end sold without regard to its inherent value, but solely with a view to what the " shorts " may be forced to pay. The profits of such " corners," thus constructed, are sometimes enormous. Yet, as in the game of faro, the most expert

dealer is sometimes put to heavy loss by the combination which
is playing against the bank; so even the machinations of the
strongest and shrewdest operators are brought to nought either
by a combination of brighter minds, by a failure to carefully
guard every weak spot, or, it may be, by very chance. The same
elements are present in both games, faro and stock-jobbing.
These corners are conceived in cupidity, carried on in deceit, and
consummated in heartlessness; yet there are not wanting those
who affirm that the commercial exchange is the very prop and
bulwark of American commerce! That the exchange, in its legitimate scope, affords an easy and safe way of doing business,
cannot be denied; that its practical operation is to foster speculation and encourage reckless gambling is equally indisputable.

This assertion seems, on its face, perhaps, ill-considered, yet
it is abundantly justified by facts. We have, thus far, considered
only the tactics of the professional " operator." Let us, for a
moment, consider the fortune (or misfortune) that awaits the
occasional speculator. The latter closely resembles the man who
plunges headlong into the Niagara rapids without even a rudi-
mentary knowledge of the art of swimming. Like a chip, he
sports upon the crest of the eddying waters of the whirlpool,
until, gradually drawn nearer and nearer to the center, he is
sucked into its very vortex, sinking to reappear no more. Yet
this comparison is weak. The outside speculator who fancies
that he can buy or sell on " pointers " (private information)
given him by parties well-posted, very nearly approaches an
idiot in the matter of intelligence. Let us take, as a single illustration, a case which fell under the author's personal observation. The experience of the victim (whom we will call Jones) is
by no means exceptional. " Mr. Jones " was advised by a
friend (?) that " old Higgenbotham " had bought up all of a
certain article and that within sixty days prices were destined
materially to appreciate. Naturally " Mr. Jones " found his
interest, as well as his cupidity stimulated. What would his
friend recommend him to do? " Buy, of course, and buy heavily," was the answer. " But I don't know how to buy," objected
Jones. " Why," replied his advisor, " that's the easiest thing in
the world, Q X & Z, one of the best houses in the street, are
particular friends of mine. Take my card and go down and see
them. They'll use you right." The unfortunate " Jones " listened to the siren song. He interviewed Q X & Z, by whom he

was received with distinguished consideration. The firm of brokers explains to him how he could, by depositing with them a "margin" of five per cent. on the par value of his prospective purchase, become the putative owner of twenty times the amount of his deposit. Of course he must buy for future delivery, this not being a cash transaction. But there was no doubt that prices would advance. Oh, certainly not.

"Mr. Jones" was naturally a little timorous, being unaccustomed to speculation. He advanced a few hundred dollars, however, by way of "margins," and at the conclusion of the "deal" found himself winner by a handsome sum. His experience was a revelation to him. He ventured again and again, with varying success. Finally he found himself heavily interested on the wrong side of the market. He was assured that prices must necessarily take a turn, and he could ill afford the sum already risked.

When the day of settlement arrived, the bubble burst and the unfortunate man found himself buried fathoms deep in dishonor and ruin. Not only was he penniless, but he realized that wherever he went the finger of scorn pointed out his every step. A temperate man before, he plunged headlong into dissipation. His wife found herself compelled to leave him, and to-day, stripped of fortune, bereft of family, deserted by friends, he walks the streets with faltering tread, aimlessly and hopelessly; hanging about bucket-shops and pool-rooms, considering that a fortunate day on which, honestly or dishonestly, he can earn half a dollar.

Better, far better, were it for the man who enters a gaming resort that his first wager prove unsuccessful; far happier would he be who determines to "speculate in futures" did his first venture result in heavy loss. In either case the influence of failure would prove a deterrent sufficiently powerful to avert years of future misery, if not ultimate destruction.

The technical nomenclature of the exchange—sometimes termed the "slang of the street"—which, as has been remarked, is incomprehensible to the uninitiated, in itself affords some key to the nature of the business transacted. Some of the most common terms are here defined, although to enumerate them all would swell the number of these pages considerably.

A "scalper" is an operator who makes it his practice to close his transactions as soon as he can see a small profit, say

a quarter of one cent. His operations are neither more nor
less than betting on a rise or fall in prices.

The " guerilla " is a species of the genus " scalper," few in
number, and makes a specialty of dealing in stocks and commodities. So unsavory is the reputation of this class that it has
fixed the appellation of " Hell's Kitchen " and " Robber's Roost "
upon certain localities in the New York Stock Exchange.

Still another class is composed of those who strive to enrich
themselves by the fictitious rise and fall of a particular stock in
which they constantly deal.

" Forcing quotations " is keeping up prices by any means
whatever. When this is accomplished by the dissemination of
fictitious news or the circulation of unfounded rumors, the operator is said to " balloon " prices.

A speculator is said to " take a flyer " when he engages in
some side venture; he " flies kites " when he expands operations injudiciously; he " holds the market " when he prevents a
decline in prices by buying heavily; he " milks the street " when
he manipulates so skilfully that they rise or fall at his pleasure;
he " unloads " when he sells the particular stock or commodity
of which he is " long;" he " spills stock " when he offers large
quantities with a view to lowering or " breaking " prices; if he
is successful in these tactics he is said to " saddle the market."

A " bear " is said to be " gunning " a stock when he employs
all his energy and craft to " break " its price. He " covers," or
" covers his shorts," when he buys to fulfill his contracts. He
" sells out " a man by forcing prices down so that the latter is
obliged to relinquish what he is " carrying," perhaps to fail.

The nature of a " corner " has already been set forth in detail. The operator or clique organizing and managing it is said
to " run " it. The day when final settlement must be made between the opposing parties engaged in such a transaction is
termed " settling day." If the " bears " are forced to settle at
unusually high prices they are said to be " squeezed." The
" squeeze " which has followed many a corner has precipitated
many a wealthy man into financial ruin. This circumstance,
however, is usually a matter of utter indifference to the manipulators. The success of a " corner " is sometimes prevented by
what is known as a " squeal," or revelation of the secrets of the
pool or clique by one of its members. Sometimes the plans of
the organizers of a " corner " are brought to naught by a "leak "

in the pool, that is, by one of the members secretly selling out his holdings. Of course, a "corner" can be formed only on what is known as a "future," or future delivery, by which is meant the sale and purchase of some stock or commodity to be delivered at some period in the future.

Yet another form of gambling very common upon the floors of stock and commercial exchanges is known as dealing in "puts," "calls" and "straddles." When a person buys a "put," he pays a stipulated sum for the privilege of selling to the party to whom it is paid, a certain quantity of some particular stock or other article, within a fixed time, at a designated price. Thus A might pay to B one hundred dollars for the privilege of selling him one hundred shares of Union Pacific stock at a stipulated price, within ten days. As a matter of course, the price named is always a little below the current quotation ruling at the time the quotation is made, that is, the day upon which the "put" is bought. If, for instance, the "put" is sold at eighty cents on that day, and the market declines to seventy-five, A might tender to B the one hundred shares, and the latter would be compelled to take them at the price. In such a case A would have gained five dollars per share, or five hundred dollars in all, provided he had "covered his shorts," that is, bought in the stock which he had already put, at the latter figure. As a matter of fact, neither party contemplated an actual delivery. The market having declined, A's net gain is, of course, only four hundred dollars, he having already paid one hundred dollars to B. This appears an easy method of winning money. As a matter of fact, however, experience has shown that very few men win through the purchase of "puts" and "calls."

A "call" is similar in its general nature to a "put," but differs from it in that the buyer of the former has the privilege of calling or buying a certain quantity, under the same conditions. The seller of the "put" contracts to buy, and of the "call" to sell, whenever the demand is made.

A "straddle" is a combination of the "put" and the "call," and is the option of either buying or selling. The cost of these "puts," "calls," and "straddles," which are known as "privileges," varies from one to five per cent. of the par value of the stock, or the market value of the commodity involved, and depends upon the time they have to run, the range covered, and the activity and sensitiveness of the market.

It is claimed in behalf of these privileges that they are, in their essence, really contracts of insurance, and as such are entirely legitimate. The general public, however, has always regarded them as a complex system of betting, and believes that they constitute one of the most pernicious features of the exchange. That they do not tend to promote commerce is shown by the fact that neither party to the transaction for a moment contemplates the actual delivery of the article bought or sold. It is essentially a wager between two individuals as to the future course of the market, one betting that prices will advance, and the other that they will decline.

Reference has been made to the very common practice of attempting to "bull" or "bear" quotations by buying or selling large quantities, or "blocks" of some particular article. There is probably no description of market in the world so extremely sensitive as the commercial exchange. A sale or purchase of any given commodity by certain, well-known operators, is often sufficient to excite its pulse to fever heat. A similar result may ensue from a report that the Secretary of the Treasury contemplates a call of a certain number of bonds; that there was a talk of war between this country and Japan; that a norther in Texas had killed a herd of cattle; that a few grasshoppers had been seen in the neighborhood of Fargo; or that the mercury was believed to be about to fall in Northern Minnesota. The great speculators, the master minds of these gigantic institutions, are quick to perceive this sensitiveness, and equally prompt to avail themselves of it. Fictitious news is as potent an agency in advancing or depressing prices as is the genuine article, and it is a sad truth that there are not wanting large operators who do not scruple to employ it. It is said—and there is good reason to believe the statement to be true—that there are men of all great commercial centers whose only occupation is the dissemination of unfounded reports, with a view of raising or lowering the prices of certain commodities in regard to which the rise or fall of a fraction of a cent may mean the gain or loss of millions. These manufacturers of fictitious news are said to "wear purple and fine linen and fare sumptuously every day." The results of their operations are to be found in the wrecking of important financial and corporate interests and the corresponding enrichment of the unprincipled manipulators who employ them.

Some years ago, there came a mysterious rumor to the New York Stock Exchange, that the directors of a certain railroad in the Northwest had decided upon taking a step which could not fail to prove disastrous in the extreme to the interests of the corporation. No one was able to tell just where the rumor originated, yet it found sufficient credence to depress the price of the road's stock, and to induce free selling. The next day came the refutation of the story; the stock recovered its tone, and the clique in whose interest the lie had been sent over the wires reaped a profit of $60,000. In the slang of Wall Street this was called a "plum." It is difficult to see the difference in moral turpitude between such tactics as these and "steering" for a "brace" faro bank.

And yet there are not wanting those who affirm, and stoutly maintain, that without the commercial exchange, business would be brought to a stand-still, and commerce paralyzed; that Boards of Trade and Produce and Stock Exchanges are prime factors in advancing the welfare of the country. And this is said despite the fact that the percentage of legitimate business done is utterly insignificant in comparison with that which is purely speculative in its character. The sales of one agricultural product alone upon the floor of a single mart of this sort for one month alone have been known to equal the production of the entire country for a whole year! Is this legitimate commerce, or is it gambling on the wildest and most extensive scale? Members of various Boards in the United States who assume to do a strictly legitimate business, sent out circulars through the rural districts, the sole object of which is to induce the recipients to speculate upon the floor of 'Change. These communications depict, in glowing terms, the ease and certainty with which ignorant countrymen may acquire fortunes in a day, through the purchase of a "put" or "call" or a "straddle." They purport to explain, fully and clearly, the methods of speculating in stocks and grain, and represent the system as simple and easily comprehensible, while the authors know that the system is in itself complex and the issue a venture—at the very best—uncertain. It is not pretended that the transaction contemplates an actual transfer of the commodity from seller to buyer. Is this frank? Is it manly? Is it honest? Is the fifty per cent. reduction sale and cut-rate drug store as deceptive?

As regards the "principles of justice and equity in trade"

which are "inculcated" by commercial exchanges generally, nothing more need be said. Were the transactions on their floors confined to actual sales at prices influenced only by legitimate means and natural causes, there can be little doubt that they would prove potent factors in the furtherance of commerce and advancements of its best interests. It is not in this aspect that the author is considering them. His reprehension of their practices is predicated upon the other, and broader side of their character, i. e., their speculative side. It can scarcely be called an open question whether it "inculcates principles of justice and equity in trade" for one man to buy up all the wheat in sight (and out of sight too, for that matter) and then force an alleged buyer, but an actual rival whom he has done his best to mislead, to settle with him at a price exceeding by 100 to 150 per cent. the actual value of the commodity.

But it is the "object" last mentioned—the "dissemination of valuable commercial and economic information"—concerning which the exchange in question has taken such a peculiar position. Originally, the "information" at its command, whether "valuable" or otherwise, was "disseminated" with the automatic regularity of clock work. Whether this dissemination was undertaken for the benefit of the public at large, or from motives purely selfish is immaterial in this connection, although the "object" may be, perhaps, inferred from the course of the directors. It was found that places far less pretentious were being opened and were doing a thriving business. Within the shadow of the great tower sprang up an "Open Board," which attracted speculators who might otherwise have conducted their operations through the channels opened by the more august body. Moreover "bucket-shops" (the pernicious character of whose methods will be explained hereafter) multiplied and flourished. The quotations of the regular exchange were as the "vital air" to the smaller concerns. "Withdraw our quotations," said the directors, "and all competition will come to naught." A wrangle ensued, followed by litigation in the courts, resulting in the triumph of the more renowned body, the " genuine, old, original Jacobs." In other words, the "dissemination of valuable commercial and economic information," came to an abrupt and untimely end, and one of the "objects of the organization, announced to the world with gravity, parade and rhetorical flourish, failed of accomplishment.

> Alas for the rarity
> Of Christian charity
> Under the sun.

And alas, too, for the sincerity and consistency of poor, weak human nature.

"Bread is the staff of life." A few years ago Patten cornered July wheat and thus controlled three million bushels of wheat which was then available. He rushed the price up to $1.27 a bushel. It is the poor who suffer from such transactions. Patten may dwell in a home of elegance and luxury provided for out of the *unearned* fortune obtained through these transactions, while the poor are struggling to raise a few extra cents with which to buy bread. It is nothing but sheer robbery for any person to so control the price of food stuff as to make its price prohibitive to the poor. God estimates character; not station and vain distinctions. He blesses those who earn their bread by the sweat of their brow, but condemns those who, with their money power, control the price of the one absolute necessity of life, thereby taking it almost out of the reach of the poor. "He that withholdeth corn, the people shall curse him; but blessing shall be upon the head of him that selleth it."—Proverbs xi., 12. It would be well for Patten and others to read the Scriptures and take them for a guide throughout life.

When Patten visited Manchester, England, in 1910, he received a very hostile reception at the Cotton Exchange. A very large proportion of the nine thousand members were present.

BUCKET SHOPS.

If the legitimate exchange presents features worthy of condemnation, what shall be said of those veritable plague spots upon the body commercial, those festering cancers which eat into the very heart of social morals—the "bucket shops?"

These institutions are peculiar to American cities. A "bucket shop" is an establishment where those whose inclinations prompt them to speculate in stocks or produce, but the scantiness of whose means forbids their operating on an extensive scale, may gratify their tastes by risking (and losing) the few dollars which they can ill afford to spare. The epithet "bucket" is a term of derision, having been originally applied to such an institution to imply that a customer might buy or sell a " bucketful " of any commodity which he might select.

Far different is the scene here presented from that witnessed on the floor of the great Exchange. There all was clamour and apparent confusion; here quiet and decorum reign supreme. The silence is unbroken, save by the sharp tick of the telegraphic instrument and the droning monotone of the blackboard marker. Yet there is one point of resemblance between the habitués of the " bucket shop," the dealers on 'Change and the patrons of the gaming hell; one and all, they win without displaying exultation and lose without manifesting regret. In the " bucket shops," however, the attentive observer may sometimes hear the heavy sigh of despair from the young man who has been tempted to risk his employer's money, as he perceives the last dollar of his margin swept away by an unlucky turn of prices; or witness a senile smile of satisfaction momentarily gleam upon the face of the feeble old man who sees himself about to be provided with the means of keeping soul and body together for another day. O, wretched picture of sordid greed, of fallacious hopes, of blank despair! O, sad illustration of the sadder truth that in the contract for the mastery of the heart of man, the evil too often outstrips the good!

But let us examine the business methods of the proprietors of these resorts where gambling is made easy, and ruin is placed within reach of the humblest. As an illustration, let us suppose that the customer wishes to speculate in some stock, say Missouri, Kansas and Texas. The blackboard shows the fluctuations in quotations as they occur on the New York Exchange. The margin which he is called upon to advance, is one dollar per share, and he may limit his transactions to ten shares, if he sees fit. It is a matter of indifference to the proprietor whether he elects to buy or sell; that obliging individual will accommodate himself to his wishes, whatever they may be. Suppose that he buys ten shares of the stock in question, at a moment when it is quoted at 16. If it rises to $17\frac{1}{4}$ he may, if he chooses, close his deal, receiving back the ten dollars which he advanced as margin, together with another ten dollars, the latter representing his profit. If, on the other hand, it drops to $15\frac{1}{4}$, he loses his margin. It is easy to see that such a transaction as this is nothing but a bet, pure and simple.

The illustration given above is drawn from the smallest description of business done. Yet these dens of iniquity are patronized by the wealthy merchant, as well as by the poor mechanic and clerk. It is on the poorer class of customers that the proprietors depend for their steady income; it is from the wealthier customers that they obtain sums of money which they denominate "plums."

While in Oil City, Pa., some time ago, I visited the bucket shops and particularly noticed some of the operations. A speculator would give an order to buy or sell a certain stock at a given figure, but for some reason or other that particular figure would not be quoted, but one higher or lower, as the case may be, would be quoted, thus compelling the speculator to either take the deal at their figure or not at all. This was done time after time. Sometimes an order would be put in to close a deal at a certain figure, and the operator would go to the ticker to send the message, but would suddenly get busy and chalk a number of quotations on the board, and then tell the speculator that he was too late. They have quite a knack of withholding quotations for a considerable while, and then chalking them the whole length of the board. In one of these places I noticed an old man who had made a deal in corn. The market was going against him, and he had to put up three margins. I remember when he put up the last ten dollar bill. The next morning he did not put in an appearance, and it proved to be the last time he ever played the market, for in a few weeks he was dead. He was a poor man, and it was probably the last money he ever possessed. In these " bucket shops " the " chair-warmers " and " pikers " would pass away the time by playing California jack for from five cents to one dollar a game. Then there would be bets on the hourly number of sales. Another class of speculators would bet on the rise or fall of certain stock for a point. In fact, they are nothing but gambling hells of the worst kind.

The manner in which traders are fleeced by the unscrupulous scoundrels who conduct " bucket shops " may be illustrated as follows: One of them will inform a confiding patron that he has received information from a source which he regards as trustworthy, that some inactive stock—perhaps Western Union —then selling at 84, is about to rise. At this suggestion the customer purchases, let us say, 15,000 shares on a margin of one dollar per share. This done, the proprietor of the " bucket shop " telegraphs to a broker to " sell 3,000 Western Union—quick,

quick," in blocks of from 83¾ to 83. The broker who receives the dispatch, either alone or with assistance, offers the stock; the offer is promptly accepted by another broker, to whom the wily manager has telegraphed instructions to buy the stock at the price named. The final quotation, 83, fixes the price, and the sale is promptly reported to the bucket shop by telegraph. The result is that the too trustful customer's $15,000 advanced as margin, is swept into the coffers of the daring rascal who has perpetrated the fraud, and whose only outlay is the payment of one-fourth of a cent commission on fictitious sale and purchase.

Let us take another illustration, drawn from a supposititious transaction in wheat. The speculator perceives from the quotations on the blackboard that some future delivery of wheat opened at 86⅛. Every minute or two new quotations are shown on the board, the apparent tendency of the market being upward. He also sees that during the preceding hour the price has been as high as 86⅝, and as low as 86. When it touches 86 again he concludes to buy, guessing that it is likely to rise. Accordingly he purchases 1,000 bushels at that price, advancing ten dollars as a margin. Perhaps the next change is an advance to 86⅛. He might now sell out without loss, as the ⅛ in his favor amounts to exactly the commission charged by the shop. The next quotation is, say 86, and the following one 85⅞. If it should continue to fall until 85⅛ is touched, he is said to be "frozen out," inasmuch as the decline of ⅞ added to the ⅛ brokerage charged by the proprietor, equals the ten dollars which he has advanced. Perhaps he concludes to "re-margin," in which case he will put up ten dollars more. Possibly the market may now take an upward turn and rise until 86⅛ is again reached. It is now within his power to close the transaction without loss other than that involved in the payment of the commissions. Let us suppose that he does so. It is quite probable that it will now occur to him that the market is likely again to recede, and he accordingly sells 1,000 bushels at 86⅛, once more advancing ten dollars as a margin. If the price continues to rise until 87 is reached, our venturesome speculator is again "frozen out," and is ten dollars lighter in pocket.

The above supposed cases are fair illustrations of the average bucket shop trading. A majority of the patrons of these establishments are "scalpers," satisfied if they can win five, ten, or twenty dollars, and close observers say that fully seven out of ten guess the market wrong. The shop always makes its regular commission, no matter what may be the result of the transaction. " Puts," " calls " and " straddles " are also sold at these places, although, of course on a far smaller scale than by members of the regular exchanges.

Such is the commercial exchange of to-day, and such the fungus-like excrescence which is its off-shoot. Call these practices which have been here described by what name you will, plain, unvarnished truth stamps them as gambling on a gigantic scale and in one of its deadliest forms. And yet the State holds over them the protecting ægis of the law, and the community at large gives them the moral support of its approving smile. For the avowed professional gambler there is no place in the political edifice. In the eye of society he is a pariah; in that of the law a culprit; in that of the church a moral leper. Yet the heartless operator who deliberates long and earnestly how he may speedily and surely accomplish the ruin of the man for whom he professes the sincerest friendship; for the selfish speculator who passes toilsome days and sleepless nights in devising schemes for forcing up the price of the necessaries of life; for the far-seeing scoundrel who concocts a cunningly devised scheme for wrecking a railroad in whose stock, it may be, are invested the funds on which the widow and the orphan depend for subsistence—for these men, society has no condemnation, the law no terrors, and the pulpit no denunciation. They build churches and found colleges; they preside at public gatherings and occupy posts of honor upon public committees. It is a trite aphorism that " nothing succeeds like success," and no more apt illustration of its truth can be given than the adulation bestowed upon men whose fortunes have been cemented by the groans of the unfortunate, and the tears of the widow. Of a truth it is time that society placed the seal of its disapproval upon gambling openly conducted in marble palaces as emphatically as upon the same vice carried on behind darkened windows and barred doors. In this, as in every other great moral reform, much depends upon the attitude and influence of the clergy, who, as a body, have hitherto kept silent as to the crying evil spread out before them.

The idea of the inception of the exchange was grand in its scope. Such organizations have a lofty mission, and it is within their power to encourage commerce, to promote honesty in trade, and to advance the best interests of the State. When an enlightened public sentiment shall compel the elimination from them of those baleful features which have been here portrayed, when the pure gold of legitimate traffic shall have been separated from the dross of illegitimate speculation, when the revival of a healthful moral tone shall have averted the danger which now menaces us, that through the influence and example of the exchange we shall become a nation of gamblers, then no longer shall phantoms haunt the imagination and fallàcies pervert the judgment of men; but there shall rise upon the eye of the world the lineaments of a republic far transcending the loftiest conceptions of Plato; a republic of which poets have dreamed and which prophets have foreshadowed; the flowerage of centuries; the bloom and perfume of a Christian civilization.

POLICY.

Policy as now run is anything but a square deal with its victims. We will assume that there are 75 numbers issued each day from the head office. They are sent out to agents, who are either barbers or saloon keepers. Some have small rooms in unfrequented alleys or lanes, but of the latter class there are very few now. The policy buyer chooses his numbers in many different ways. Some who have been inveterate followers of this mode of gambling rely on dreams, others depend on some little incident by which certain numbers are brought to their mind, some shake dice, and there are a thousand different ways in which the policy gambler guesses the lucky number. When he pays for them he pays anywhere from five cents to ten dollars a number, as his pocket money will allow; it makes no difference to the agent. When the result of the drawings are made known the lucky numbers are printed on the slips of paper, and if any one of the numbers held by the buyer appears three times in the list he wins ten times the amount he pays for his number. Policy agents are now scarce, but what are termed "bookmakers," or solicitors are more numerous. These men are virtually subagents, and are usually salaried.

Winners in policy are few and far between, but there seems to be a sort of mania for it among a certain class, which grows stronger the longer they deal in it. With some business men it becomes a hobby, which they fall into in a quiet and almost unconscious manner, but it is seldom played by any but men of small means, in fact, it is impossible to learn of a single case where a wealthy man has been known to buy policy tickets. Bookmakers can generally be found in saloons and concert halls, and around

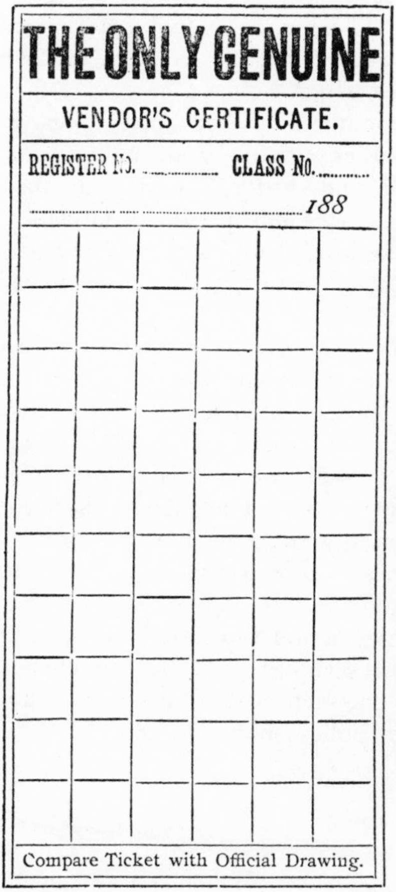

THE ONLY GENUINE

VENDOR'S CERTIFICATE.

REGISTER NO. .... CLASS NO.............

...................................188

Compare Ticket with Official Drawing.

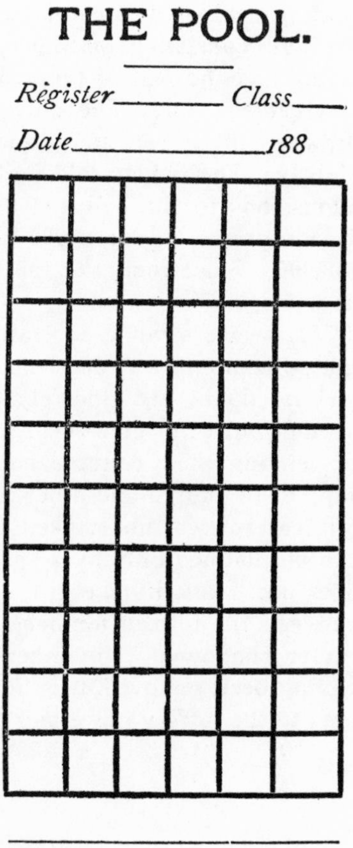

THE POOL.

Register_____ Class____,

Date_____188

theatre entrances. The regular buyer is quick to discover his business, and his purchase is made quietly and secretly. Detectives are constantly on the watch for these transactions, and should any mysterious movement be made by two men on the street, which would give rise to the suspicion that they were policy men, they are carefully shadowed until caught. After once being caught they are interviewed by the officials, and ever after made objects for surveillance. Thus in a measure they are fugitives and outcasts from all society. Still, their calling is a lucrative one, often netting the bookmaker $15 a day, and they become wealthy in time.

Church fairs are frequent in many localities. At one fair held for a whole week, the proceeds were devoted to paying the floating debt on a Music Hall. There were offered 1,500 prizes, the bait consisting of $1,000, $500 and $100 in gold, an $800 piano, and the rest of the prizes being pictures, barrels of flour and cement, etc. The entertainments offered were upon the drawing of prizes, and drew a crowd of 40,000 and upward nightly. The tickets sold for $1, and entitled the buyer to three admissions to the hall and a chance—one in nearly 50,000—to draw a prize. About 48,000 tickets were sold and the fair netted $46,000. Since then, say the lottery agents, their sale of tickets have largely increased.

It seems strange—or rather, it would seem strange were it not so common an experience—that citizens who profess to be, and no doubt are sincerely opposed to lotteries on principle, should indirectly give them moral and material aid and support by lending their countenance to schemes of this nature. The support of church and other raffles, gotten up in aid of charity or gift enterprises, undertaken for any purpose, however worthy, can be justified only by a species of moral casuistry. The altar does not " sanctify the gift," and the line of moral demarcation between the lottery for benevolence and the lottery for gain, is rather shadowy. The inherent scruple as to buying chances having been removed, it is but one step farther, and that a short one, to the lottery office and the policy shop.

THE GAMBLER'S WIFE.

By Regnel Coates.

Dark is the night. How dark! no light! no fire!
　Cold on the hearth, the last faint sparks expire!
Shivering, she watches by the cradle side,
　For him who pledged her love last year a bride!

Hark! 'tis his footsteps! no! 'tis past! 'tis gone!
　Tick! tick! how wearily the time crowds on!
Why should he leave me thus? He once was kind!
　And I believed 'twould last! How mad! How blind!

Rest thee my hope! Rest on! 'Tis hunger's cry!
　Sleep! for there is no food! The fount is dry!
Famine and cold their wearying work have done,
　My heart must break! and then the clock strikes one.

Hush! 'Tis the dice-box! yes, he's there! he's there!
　For this! for this he leaves me to despair?
Leaves love, leaves truth! his wife! his child! for what?
　The wanton's smile—the villain and the sot!

Yet I'll not curse him, No! 'tis all in vain!
　'Tis long to wait, but sure he'll come again!
And I could starve and bless him but for you,
　My child! his child! oh, fiend, the clock strikes two.

Hark! How the signboard creaks, the blast howls by;
　Moan! moan! a dirge swells through the cloudy sky,
Ho! 'tis his knock: he comes! he comes once more!
　'Tis but the lattice flops! thy hope is o'er!

Can he desert us thus? He knows I stay,
　Night after night in coldness to pray,
For his return—and yet—he sees no tear!
　No! no! it cannot be, he will be here!

Nestle more closely, dear one to my heart,
　Thou art cold; thou art freezing; but we will not part;
Husband! I die! Father! It is not he!
　O God, protect my child! the clock strikes three.

They are gone! they are gone! the glimmering spark hath fled!
　The wife and child are numbered with the dead!
On the cold hearth; outstretched in solemn rest,
　The child lies sleeping on the mother's breast.

The gambler comes at last!
　But all was o'er;
Dead silence reigned around
　When the clock struck four.

113

DICE AND THE DICE BOX.

The origin of dice is shrouded in obscurity, but it is certain that their use has come down to modern days from a period of remote antiquity. Dice throwing has always been one of the most popular forms of gaming, and in days gone by immense fortunes have been staked and lost upon the throwing of the cubes. At the present day, judging from the various new contrivances being manufactured for the use of dice, it would still seem to be a very popular form of amusement.

Dice are among the time-honored tools of the "professional." The honor of their invention is ascribed to the Egyptians, and in some of the bas-reliefs that have been disinterred in the land of the Pharaohs, figures playing with something closely resembling dice are discernible. The Ethiops of three or four thousand years ago were, it is believed, addicted to gaming of this sort, and in this connection it may be remarked that gambling is quite as much a barbaric as a civilized vice. In fact it may be questioned whether the Troglodytes did not gamble in their caves, and swindle one another out of the spoils of the chase before they had learned to construct huts in which to live.

It is not my intention to describe all the games of dice which may be played, but to explain those most commonly used by sharpers to defraud the ignorant, and to show some of the more modern games now in vogue.

Chuck-a-Luck. This is a simple little game of dice, yet one of the most fascinating of all games of chance. It is sometimes designated as " the old army game," for the reason that soldiers at the front were often wont to beguile the tedium of a bivouac by seeking relief from monotony in its charms.

The outfit requisite to play the game is so simple and inexpensive, consisting of three small dice, a dice box, and a cloth on which are inscribed the numbers one to six, corresponding to the dots or "pips," on the six faces of the cubes.

Bets are made by placing the money wagered on the num-

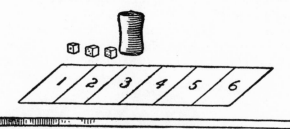

bers on the cloth. The dice, having been placed in the box, are shaken and thrown upon the table. Bets made upon either of the three numbers which come uppermost are won by the players. Money staked on either of the remaining numbers are won by the bank.

On its face, this game appears to be one of pure chance. As played upon fair and circus grounds, however, there is very little chance about it. The "banker" does not throw the dice fairly. Through long practice, he is able to retain two of them between the fingers of the hand which he holds over the inverted dice box. The other die he allows to remain in the box, and rattles it against the sides, occasionally knocking the box itself against the button of his coat in order to simulate the sound produced by the shaking of three dice. When he removes his hand from the mouth of the dice cup, he drops upon the table the two dice which he held in his hand and permits the third die to fall by chance. The reader will readily perceive how great is the unfair advantage thus obtained.

Hyronemus. This is, perhaps, one of the most successful games of dice—considered from the standpoint of the operator—known to the gambling fraternity.

The illustration affords a view of all the paraphernalia employed in conducting it, as it was played until more recent years. The use of electricity has caused the necessity for changes in the equipment, but the method of play is the same. On a cloth-covered table rests an inverted tambourine, above which stands an implement substantially of the form depicted in the cut. The latter may be best described as consisting of two wooden bowls, the smaller ends of which are placed opposite each other and

connected by a hollow tube as shown in the diagram. On the
cloth which covers the table are painted numbers from one to six.
Three dice are used in playing, differing from ordinary dice, only
in being larger and in having figures painted on the faces, instead
of the small black dots commonly employed.

The mode of playing is as follows: Players select the number or numbers on which they wish to bet, and place their wagers
on the corresponding squares on the cloth. The dice are then

placed in the upper bowl and permitted to drop through the tube,
and fall upon the tambourine, directly under the inverted bowl.
The bowl is then raised, and if the bettor happens to have placed
his stake on the number appearing on one of the upper faces of
the cubes, he wins the amount of his bet. If the number which
he selected appears on two of their faces, the proprietor of the
bowl pays him double. If the three dice all show the same number and he has happened to place his wager thereon, the operator
pays him three to one.

The "percentage" against the players in this game is so
large that the proprietors are ordinarily content to play it on the

"square." It sometimes happens, however, that the operation of the recognized laws of chance seems to be reversed, and a player wins over and over again. Of course, this is not to be tolerated. The proprietor of the game is running it for his own pecuniary profit; the idea of conducting a scheme for the bene-

Hyronemus Tub and Layout.

fit of the general public has never occurred to him. Sometimes instead of taking all three dice from the tambourine, he removes only two, thus retaining a knowledge of at least one of the winning numbers. I have also known a device of this kind to be resorted to. When a certain number is winning repeatedly, the operator, having (apparently by accident) knocked the dice off the table, while stooping to pick them up will substitute another set of three cubes, none of which contains the tubes in question.

But the most contemptible form of swindling consists in replacing the tambourine by a thin board, which may be so agitated, by means of a concealed spring, as to overturn the dice after the manipulator has ascertained the numbers shown by looking through the tube.

Sometimes the operator provides himself with dice having all the faces marked with the same number, by substituting one or more of which he is able to cast whatever throw he pleases.

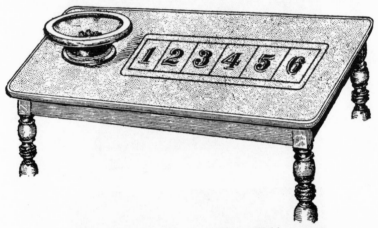

Improved Electric Tub and Table.

The Electric Tub, as shown in the illustration, is one of the latest inventions, and is used for hyronemus, chuck-a-luck, and for all kinds of hazard games. It makes the game a sure winner for the operator, and large amounts of money are staked on this game. It is expected to supersede, in the near future, the cage and all other devices.

The dice are made to come treys or fours, at will, without touching dice at any time.

The tub can be controlled without fear of detection.

This device has been made expressly for the use of privilege men who follow the fairs and circuses. Many of the public parks and resorts are found to be desirable locations for the running of this game. The operator generally gets into some shady nook or quiet corner, where he can run his " shady " game without fear of molestation. The " suckers " find this much to their advantage, as they do not generally desire to play against these games in full view of the public.

The cage is operated by turning the handle, thus causing the cage to swing around, when the operator bringing it to a stop, the dice settle, and the numbers counted. The wins and losses are counted the same as on the other forms of hyronemus.

This machine can also be used with electrical attachment.

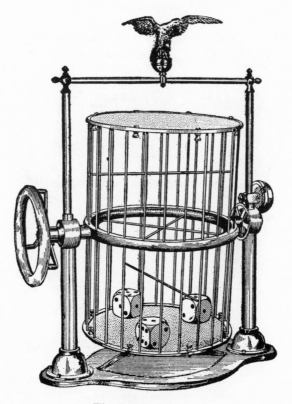

The Jumbo Cage.

When using an outfit of this kind it is impossible for the players on the outside to beat the one running the game, even though they are permitted to "double-up." The electric magnet is placed in a money drawer that can be placed under any table and the cage can be set up directly over it. Of course electric dice must be used with these magnets.

Klondike. In this game the player tries to beat a pair of sixes with one throw of two dice, and also tries to beat the game-keeper.

Sometimes the game is played with five dice. The player bets the gamekeeper that he will beat his throw, or he can bet the opposite. Should the player throw a straight or ties, the gamekeeper takes the money. This is the percentage the house claims for itself.

The layout is spread on top of a table and the battery, when one is used, is placed under the table. Sometimes a copper wire runs down through the leg of the table and is bent over the bottom end of the leg. The table is then set in such a position

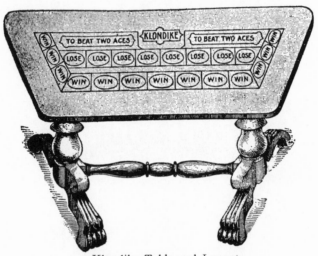

Klondike Table and Layout.

that the leg rests on a brass screw in the floor and the circuit is completed, the current being supplied through the screw and copper wire. It is a simple matter to lift the table and show that it has no wire connections, in case any one expresses a doubt as to the fairness of the game, but it is only necessary to replace the leg on the head of the screw to be in a position to continue the electric control of the dice.

In this game the dice are made to come sixes when the current is on, thus giving the banker the highest possible hand; the aces turn up when the current is off, as the lead load is set in the dice right back of the sixes, thus causing the sixes to rest down, and the opposite side, the aces, to rest up when the current is not applied.

Loaded Dice. Although many kinds of loaded dice are used, there are comparatively few among the guild of professional gamblers who are experts in their use. The sharper who does not travel, preferring to wait, at home, such victims as the antipodes of Providence may send him, is satisfied with employing occasionally, a set of high dice. But the peripatetic scoundrel who, like Satan, "wanders to and fro upon the earth," seeking for victims, usually provides himself with three sets—one "high," one "low," and one "square." The fraudulent dice are loaded with quicksilver, the interior of each dice being hollowed out in such a manner as to cause the weight to fall upon the opposite

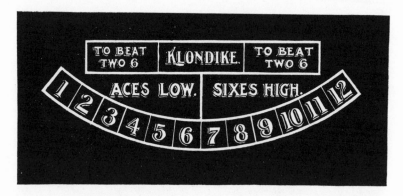

Klondike Layout.

side to that intended to come up, the weighted side being, of course, always undermost.

The professional, in using these dice against a single adversary, usually works very rapidly, distracting the dupe's attention, as far as possible, from his operations by story telling or some other interesting conversation. He changes the cubes swiftly and often, "ringing in" the "high" ones for himself, and the "square" ones for his opponent or the latter for himself and the "low" ones for his victim, occasionally, however, using the fair dice for both, in order to disarm suspicion.

Craps. This is a favorite game among steamboat men, and is particularly popular among colored people. I first became acquainted with it on board the steamboat "City of Chester" on the Mississippi river. I was travelling in partnership with a man named Martin, and we had succeeded in fleecing one man out of some $800 at poker, in the cabin. I went out on deck, and my attention was arrested by hearing a negro crying in a stentorian voice, "come 7 or 11," then another man calling out, "chill'en cryin' fo' bread." This was followed by the sound of something rolling on the floor. My curiosity was aroused, and I went below to learn what was going on. Here I first saw the game of " craps " and my introduction to it cost me precisely $15. I went upstairs and informed my partner that I had discovered a new game. He was anxious to see it, and together we returned to the main deck where the game was in progress. He dropped $10 to the " crap " roller, expressed himself as satisfied, and we returned to the cabin. I did not at the time understand how I was

Crap Layout as used in Chicago and the West.

cheated, although I was perfectly well satisfied that the cheating had been done. Since then, I have discovered all about it.

The game is played with dice about half the size of the cubes ordinarily used in other games. Only two are employed and they are held in the hand and thrown forward upon the table or whatever surface may be convenient. The numbers 7 and 11 are called " craps." After the dice have ceased rolling the spots on both sides are added together, and if the sum is equal to 7 or 11, the " crap " thrower wins all bets which have been made against him. If the same amount to two, three, or twelve, he loses, and is required to pay each player the amount of his stake. Should the sum of all the spots on the two dice amount to four, five, six, eight, nine or ten, he is entitled to continue throwing, until he has either cast the amount thrown again, or throw a seven. In the former case he wins the player's bets; if, however, the sum of the spots amount to 7 before the number first thrown turns up again, he loses.

The game commences by one player throwing the dice until he loses, when the next player at his left takes the cubes, and so on in rotation.

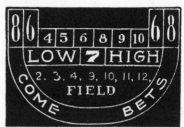

The favorite method of cheating at this game is by the substitution of unfair dice. For this purpose, loaded dice are sometimes used, and sometimes dice specially prepared, on the faces of one of which, are painted two aces, two twos, and two sixes, while the other dice is inscribed with two threes, two fours and two fives. If the reader will take pains to figure out the combination of numbers which may be made with two dice so prepared, he will see it is an utter impossibility for the thrower to make either two, three, or twelve, the numbers which will

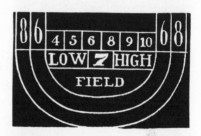

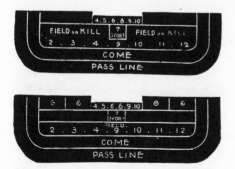

Crap Layouts.

be a loss to him. In addition to this circumstance it is also apparent that the chances of throwing 7 are very greatly increased by the arrangement of two fours on one dice and two threes on the other, as well as two fives on one and two twos on the other. The small size of the dice employed in playing this game and the fact that they are thrown from the hand, renders the substitution of unfair dice a comparatively easy matter.

Although the game, as I have said, is an especial favorite among negroes and deck-hands, nevertheless, it is frequently played by " high toned " gamblers for large stakes.

A story is told of a raid once made in Chicago, the players anticipating interference on the part of the police, had their little cubes made of cut sugar, and when the officers of the law made their appearance, swallowed the dice, and there being no gaming implements found, the case against them was necessarily dismissed.

 This cut shows the new " crap " dice now being produced. " It is an invisible double-shaped dice, the dice being made to show ace, deuce and six, instead of ace and six as in the old style; which gives the banker much greater percentage. These dice are all made by machinery, which makes them absolutely mechanically correct. A 32nd off with our process, gets the result of a 1-16 the ordinary way. These dice are intended for a game that has the same patronage every day. We guarantee them to please you and at the same time to hold your play. 5-8 red transparent is the best size and color to use. Price per pair, $2."

Such is the description given by the manufacturer. It is high time that the general public became acquainted with the deception and fraud that is being practiced. Presuming that it was allowable by law, to gamble, the man who would go into a game of this kind would naturally want an even chance for his money. But as there is no law in the United States which permits it, and there are many laws against it, I say it is the duty of every government in this country not only to forbid gambling, but to enact laws that shall make it illegal to manufacture crooked gaming devices of any description whatsoever.

A " Black-Hand " Game. " Shooting craps " may be a negro game, and playing cards a white man's game; but nevertheless the Supreme Court of the Lone Star State refuses to recognize any such fact. Recently a negro was fined $10 under a statute which prohibits " shooting craps," but does not make it

an offense to play an innocent game of cards. He now appeals.
Sparks v. State, 142 Southwestern Reporter, 1183. His conten-
tion is that the statute is a discrimination against the negro.
Craps, he claims, is a negro game, while cards is a white man's

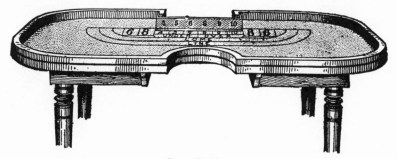

Crap Table.

game, and this the legislature well knew in taking this good old
amusement away from him, and therefore the statute is unconsti-
tutional. The court answers: " Appellant's position is a unique
one, but we cannot agree with him. It is unnecessary, we think,
to discuss the question."

Grand Hazard. Three dice are used in this game. Sometimes they contain spots, as do ordinary dice, sometimes on the

faces are painted representations of birds, animals, or reptiles,
such as a horse, an eagle, a rattlesnake, etc. On the table upon
which the dice are thrown is spread a cloth on which are depicted numbers or figures corresponding to those upon the faces
of the cubes. Bets are made by playing the stakes upon whatever square or squares the player may select. The dice are
dropped through a funnel-shaped cup, as shown in the illustrations, and the gains or losses of the bettors are determined by

inspecting the face of the dice which lie uppermost after they

have fallen upon the table. If any player has wagered his money, for instance, upon the number six, and one of the dice shows a six-spot on its upper face, the bettor is paid the amount which he has ventured. In case the three dice should all show the same number. or figure when they fall, the proprietor pays to the bet-

tor, who has placed his stake upon the corresponding square on the cloth, 180 for 1.

In this, as in all other fraudulent games with dice, gamblers resort to the substitution of "ringers" for fair dice, and

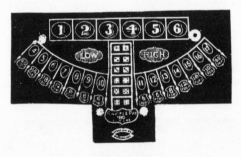

have the poor fools, who risk their money on such schemes, practically at their mercy.

Poker Dice. This game is usually played in saloons for drinks or cigars, though sometimes for money, and occasionally for higher stakes. As a general rule five ordinary dice are used, but sometimes dice like those shown in the accompanying illustration, and which are known as "octahedron poker dice," are used instead. The only other equipment necessary is a dice cup. Each player has three throws. The highest score which can possibly be made is five aces, the next, five sixes, then five fives, and so on. Next to five familiar spots, the best throw is four of one kind and an odd number, the relative value of such throws being measured by the number of spots upon the top of the four dice, aces ranging highest. The game is called " poker " dice, because of the general resemblance between it and " bluff."

so far as the value of the throws is concerned as compared with that of the hands held at poker.

High and Low Dice Tops. These little implements are used chiefly for winning drinks or cigars, or small sums of money. They are eight-sided spinning tops made of ivory, the respective sides being numbered one to eight. Sometimes they are made fairly, but dice tops of the latter description are not in favor with the professional gambler, who uses a top having a

movable iron peg which the sharper may so arrange as to cause the high or low numbers to fall uppermost when the top comes to rest, after being spun. If the peg be turned one way a high number will come uppermost; if the other, a low number. Of course the greenhorn, not being aware of this little peculiarity of the top, it is comparatively an easy matter for the confidence man or other cheat to arrange the peg in such a way that when he spins for himself he turns up a high number, and when his opponent takes the same article in hand, however, he invariably turns up a low one. It may be seen that the former has it in his power to win as often as he chooses, but in order that his luck may not appear to be positively miraculous, he sometimes permits his dupe to win.

Eight-Die Case or Derby Pool. This is a favorite game with travelling sporting men, who introduce it at county fairs, etc., where there is a large crowd. The diagram represents the arrangement of the interior of a glass covered case showing the value of the prizes. The divisions in this case are numbered from eight to forty-eight, inclusive, to correspond with the numbers which may possibly be thrown in casting eight dice, which the proprietor carries with him, together with a dice box. For a stipulated consideration, he permits any one who may wish, to throw the dice upon the glass cover of the case. The sum of the spots on the upper faces is taken, and the player is given whatever prize the number may call for.

Used as a cigar game, the proprietor usually charges five or ten cents for a throw, according to locality. The player may be successful in securing from one to one hundred cigars, or he may get what the boy shot at—nothing.

An examination of the diagram will show that the higher prizes are invariably placed in squares corresponding to a number which it is almost impossible for a player to throw. Thus, a one hundred prize is placed in the square numbered eight. To win this, it would be necessary to throw eight aces. Those numbers which may be easily thrown are always attached to squares containing small prizes, or a blank.

This game is said to increase the business at the cigar stand at least twenty-five per cent, and to take off more money than any hundred dollar slot machine ever made.

First Flop Dice are used where the dice are shaken for drinks, cigars, or money, specially to protect the proprietor against his customers. A fair deal is not to be thought of in this line of business. He fully believes that, in his case, " Self-preservation is one of the first laws of nature." These dice are so

" fixed " that it is almost impossible for the uninitiated to throw a bigger hand than the proprietor, he being able to throw the five aces if he so desires.

In my exhibitions I challenge the audience to compete with me in throwing with the same dice and the same box, and offer the sum of $500 to any charitable institution in the town, my opponent cares to name, should he be able to beat me. I have been offering this for the past twenty-six years, and no one has ever been able to claim the money yet.

While demonstrating at Maskelyne and Devant's, London, England, where I was engaged for ten weeks, giving my practical demonstrations on crooked gambling, a man from South Africa came upon the stage and shook dice with me. After several throws he succeeded in throwing four aces and a six. The audience were all attention awaiting my next throw. I now had to do the work or stand a good chance of forfeiting the $500. I took up the box and with a slight turn threw out five aces on the board. My opponent was amazed. He asked me to throw the same on the bare table, which I was successful in doing. He then asked me to throw on the floor, which I did, being quite willing to accommodate the gentleman. Five aces again showed up. On seeing this he staggered, and had to be supported, and exclaimed, " My God! is it possible that I have been robbed of my money?" He came to me and told me he had lost quite a fortune at dice, and thanked me for my demonstration.

The Electric Magnet is put up in the form of a cigar moistener, and it is impossible for the casual observer to note any distinction. Of course the dice used with these magnets must be " electrified." Several dry batteries are used, together with a few small magnets, some wire and the push button. All the operator has to do is simply to " push the button," thereby completing the circuit, and all that remains to be done is to roll the dice.

The operation is swift, sure, and silent. " Silence is gold;"

yes, it is in this case. The squeeze is pressed and the magnet does the rest. The change pad is laid over the magnet when the dice is being shaken, and the magnet works through any material except iron and steel. In order to throw a " big throw " all that is necessary to be done is for the operator to press the secret squeeze and throw the dice over the magnet, and it will beat any throw the opponent might make, and thus with the same dice he uses, without any juggling of the dice or box. The dice roll perfectly natural at all times, and no one can see any difference when the " current " is on—only in the size of the hands thrown.

Electric Case Magnet.

This is without doubt the most useful article ever put into a cigar store, saloon or other place, where people will " shake for the cigars or drinks," and probably later for money.

It is surprising that with all the educational facilities that men have, that they do not stop to consider why it is that the general run of cigar salesmen and bartenders can beat them so frequently at the game. The average man will say, "It's just my luck," while, in reality, " luck " has nothing at all to do with it; and so the bartender " goes on smiling."

The scene represented on the following page will be familiar to many readers of this book. Go to the cigar stands in the largest hotels in almost any city where dice shaking is permitted, and it will be no uncommon thing to find a young woman behind the counter, shaking dice with men. To my mind, this is

one of the most disgraceful sights ever permitted by city administrations, for it not only places the young woman in a position where she is compelled to hear language which the men

who patronize these stands, would not use in the presence of
their own mothers and sisters, and is not only thus humiliated
thereby, but she oftentimes has to act the part of a sharper.

If you look at the open door shown in the illustration, you
will perceive the batteries in the cupboard, all ready for operation. Having read the explanation of the electric magnet, you
will readily understand that the proprietor who uses such, would
have no scruples in placing a young woman behind the cigar
counter and leaving her in charge during his absence, for she
would not require any skill whatever to beat all who would
come to shake dice with her for cigars. Then again, she would
prove to be an " extra added attraction."

Some men seem to have no souls. They know that there
are numbers of young women looking for work, and where there
is one that would refuse to stoop so low in the gutter, there are
a dozen others who would do the work from " necessity."

While staying at a very prominent hotel in Cleveland some
time ago, I accosted the girl at the cigar counter, and I asked
her why she did not try to get something more respectable to do.
She told me that it was winter and very difficult for her to ob-

tain the kind of work that suited her, and at the same time make a living.

I wish the W. C. T. U's and Y. W. C. A's all over the country would take up this question. If they cannot do what is required by gentle persuasion with the proprietors or the girls themselves, then I would like to see them combine their forces and bring pressure to bear upon the local administrations, urging them to pass by-laws prohibiting women from serving at the cigar stands. If their efforts in this direction prove futile, I suggest they work for the enactment of state laws which shall prove effectual.

We want the conditions of our American womanhood to be that of the best. How can we expect the young women to attain to the highest state of womanhood,—that is, by being fit to hold the honorable position of a true motherhood to the future generation of this our country,—if they are permitted to eke out an existence in this manner, which is most degrading to our nation.

We are disgusted when we hear of women serving behind the bar of a saloon, and such an one is ostracized by society. Then why not take upon ourselves the responsibility of seeing to it that these girls be removed from the temptations that surround them.

Electric Transparent Dice.

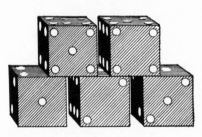

It has taken many years of experimenting in perfecting this most mystifying gambling device ever invented. The work put into these dice absolutely defy detection by looking at them. The magnet alone is the only possible means which can be used to discover that they are " faked." These dice are made to come any combination the sharper desires. They are guaranteed to do the work and to get the money. They are sold at $15 the set of five. When the " sucker " finds transparent dice being used it naturally disarms him of all possible suspicion, for he can look them over and never discover anything wrong with them.

The electric transparent dice are becoming more popular with the sharper than any other dice used. They look "square," but they are not "square."

Electric Money Drawer. The diagram here shows the money drawer all complete and ready to screw under the table. It is used especially for Klondike, Hazard, first flop, chuck-a-luck, and for all kinds of dice games. It is said to be swift and sure, and the greatest money maker on the market.

The outfit consists of one drawer 23 inches long, 14 inches wide, 5 inches deep, one magnet, batteries, switch, and one set of five electric dice made for any combination desired. The complete apparatus can be had for the sum of $25, and guaranteed.

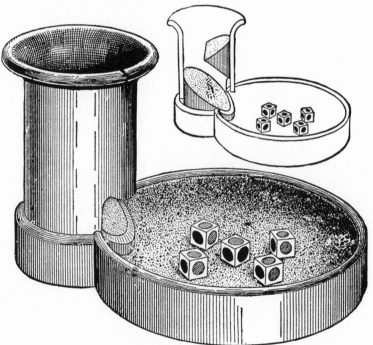

The New Cube Game.

The cube game consists of one mahogany stand with a base of ten inches in circumference, with a four and a half inch cylinder, seven inches high. If you look at the smaller diagram you will perceive that in the cylinder is placed slanting shelves, which cause the cubes when thrown into it to be thoroughly tumbled about. The dice fall into the saucer shaped bowl or base, where they are easily seen and easily picked up for the next throw. On each of the five cubes is six colors—red, black, green, yellow, blue and dove color.

This game can be run in innumerable ways, one of the most popular being 25 throws for 25 cents. The player selects his color, and if he succeeds in throwing 26 of color named in 25 throws, he gets $1 in trade; if he throws only 11 or less he gets $1 in trade; if he throws 33 or over he gets $2 in trade.

This is called an "innocent amusement." In looking at the method of play a little more closely, you will observe that if he throws any number between 11 and 26 the player gets nothing; if he throws any number between 26 and 33 he gets nothing. The numbers he is likely to be successful in throwing, have no prizes provided for them.

Sometimes only three cubes are used. In that case the player selects his color, drops the three cubes into the top of the cylinder, and lets them settle in the bowl. If one cube comes with his color up, he receives twice the amount played in trade; if two cubes with his color come up, three times amount played in trade; and if three cubes come up with his color, five times amount in trade. Whether he wins or loses the house always takes the amount played.

Another method used to induce play is for the house to offer $100 for a dime to anyone naming a color and throwing five of them.

This game is said to be able to run where slot machines and dice games are barred, and to possess many great advantages over the ordinary slot machine, which player can only play for a certain amount, while the cube game can have any limit put upon it the owner sees fit to offer.

THE NEW MATHEMATICAL BLOCK GAME; OR, ROLLING LOG.

This game consists of four logs, three fair, one "ringer;" one tray, and a chart with numbers ranging from four to twenty-three inclusive; ten spaces for small prizes and ten for larger

ones. This is when it is fixed up as a "gift enterprise." At other times blanks take the place where the small prizes are arranged. The game is operated by placing three logs in back of tray, player or dealer elevating same to allow the three logs to roll down the table. When they come to rest the spots that are on top are counted, and the sum total shows the number which tells the reward. It is so made that the operator can make it come big or little prize at will. The "ringer" is brought into play whenever he deems it necessary.

DIE PINS.

This game is on the principle of the eight-die case. Each pin is numbered one to six, and the usual chart with numbers is furnished, showing the value of the prizes offered. The pins are knocked down by the hand, and when they come to rest the numbers on the top of the pins are counted, and the sum total shows the number which tells the award. Of course there are numerous ways of placing the bets on this game, and it is no uncommon thing for the operator, with the aid of " cappers," to get the " sucker " to " double-up " and thus take his money away from him.

STAR POINTER.

This is one of the latest and cheapest machines ever put on the market for use in cigar stores, etc. It is specially recommended for raffling purposes and as a trade stimulator. The wheel is only seven inches in diameter, made of cast steel, handsome enamel finish with gold figures, also celluloid indicator. It is used in a similar manner to the paddle wheel, as shown in another part of the book.

THE STRIKER.

This cut illustrates what is known as "The World's Fair Striker." This machine appears to the uninitiated a very simple contrivance, and is readily induced to try his "luck" as the amount for a chance is small, and he naturally thinks that if he loses he cannot lose very much. This machine is under the control of the operator to such an extent that he can make it come either a large or small prize, or even a blank. There are no

suspicious moves, no stalling, and every movement is so natural, that the moment the indicator is let down it is all ready for the next play. I am often asked at various places where I go to give my demonstration, whether I have a striker with me, and it generally happens that the person who is so anxious to know, is in the habit of using one of these machines.

DROP CASES.

These machines work on the principle that "the more you drop down, the less you pick up."

If there is any class of gamblers that could possibly be called robbers, then I say that the men who handle machines of the description here shown, are nothing but daylight robbers. There is a certain amount of respect (if it could be called by that name) for the man who will guess on even chances, but there is nothing but the most utter contempt and severe condemnation due the man who deliberately undertakes to fleece the ignorant public in this manner. By this I do not mean to exonerate the public for going up against these machines, for they should know, if only they would stop and think, that as these are not games of skill, then the element of chance must be very strong.

To all appearances these machines are perfectly " square,"

and the high prizes denoted on the charts and layouts are very tempting to the city youth and the young man from the country.

The operators are usually very cautious in opening up these games, but become emboldened as the play goes on. They generally put up their stands in a small tent or side show at fairs and carnivals, etc. When on the race track they are often to be found underneath the grand stand. They rely very considerably for the success of their venture upon " cappers," some of whom are picked up in the town in which the fair is being held, as this greatly lessens any suspicion that might arise. Wherever fairs and race meets are held regularly, the " fakirs " have no difficulty in securing the necessary numbers of " cappers." On one occasion when the sheriff of a certain county went to look at a certain game being operated on the fair ground, who should come forward to remonstrate with the sheriff but a former deputy, telling him there was nothing crooked about that particular game. Some people have the erroneous impression that if the games are not "crooked" that the games ought to be allowed to run, irrespective of the fact that they are gambling implements. The public cannot tell by looking at the outward appearance of the machines that they are crooked, and they are loth to believe what they cannot see.

Nevertheless, hundreds of "suckers" have rued the day when they first dropped the nickel or marble into one of these machines.

The young man who goes to the fair is usually looking for some kind of amusement, and if he happens to be from the country, he brings with him the nice little roll of pocket money he has been saving up for the occasion.

The desire to get "something for nothing" is implanted in his mind, although perhaps not so strongly as in the mind of the man who deals in pools on the race-track, or the man who speculates on the stock exchange.

When he first enters the fair ground he has no idea whatever of gambling. He has probably heard very little about gambling, and what little he may have heard would be associated with card playing. Naturally curious, he is a fit subject for the " capper."

The " capper," being a man of " experience," readily discovers the class of men likely to nibble at the bait and thus fall into the trap. He has a happy way of making up an acquaint-

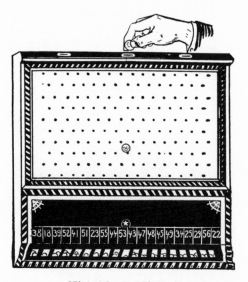

Nickel-in-the-Slot.

ance with a stranger. Sometimes he has to resort to stratagem. Approaching a countryman, he offers to " divide risks " with him; i. e., to advance half the money and share equally in the gains or losses. This seems to be a fair proposition, and the countryman thinks he cannot lose very much any way, so he falls in with the scheme. As long as the " capper " and the " sucker " play together, they invariably lose. Should the dupe become disgusted with his " run of hard luck," the " capper " continues to play alone. The operator works the lever and his confederate soon wins a prize; the greenhorn (who always stands near, to await the issue) at once feels encouraged, and it usually requires little persuasion on the "capper's" part to induce him to make another venture.

Should business be a little dull, it will sometimes pay the operator to "allow" the dupe to win, as this not only encourages him to continue playing, but he will go and tell his friends of his success. When he returns, however, there is a different story to tell, for he loses what he had previously won.

Occasionally a number of "sports" will surround the machine, but not being content with just ten cents a chance, will propose to raise the amount staked to fifty cents and even a dollar, in order to get high play. The operator being willing to accommodate them, and to show he is willing to sport, readily agrees. Of course he knows they wish to show him that they are pretty good sort of fellows, and that there is nothing mean about them. They become delighted with the occasional success they meet with, but are totally unaware that whatever success they may have is entirely at the option of the operator. This gentleman, of course, is a most affable being. If the victim loses heavily, he tries to cheer him up by telling him that he will have better luck next time, and urges him to make another venture. To the man who has won a prize, he is equally anxious for him to return to the play, even though he should be a "capper."

The majority of the drop cases are made so that they fold up like a travelling case. This is exceedingly convenient in case of it being necessary to make a quick removal. Where the county and city officials do not agree as to the administration of the law, then either one or the other will take it upon themselves to enforce the law and arrest the gamblers.

I once had such an experience in a Missouri city. When the policeman placed his hand upon my shoulder and informed me that I was under arrest, my first impulse was to get away, and

I twisted my body into as many contortions as are discernible upon the face of a man who is shaving himself with a dull razor. I soon found that escape was impossible. The blue-coated minion of authority held me with a tenacious grip. Then I began to appeal to the finer instincts of his nature. I told him that I was innocent; he laughed at me. I told him of my poverty, talked to him of my family, and otherwise appealed to the gentler side of his character. He listened to all I had to say in silence, and with a smile that Artemus Ward would have described as "coldly cynical." Inserting the thumb and forefinger of my right hand in my vest I drew out a ten dollar treasury

Zig-Zag.

note, which I quietly slipped into the hand of the protector of public morals. His large fingers closed over it with the same firm grasp with which they had prevented my escape. Stepping back from me one or two paces, he looked earnestly into my face and exclaimed, " Well, begorrah, an' Oi believe O'ive got the wrong man."

It is not all honey for the gamblers.

These drop cases are sold from $25 and up. The one I will first describe is one that I have in my possession, and which cost $350. It was captured one Sunday morning in a raid at Coney Island, after one man had lost $1,600 on it before breakfast. After reading the description of this infernal machine, the reader will easily understand how that amount of money could

be lost in so short a time. " The fool and his money soon parts."
This machine is illustrated on page 138.

The diagram shows the letters of the alphabet from " A " to
" Z " inclusive. A chart showing the prizes and blanks go with
the machine. Some letters represent a star, which means that
the player has to " double-up;" the letter " L " represents two
stars, which means that the player must put up four times the
amount of his bet; the letter " N " represents three stars, which
means that he must put up eight times the amount; and the letter " M " represents the only blank on the board.

Suppose I am operating this machine. A young man from
the country—a farmer's boy—comes up and takes a look at the
machine. He asks me what it costs to take a chance on it and
I inform him that it will cost $1. Understand, in the first place,
that he bets one dollar against my dollar. And whatever amount
he may put up all he can hope to win in the end is just that one
dollar.

He places down his money and I hand him a marble which
I tell him to drop into any one of the five apertures you see at
the top of the machine. I size him up and conclude that he has
about $15 in his possession, so I plan to get that amount away
from him. He is a farmer's honest boy and has been given $15
to spend and have a good time. Before handing him the marble
I have the machine already set, so that when he drops the marble
in it rolls down between the needle points and falls into one of
the grooves, over which is a letter representing a star. As this
is neither a winning nor a losing letter, the money he has put
up is " in chancery." But to get it back he must go on with the
play and double-up. He now puts up $2 on the condition that
if he wins a prize, he gets his money back also. Again the
marble is dropped, meeting with the same result. He now has
to put up $4. The same operation is performed, but without
his having met with any success. He has now put up $7 in all,
and the money is still in chancery. I calculate that he has now
$8 left out of the $15, so in order to get that I open the side
drawer and pull out a roll of bills. In doing so I perform a little
operation of my own and the machine is " fixed " to make him
lose all of his money. I now offer him as a special inducement
to put up the other $8, a conditional prize of $100, that if the
marble comes on to a winning prize, he gets the prize, the $100,
and his own money back. This looks rather good to him as he

has been wondering in the meantime what he shall tell his father and mother what he did with the money, so he puts up the last $8 and watches with feverish excitement the rolling of the marble until it rests in the groove over which is painted the letter " M." We all look eagerly at the chart to see the result, when we discover it represents the only blank on the board. He goes away disheartened and all the enjoyment that he hoped to get at the fair, has vanished.

Surely this cannot be classed as anything but robbery. Yet this very thing is occurring almost every day.

In each of the machines illustrated the system is very similar. Those machines which do not " represent" are simple prizes and blanks. Where this is the case there is a slide which can be moved by a very slight pressure, thus placing it under the complete control of the operator.

" Honest John " works absolutely certain at all times. Certain that the operator will win, which naturally follows that the " sucker " will lose.

FISH POND.

This is a very popular game with the children. The illustration shows a complete outfit. A very attractive board loaded with jewelry is displayed, the value of which does not average one cent a piece, and vary from a pocket mirror to a nickel

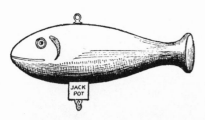

watch. The players pay ten cents for the use of a rod and line with which to catch a fish. T h e diagram represents a "two-way fish" that is a marvel of mechanical ingenuity. Each fish can be made to show prize or blank at will. "No thumbing of numbers." Nothing unnatural. Player selects fish, it is handed to him; he pulls out the slide on bottom which displays number that designates prize he has won, unless it should happen to be a blank, which is not at all unusual.

SINGLE ARROW CHUCK-A-LUCK SPINDLE AND TABLE LAYOUT.

As will be seen in the illustration, this game is a combination of chuck-a-luck and spindle games. Reference has been

made in another place to chuck-a-luck, but it is claimed for this game that it will win a larger amount of money for the operator than if he used dice. The percentage is said to be twice as great. By means of the "squeeze" when used the operator can make the percentage whatever he thinks proper.

NEW IDEA CIGAR MACHINE.

This is called a "Trade Stimulator," and is used for raffling purposes. The word "gambling" is becoming obnoxious to many. If a young man who is just commencing to enter pool-rooms and cigar stores is told that these machines are gambling machines, he will probably pass them by. But when he is told that it is not gambling but is only a trade stimulator, he will usually take a chance on one of these machines. Sometimes to

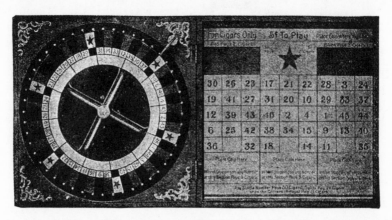

avoid suspicion the operator will give some little rosette with each play, but it is very rarely the player gets anything like value for his money. This wheel can be played for either red or black or numbers. The player places his coin on one of the colors or numbers as shown in the illustration, and a number of players may play at one time. It will be noticed that this machine is made to fold up like a travelling case. This is for the convenience of those who wish to operate them on fair grounds, etc., as they are the least suspicious looking articles when folded up, and are not cumbersome to the owner.

GRAVITATION BALL GAME.

These games vary in size and make-up. The one here shown is a three-ball game, the three balls usually selling for ten cents. The cage looking case is provided with three holes in the top, and there are three wooden rings at the bottom of the cage corresponding with the holes at the top. The cage is usually about six inches deep. The player, in order to gain a prize, must succeed in dropping the ball into the wooden ring so that it will remain there. The ball is made of wood also. It is claimed to be a game of skill. As the ball drops down through the hole it generally gives a bounce—not on to the ring, but away from it,

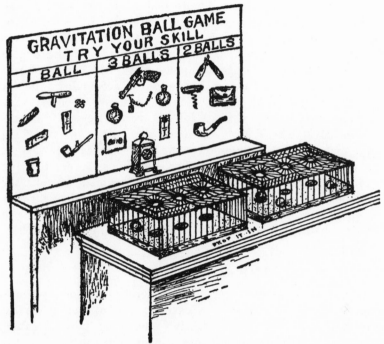

and it is almost impossible for the ball ever to stay on the ring. Then again, to make it more difficult, the rings are sometimes so placed that they are not exactly in line with the hole above, although it may be but a fraction of an inch, and unless the player had a very straight eye and was looking for such a contingency, he would not discover anything wrong. The result is that the operator does not have to invest much of his surplus cash in purchasing articles for prizes.

CANE RACK.

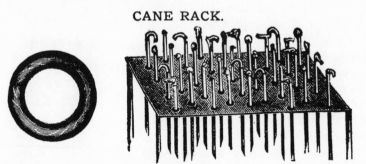

The casual observer at the county fair will stop and look at the cane rack with interest, finally making up his mind to try for one of the canes. In different localities the price varies for the number of chances given for your money. He probably pays five cents for six throws. To be successful in securing one of the canes the ring must go completely over the cane and rest on the table. This is almost impossible to accomplish, and for several reasons. The ring, which is made of wood, is very light, and therefore too delicate for the average person to handle conveniently. Three sizes of rings are made, viz., 1⅝, 1¾ and 2 inches. The handles on some of the canes will vary in size up to about four inches, so that it is impossible for the ring to go on them. Indeed, very few canes are made to take the ring, and the operator of a cane rack stand can often go through the whole season with an investment of not more than $10. For that amount he can get a complete outfit, including 240 canes.

THE O'LEARY BELT.

Like the other swindling devices herein described, the mechanism of this contrivance is easily operated, and, when explained, readily comprehended. It is, however, what is called, in the slang of the street, "a sure winner" for the manipulator. Thousands of dollars have been won through its operation in a single day, and one used on the streets of Cincinnati won $125,-000 in six months.

In order to work it successfully, it is indispensable that the top of the machine be raised high enough above the heads of the surrounding crowd to prevent the by-standers from seeing the interior, inasmuch as such a view would disclose the apparatus by means of which they would be robbed of their money. With this end in view, the operator generally operates it from a buggy, the upper part of the machine standing about three feet above the floor of the conveyance.

As will be seen in the cut, the device consists of a hoop-wheel, a supporting rod and a box platform, supporting the rod and wheel. The apparatus may be taken apart and neatly placed in this box. On the box is placed a valise containing money. The wheel, or "belt," is made of brass, and is about sixteen inches in diameter and four inches broad. It contains thirty-two compartments, each one containing a card, which is held in position by a small fold of metal on each of three sides. These cards may be perfectly blank, though usually they contain pictures of famous celebrities. The valise, which is shown in the illustration at the foot of the upright rod, contains money. Inside the metal hoop is a leather belt, of which, at equal distances, are painted numbers representing sums of money, so arranged that one will fall behind each alternate compartment. When the cards are raised, the belt is seen through a rectangular opening at the back.

The driver of the buggy carries a number of whips. As soon as a crowd has gathered around him (which is certain to happen in a very few moments), he informs the spectators that any one or more may, for $1.00, purchase a chance to win a money prize, varying in amounts from $1.00 to $20.00. Some one having expressed an inclination to buy, the proprietor takes his money and hands him a whip, with which to point to any one of the thirty-two sections of the "hoop" which he may select. The purchaser having rested the whip on a compartment, the operator removes the cards which he has touched. Underneath is shown either a blank space on the belt or one inscribed with a certain sum. If it happens to be the latter, the buyer is given the amount indicated; if the former, he receives nothing.

The name of this device is supposed to be the same as that of the inventor. A well-known confidence operator by the name of O'Leary flourished some years ago, who was recognized among his companions as an expert manipulator of this apparatus, and it is generally believed among the guild of peripatetic gamesters that the idea of its construction was conceived in his fertile brain, through the direct inspiration of the antipodes of Providence.

SHELL GAME.

In some of its salient features this game resembles "three card Monte." The only implements necessary are three hollow shells and a small rubber ball, about the size of a buckshot.

Halves of English walnut shells are the ones commonly employed, although any hollow hemispheres will answer; sometimes operators use halves of potatoes scooped out. The simplicity of the apparatus enables the " shell " man to carry his outfit with him in his vest pocket wherever he may go, and he

is accordingly able to ply his vocation at any spot where he may be able to gather a crowd.

The operator, after rolling the ball, places one of the shells over it in such a way that the edge of the latter shall be slightly raised, thus affording a plain view of the ball underneath. He then moves the shells around, after which someone is invited to tell under which shell the ball is to be found, and a bet is made. The operator wins big money on this game, for the " outside " invariably loses, as the ball is never under any of the shells when the bet is made. It looks simple, but is not nearly so simple as the one who goes up against it.

One of the best known " shell men " in the country for many years was " Jim " Miner, better known as " Umbrella Jim," who was fond of introducing his games by singing the following doggerel:

> " A little fun, just now and then
> Is relished by the best of men.
> If you have nerve, you may have plenty;
> Five, draws you ten, and ten, draws twenty.
> Attention giv'n, I'll show to you,
> How umbrella hides the peek-a-boo.
> Select your shell, the one you choose;
> If right, you win, if not, you lose;
> The game itself is lots of fun,
> Jim's chances, though, are two to one;
> And I tell you your chance is slim
> To win a prize from ' Umbrella Jim.' "

TIVOLI OR BAGATELLE.

The gambling device known by this name is shown in the accompanying illustrations. The table is made of wood usually

about 3½ to 4 feet in length and 2 feet broad. Running length-
wise through the center of the
table is a wooden partition, dividing it into two equal parts. At
the lower end of each division
are ten compartments, open at
the top, each set being numbered
1, 2, 3, 4, 5, 6, 7, 8, 9, 0. At the
upper end of each division is a
gate, lettered on the diagram c. c.
Between the gates and the numbered compartments are placed
metal pins or pegs, arranged substantially as shown by the dots
on the diagram. Directly below
the lower row of pins and extend-
ing over the upper ends of the
compartments is a board, which
runs entirely across the table,
but only one-half of which is
shown in the illustration.

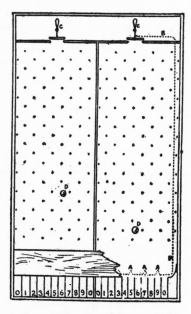

The chart shows the winning and losing numbers. The
letters " rep." are an abbreviation for the word " represent," and
show that the player who happens to make the number in that
square must, if he does not wish to lose his stake, double it and
play again.

It is utterly impossible for a chance player to win at this
game. You will notice in the illustration the dotted line running
the entire length of the board. As this is being manipulated by
the operator a row of ten triangular metal points, marked a, a, a,
are so arranged that one shall stand in front of each alternate
compartment, thus throwing the marble into one of the adjacent
divisions. Of course the compartments closed by the points always contain the winning numbers.

The assistance of " cappers " is indispensable to running
this game, for interest is certain to be supplanted by a sense of
discouragement, as the dupes who stake their money in good
faith are never permitted to win.

TIVOLI OR BAGATELLE.

Jewelry. 20	$5.00 47	$2.00 79	$10.00 11	$1.00 71	$10.00 25	Jewelry. 6	Blank. 16
Rep. 96	Jewelry. 26	$10.00 97	$10.00 29	$5.00 83	$5.00 39	$10.00 59	Jewelry. 32
Blank. 00	$5.00 85	Jewelry. 34	Rep. 58	$2.00 41	$5.00 21	Rep. 68	$1.00 55
$1.00 91	Blank. 40	$5.00 5	$1.00 75	Jewelry. 62	$5.00 93	Blank. 72	Rep. 14
Rep. 22	Jewelry. 80	Rep. 54	Jewelry. 28	Rep. 84	$2.00 57	Jewelry. 64	Rep. 42
Jewelry. 66	Jewelry. 30	$10.00 45	$2.00 2	$10.00 35	Jewelry. 78	$5.00 7	$2.00 27
Blank. 18	Rep. 88	Rep. 38	Blank. 10	Jewelry. 92	$5.00 53	$20.00 17	Jewelry. 48
Jewelry. 50	Rep. 74	Jewelry. 94	Jewelry. 24	$25.00 33	$2.00 99	$1.00 81	$1.00 23
$1.00 65	Jewelry. 86	$2.00 61	$5.00 49	$5.00 63	Jewelry. 76	$5.00 69	$2.00 37
Blank. 46	Rep. 56	Jewelry. 36	$1.00 77	$5.00 43	$5.00 19	Jewelry. 60	Rep. 12
$2.00 95	$5.00 1	Jewelry. 52	Jewelry. 82	Rep. 70	$5.00 81	$5.00 13	Rep. 90
Jewelry. 8	Jewelry. 4	Jewelry. 98	$2.00 73	Rep. 44	$5.00 9	$5.00 51	$5.00 87
		$2.00 15	$5.00 67	$2.00 89	$2.00 3		

THE JENNY WHEEL.

This device is most commonly used by the "small fry" gamblers. It is a "fake," pure and simple, and the apparatus for cheating is so simple in construction that it could be easily detected should a victim ask for the privilege of examining it. Should such an inconvenient request be made, however, the

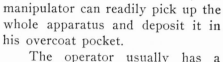

manipulator can readily pick up the whole apparatus and deposit it in his overcoat pocket.

The operator usually has a small case containing articles of cheap jewelry, each one bearing a number. The player pays ten cents for the privilege of twirling the saucer containing the marble and taking his chance of winning a prize. If the marble falls into a compartment numbered to correspond with the number attached to any one of the prizes exposed in the case, the article so numbered is given to him. If, unfortunately, he draws a blank, he receives nothing.

BEE HIVE.

The accompanying illustration gives an excellent idea of the general appearance of this device. It consists of two cones, the inner one of which is placed upon circular pieces of wood, around the rim of which are thirty-two compartments, numbered from one to thirty-two, and separated by thin metal plates. Driven into the surface of the inner cone are small nails or metal pegs, the arrangement of which is a matter of comparative indifference, although they are usually rather close together and approximately equi-distant. The outer cone serves as a cap or case.

An unsophisticated player can never win except through the consent of the operator. In order to encourage the crowd in playing, "cappers" have to be employed, who are always on hand to draw prizes. It sometimes happens, however, that the verdant looking countryman, after receiving the dollar from the "capper" and winning a prize for the latter, forthwith "makes

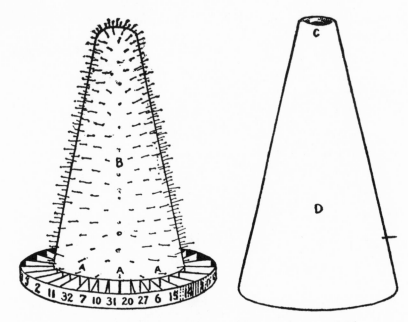

cracks " for parts unknown, leaving the proprietor and his astute confederate to mourn the loss of their money and to bewail their own misplaced confidence in human nature.

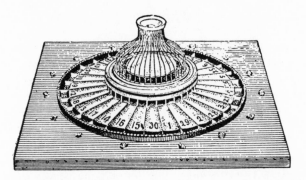

This is an illustration of what is known as the " Improved Bee Hive," and is of the latest design and construction. It is stated that it can be run where all others are barred. The ball is in sight from start to finish, so that while the player can see the play and know just where the ball stops, it is impossible to detect the secret workings of the machine.

This machine is specially made to catch " suckers " and is

full of honey, but the "suckers" don't get any of the honey; they are lucky to get a piece of beeswax.

"The little bee sucks the blossom,
The big bee gets the honey,
The sucker does the work,
And the gambler takes the money."

SQUEEZE SPINDLE.

This device has been successfully employed in defrauding the unwary for nearly sixty years, and is still to be found on every fair ground where the directors are men of sufficiently easy morality to permit unprincipled sharpers to fleece their townspeople for a consideration. I have myself won thousands by this very means.

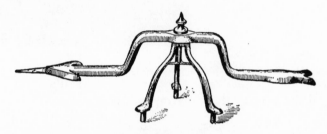

This illustrates what is known as the Improved Camel Back Spindle. Notice the description given to induce the public to become purchasers of this machine. " This spindle has the most perfect creep ever made, next to perpetual motion arrow 22 inches long, stands 4 inches high, weight 7 pounds. The only controlled spindle ever made without a gaff. WE GUARANTEE DETECTION IMPOSSIBLE, EVERY LEG A SQUEEZE. Yet all legs are fair as the tripod is one solid casting. Spindle works so accurate that operator could split a hair."

Coney Island is the favorite resort where the squeeze spindle is chiefly operated. I have in my possession at the present time one of the old veterans, and can vouch for it that thousands have been lost on this machine. The majority of men who witness my demonstrations on crooked machinery are familiar with this kind of a machine, but after witnessing my demonstration many come to me personally and promise never to go up against it any more.

Another form of the squeeze spindle, is known to the profession as the "three spindle" machine. It differs from the

above spindle, only in that it contains three arrows instead of one, two of which are under control of the operator through the employment of friction at the pivot by means of precisely similar contrivances. It is not difficult, however, to perceive the very large preponderance of chances in favor of the sharper, who always has it in his power to determine who shall win the large wagers. As a rule small bets are placed on these machines, but the sharper can average as much as $400 a week. The illustration here shown is known as " the old army game."

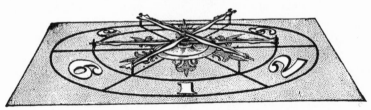

It is claimed for the above machine to be the most popular and fascinating spindle ever put upon the market. " The Winner of the Day " Chuck-a-Luck percentage Banker. It is got up very attractively, and the layout is richly ornamented in colors and gold. Works on the same principle as that shown in the preceding illustration.

On this machine each player places the amount he wishes to bet on the color or horse which he selects. The proprietor gives odds of ten to one on the horses and even bets are made on the colors. That is to say: if a player wagers a dollar on the red and wins, the proprietor pays him a dollar and returns his stake. If he bets a dollar on a horse and wins, he receives $10 in addition to his original wager.

Here again the player cannot win without the proprietor's consent. At the point of four, as shown in the diagram, is placed a metal disc, resembling a button, which is attached to a stout wire rod, which in turn is sunk into the wooden top of

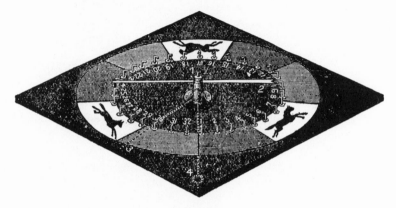

the table and entirely concealed from view by the cloth covering the latter. When this metal button is pressed, it operates the rod, the other end of which, by creating friction at the central pivot, gradually stops the movement of the arrow, and the operator is enabled to bring the latter to a standstill at whatever point in the ellipse he may see fit. He can operate the rod

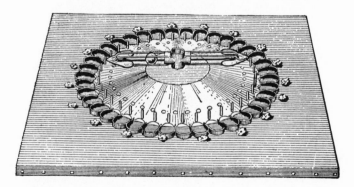

by the hand, but if anyone objects to his hand being on the table, another contrivance is attached, the location of which is indicated on the diagram by figure three. The latter contrivance is worked by pressure from some part of the body, usually the hip.

The Ball Spindle is of the latest design, and is considered to be the most ingenious device ever invented in the spindle line, and stands for any kind of inspection the operator wishes to submit it to. In appearance it is fairness personified. It is the only spindle made that indicates with loose ball, carried by the arrow while arrow is moving; when arrow stops, ball falls out, rolls between pins and into pocket. Guaranteed not to blow. Big and little prizes are usually given on this machine, and in case of emergency it can be set as a fair " joint." This spindle has 38 pockets, same as a roulette wheel. It can be framed up for many different games such as red, black and star, or for chuck-a-luck, etc., or as a " represent " game.

One of the most expensive spindles ever placed upon the market is that shown in the illustration below. The manufacturers claim to have spent ten years of time in experimenting, and the expenditure of hundreds of dollars, in perfecting what they term " the greatest spindle ever invented." Why so much time and money expended on such an article with which to fleece the unsuspecting public? I have seen boys and girls from ten years of age and upward pay their dimes to take what they think is a chance of winning a big prize. They are ignorant of the

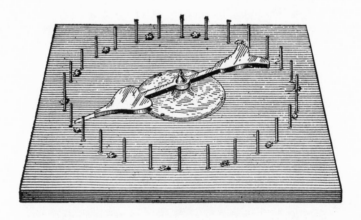

real nature of these implements, and to them it looks big to have the chance of winning a dollar (?) watch or some such article. Such a glowing description is given of this machine. It is sold for the small sum of $50. " Stops natural, looks natural, can be made to come either blank or prize at will, can be turned either way to win or lose. No suspicious moves. Nothing unnatural.

Will be allowed to run anywhere and will always get a play. Can be used as a grinding joint or for money. The greatest money getter ever invented."

The operators of spindles will often give a small artificial rosette to those who are not "lucky" enough to win one of  the larger prizes. They do this to shield themselves in the eyes of the law, for if they are arrested they claim it is not a gambling implement, but a "gift enterprise," as they give something on every p l a y. What is the value of this beautiful rosette? It does not cost more than one quarter of a cent. The fact that they give more or less than an equivalent constitutes it gambling.

The Jewelry Spindle is probably the least suspected of all.

The crowd may have doubts of the fairness of other spindles, but when they see such an array of jewelry exhibited as you see outlined on the illustration, they immediately conclude that it cannot be anything but fair. They lose sight of the fact that the fellow who operates the machine is not there to sell them value for value received, neither is he there for the fun of it, nor for his health. The crowd may be there for " the fun of the fair," but not this man. Let us see what he really gives in re-turn for the dime that is paid for a chance. Remember he gives something every time. You may get in return, anything from a pocket mirror to a nickel watch. You may possibly get a set of spoons; and if you are a young man you can then take your girl out and have a dish of ice cream with two spoons in it. The manufacturer declares he has been compelled to turn out a $50 spindle, which, by reducing cost in some unimportant parts, and making in a large quantity, he can offer it at an unheard of price. And so this spindle, together with 2,615 pieces of assorted jewelry, are sold for $31. This gives the operator a profit of $230.50 at ten cents a roll. Figure this out for yourself and see what value you get for your money.

You will notice on the diagram that the numbers one to six appear four times and that there are four stars. This makes it possible for 28 to play the machine at one time. It is only in such an instance that anyone secures a large prize, and even that cannot be of much value.

The above illustrates a jewelry outfit such as is used by the fakirs who follow the fairs and circuses. It costs very little cash to start up in that line of business, but I would advise them to try some honest means of securing a livelihood. It will be a great blessing to the country at large when it becomes impos-sible for officials to accept a rake-off from this class of people.

Let me relate an incident that occurred upon a Missouri fairground. A sharper, who had interviewed the directors, convinced (?) them that his machine was entirely honest, and arranged matters satisfactorily all around, felt serenely secure in the operation of his " privilege." (And right here I again condemn the granting of such " privileges." A " privilege " to do what? To prey upon the ignorant; to dupe the unwary; to victimize the unsuspecting; to debauch the young; and to scatter broadcast the seeds of corruption, whose fruit will be misery in every home.) But this is by the way, so I will return to the narrative. The " privileged " gambler had set up his wheel, and to use a slang phrase, " was doing a land-office business." A verdant countryman approached the machine. Over and over he tried his " luck," which every time—as a matter of course—rested with the " privileged " monopolist. This went on for some time, and I, as a disinterested spectator, watched the game. The agriculturist quit a loser to the extent of some $50. The blackleg's face was impassable. The countryman thrust his hand into his pocket; when he withdrew it, it clasped a long-bladed knife, the blade reflecting the light. " Stranger," said he, " I want my money back. I don't know how you did it, but you've cheated me, and I'm going to get even. Give me back that money!" Only the unnatural pallor on the old man's face indicated the extreme tension of his feelings. The swindler looked at him. At least seventy-five or a hundred persons were standing around; something had to be done, and promptly. " Why, old man," said the proprietor, " there's no use in your cutting up rough. Of course you can have your money. I was only joking." And with these words he returned the dishonest winnings.

NEEDLE WHEEL.

This machine consists of three parts. The outer rim, which is stationary, contains thirty-two metal grooves, numbered, apparently without special arrangement. Inside this rim is a circular piece of wood, resembling a wheel, but without spokes, which is covered with a cloth. Above this is a saucer-shaped piece of wood, in which are bored three holes. On the table on which the wheel is placed stands a wooden box, containing thirty-two compartments. These numbers are divided equally into prizes and blanks.

The player, after paying his money for a chance, places a marble in the upper wheel or saucer, which is given a twirl, the lower wheel being usually set in motion at the same time, but in an opposite direction. As the upper wheel revolves, the mar- ble flies around a n d finally falls through one of the holes on to the lower wheel. The latter slopes gently from center to cir- cumference and the mar- ble naturally rolls down to one of the compart- ments in the outer rim, where it stops.

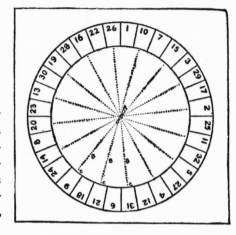

The " fake " consists of a rod which runs through both wheels, ornamented with a knob on the top. This knob actually operates a thumb-screw which sets in motion a system of six- teen wire levers, lettered b, b, b, on the diagram, which force up through the cloth covering a like number of fine needle points, c, c, c. These have the effect of sending the marble into one of the blank compartments.

CORONA OR MASCOT.

To operate this machine two men are necessary, in addition to a number of " cappers." The apparatus consists of a circular piece of wood, at the outer rim of which are painted numbers from one to sixty. Inside this is placed a round piece of heavy glass, on which is painted either an arrow or a small pointer. This inner plate revolves upon a central pivot. Prizes of money or jewelry are placed upon the numbers. Those who wish to win any of them buy tickets, on each of which is inscribed a num- ber, the purchaser selecting his ticket at random, from a large number which are placed in a box. At the right of the ostensible proprietor sits his confederate, who poses as " book-keeper." In order that no " sucker " may, by any chance, win a prize of any value, a lever, similar to that used in the squeeze spindle, is sunk into the table and concealed by the cloth cover. The " book-keeper," by pressing on the end of the wire rod, which is directly underneath his book, can apply friction to the pivot and cause the wheel to stop at any number which he may choose. It is hardly necessary to say that the box from which the purchaser takes his ticket contains none bearing the number which would

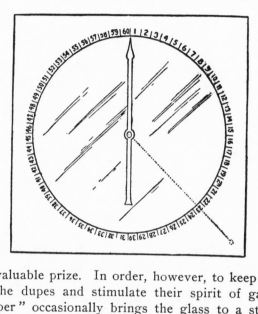

call for a valuable prize. In order, however, to keep up the interest of the dupes and stimulate their spirit of gaming, the "book-keeper" occasionally brings the glass to a standstill at a point where the arrow indicates a money prize. Instantly a "capper" steps forward from among the crowd, presents a ticket, and claims the prize. The unsuspecting fools thus become encouraged and continue to play with fresh zest.

In case any of the players should become suspicious, and demand a sight of the tickets remaining in the box, in order to satisfy himself that the numbers corresponding to the money prizes are actually there, the proprietor cheerfully assents, readily producing the box, into which he has surreptitiously transferred the necessary cards from his pocket.

BOX AND BALLS.

This is a device by no means common, there being very few of the "fraternity" who can operate it successfully. In the accompanying diagram, figure "1" shows the exterior of the box.

Inside this box " B," are placed thirty ivory balls or marbles, each of which are numbered. Near the operator stands a table

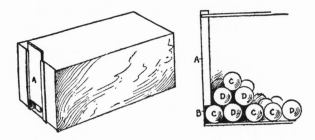

on which is a show case containing twelve prizes, part of which are articles of jewelry and the remainder sums of money. When a sufficient number of chances have been sold the operator

$10.00	Jewelry.	Rep.	$10.00	Rep.
1	8	12	29	4
$52.00	Jewelry.	Blank.	$20.00	Jewelry.
15	24	28	17	10
Jewelry.	$10.00	$5.00	Jewelry.	Jewelry.
6	21	3	22	14
$5.00	Jewelry.	Rep.	Jewelry.	$5.00
11	27	30	26	7
Rep.	$5.00	Rep.	$10.00	Jewelry.
18	25	20	19	16
$10.00	Jewelry.	$5.00	Rep.	Jewelry.
5	13	23	9	2

Chart for Box and Ball Case.

shakes the box, causing the balls to roll from one end to the other. Letter " A " on figure 1, represents a slide at one end of the box. This slide is raised by the manipulator and allows one ball to escape at a time. The number of the marble is examined and he receives whatever it represents on the chart.

The fraud consists of two elements, one relating to the marbles, and the other to the box. In the first place, the ivory spheres are not all of equal size, the twelve whose numbers correspond to the valuable prizes being the merest trifle larger than the eighteen which call for articles of no value. The "fake" in the box is in the slide, "A," and is shown in figure 2, which gives an enlarged view of this part of the apparatus. In this figure the line "B" represents a shoulder, whose height above the bottom of the slide (which is shaved almost as thin as paper), is so delicately adjusted that it stops the larger balls, and allows the smaller ones to strike against the thin wood. The sensitive finger of the manipulator readily discerns the striking of a ball against this part of the slide. If he feels it he knows that he must raise the slide and allow one of the smaller marbles to escape, inasmuch as the latter calls for no article of value.

THE SWINGING BALL.

This is a very simple contrivance. The lower line represents the support on which rests a frame, composed of two uprights, and connected at the top by a cross-piece. From the center of the latter hangs a string, at the end of which is a wooden ball, lettered "C." In the center of the lower support there is placed a triangular pin, lettered "D" on the diagram.

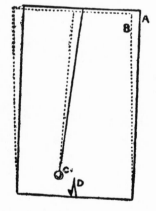

The player pays ten cents for a chance to swing the ball. If, as it swings back it overturns the peg, he receives back his ten cents, together with a dollar.

To prevent such a catastrophe, the ball is usually slightly deflected toward either the right or left as it leaves the hands of the player. If the upright remains perfectly perpendicular, the chances are that the ball, on its return, will strike the peg through the operation of the law of gravitation. Just here is where the operator does a little " fine work." The uprights are always made a little loose, so that by a very slight pressure from the shoulder on the part of the manipulator, at the point " A," they may be bent from a perpendicular position to that indicated by the dotted line " B." The inevitable result is that when the ball swings back, the force of gravity draws it on one side of the peg, and the unfortunate speculator sees that the money which he paid for the privilege of throwing it, has been lost.

" DOLLAR STORE " OR " DROP CASE."

This outfit consists of a wooden case, holding one hundred or more envelopes, together with the usual chart showing the amount of prizes. It is a great money making scheme.

The " capper " and the intended victim each pay for a draw, the former drawing number " eleven." The operator then slips the envelope containing the ticket marked " eleven " into a secret pocket, from which at the same time he draws another envelope holding a ticket marked " forty-four." He then places

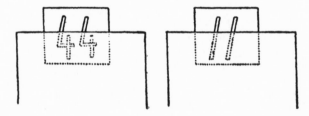

this envelope, together with the one held by the " sucker," in the box, in such a way that the edge of one of them rises a little above the rest. Both the " capper " and the greenhorn perceive this circumstance and the latter supposes it to have been the result of accident. The " capper " then draws the envelope whose corner is raised and the dupe takes the next one to it. The " capper " puts up say twenty dollars, and then opens his envelope. He curses his luck when he discovers he has drawn a blank. While the proprietor turns his head, the confederate snatches the envelope away from the dupe, hastily raises the flap, pulls out a small portion of the ticket within, thus showing the tops of figure " forty-four," which leads the dupe to believe he has drawn the lucky " eleven." Until the money has been paid he is not allowed to examine his ticket. When, having paid the cash, he opens the envelope, he discovers that instead of the magic " eleven " he has drawn " forty-four," having been misled by the resemblance between the upper ends of the figures " four " and " one," shown him in the momentary glance which the " capper " gave him of the card. Of course, he is utterly without redress, and has to bear his loss with such degree of equanimity as he may be able to command.

KENO.

This game is a favorite one with nearly all non-professional gamblers, not only because the risk of loss involved is not large, but also because of the popular impression that it is always played " on the square." As a matter of fact it is usually conducted fairly, although, as will be explained, sometimes barefaced swindling is resorted to by the proprietors. The game very closely resembles the children's game of " lotto." Any number of persons may play. Each one desiring to participate in the game buys a card on which are three rows of five numbers each, arranged together with regularity. The price paid for the card varies from ten cents upwards, although sometimes very high stakes are played. None of the cards contain a higher number than ninety-nine. The conductor of the game—who is known as a " roller "—takes his position, usually upon a raised platform, in full view of the players. Before him is placed a globe containing ninety-nine balls, numbered consecutively from one to ninety-nine, to correspond with the figures on the players' cards. The balls having been thoroughly mixed, the " roller " presses a spring at the bottom of the globe, opening an aperture just large enough to permit one ball to drop at a time. As soon as the first one has fallen, the aperture is closed and the " roller," in a loud voice, calls out the number inscribed upon it. If a player finds the number in either of the three horizontal rows on his card he places a button over it. When any player has all five numbers in any one of his rows thus called out, he exclaims " keno," after which the " roller " takes no more balls from the globe. His card is then inspected by one of the " collectors "—of whom there are usually two—and if his tally is correct he is given the entire amount of money paid by all the

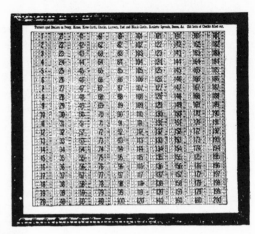

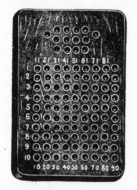

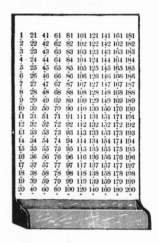

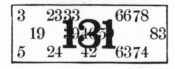

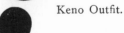

Keno Outfit.

players (which is called the " pot ") less a discount of fifteen per cent., which is retained by " the house " as its " percentage." Thus, if there are a hundred players, each of whom has paid ten cents for a card, the winner receives eight dollars and fifty cents, the bank reserving to itself one dollar and fifty cents as " percentage."

Matters having been thus arranged, fresh stakes are advanced by those wishing to play again, the balls put in the globe and the game resumed.

It may readily be seen that the " bank " incurs no risk whatever, and its sure percentage on the stakes is large enough to satisfy the cupidity of most gamblers. Fortunes have been made by the proprietors of these games, one concern in St. Louis having made $190,000 thereby. Still, the instinct to cheat is strong in the breast of the professional sharper; and sometimes a confederate of the proprietor plays in the game and wins the " pot," through the co-operation of the " roller." The latter withholds from the globe several balls, which he substitutes from time to time, for the ones which he should have taken from the globe. The numbers on these withheld and substituted balls correspond to those necessary to fill out one of the horizontal rows on the confederate's card and the latter is thus enabled to win through fraud.

THE GAMBLER'S LUCK.

To prove how matters will go wrong,
When gambling ways you start along,
    Just listen to this tale:
I tramped for many a weary day,
And funds were gone, and skies were gray,
    For trade was flat and stale.

My blood seemed chilled, the outlook black,
As I came hoofing down the track
    And reached a country town;
I did not know a single soul
To ask for hash, or beg a bowl,
    And I was done up brown.

I earned a dollar in that town,
And in a faro bank sat down,
    And took a little horn;
The checks they used, my gentle youth—
You may not think I tell the truth—
    Were grains of Indian corn.

I scanned the players there awhile,
A pleasing thought soon made me smile,
　　Mused I: " Here's luck for me."
I knew a few miles further back,
There stood a corn-crib by the track,
　　As full as it could be.

Though dark and wet, I left the place,
And turned my eager, hopeful face
　　Towards that brimming bin.
Footsore, I reached the happy spot
And felt among the lucky lot,
　　And took a big ear in.

I shelled it as I went along,
And sang the only happy song
　　I'd sung for many days;
I stuck my stake into my clothes,
And in that bank I stuck my nose,
　　For I had made a raise.

I watched the game an hour or two,
And tried to look as green as you,
　　And thought I'd played it fine.
I walked up like a country jake,
And took a handful of my stake
　　And placed all on the nine.

The dealer turned his eager eyes
On mine, which caused me some surprise,
　　And said in tones quite bland:—
" My friend, it may not look quite right,
But no ' reds ' here are played to-night."
　　And that's the way it panned.

I trudged along the track next morn,
And there I saw old Farmer Thorne,
　　Empty his bins with care.
In that large crib, chuck full of grain,
The sight of yellow ears brought pain,
　　For not one " red " was there.

MONTE CARLO: THE DEVIL'S UNIVERSITY.

If you travel along the northwest of Italy, you will eventually reach the little principality of Monaco, and the notorious Monte Carlo. Leaving the city of Nice, by train, and passing through a tunnel, you come full upon the beautiful bay of Villa Franca. Go under ground, again, and you presently emerge upon a rocky headland jutting out into the sapphire sea. This cape bears aloft the little town of Monaco. On the extreme southern side of the headland is a deep bay, beyond which, at a distance of half a mile stands Monte Carlo, on another and lesser promontory. The famous Casino crowns the slope of Monte Carlo, and contains the gambling rooms, concert hall, and theatre. The Casino was established by the late M. Blanc, after his enforced departure from Baden-Baden. But in reality this stately palace was erected, and the surrounding grounds laid out, at the expense of the dupes, the blacklegs, and the courtesans of Europe. M. Garnier, who planned the grand opera house, at Paris, designed the architecture of the Casino in its sensual detail. But this devil's university of Monte Carlo, with its classic rooms, and chairs for Professor Belial and Mammon, is, in sober truth, the erection of those named. The fortune is always with roulette and rouge-et-noir.

There are six tables in the Casino for roulette, where the lowest stake is twenty-five francs. Two rouge-et-noir, where the lowest stake is twenty francs. These tables are always crowded, Sundays and week-days alike.

By some Europeans, it has been insisted that while Monte Carlo may not have moral or elevating influence, yet men will play, and it is not worse there than at the club. This plea is specious and superficial. The club is private; it is not open to women and children. The mischief that might occur there is not an example for the public, and therefore not contagious. The club does not exist for the sole purpose, and is not supported by the profits of the play. It is not an instrument of wholesale demoralization, as is Monte Carlo. The latter is a curse, a public scandal, and an unmitigated evil. In these times of spirited foreign policy, a more wholesome exercise of diplomacy cannot

The Casino at Monte Carlo, Monaco.

be imagined for some European power, than bringing pressure to bear on France for the extinction of Monte Carlo. It is a disgrace to the French Republic that under its protecting wing this pandering to European vice should be allowed, or that Monte Carlo should be a shelter for the sharpers expelled from other haunts on the continent, there to fatten on the wages and spoils of iniquity. If Monaco and Monte Carlo were cleansed of this blot, they would be among the most alluring resorts in the world. The demoralizing tables, and the vicious crew should not be allied with such delightful scenery and salubrious climate.

M. Blanc, now dead, obtained the lease of the place from the Prince of Monaco, agreeing to pay him an enormous rental, one-tenth of the profits of the game, and to defray the expense of maintaining the standing army, the police, and the menials of the principality. The interior of the Casino presents the appearance of a grand drawing-room fête. Monte Carlo is the last and sole representative of the class of gambling resorts of which Baden-Baden, Wiesbaden, Homburg, and Ems, were formerly notable examples.

It is said that the game at Monte Carlo is undoubtedly fair. This may be true. The eyes of the greatest scoundrels in Europe, it is argued, are bent upon the dealers, and that ought to be a sufficient guarantee against any fraud being practiced. But this does not certainly follow. The powers of a Professor of Legerdemain are admitted, and knowing this, it would be childish to guarantee the integrity of any professional gambler.

At the Casino eight roulette and two trente et quarante, or rouge-et-noir tables, are kept running. Roulette is not played precisely as in America, the player has less odds against him, from the fact that the tables have only one zero instead of two. The heaviest play occurs at the trente et quarante tables. This game is played with six packs of cards of 52 each. Having shuffled the cards, the dealer passes them to the nearest player, sometimes the nearest female player, to be cut. It is a gambler's superstition that bad luck attends the one who cuts the cards, and accordingly the professionals often shirk that duty. The pack is not cut as in the United States. The operation consists of inserting a blue card in the sextuple pack. Two rows of cards are dealt on the table, the first representing black and the other red   The ace counts as one, and court cards as ten each, and the tailleur, or dealer, continues to turn cards for the black row until the aggregate number of their spots exceeds thirty. Suppose he deals three " court " cards, or tens, he must deal another. If it is a deuce he calls *" deux,"* and then proceeds to deal the red row, which, perhaps, aggregates thirty-five. *" Cinq,"* exclaims the dealer. The black row being nearest to thirty wins, and accordingly, all who have bet on the black win the amount of their stakes, and the bank rakes in all that has been bet on the red.

Should the two rows tie, on thirty-one, the bank takes half of the stakes, but ties on any other number are considered as a stand-off and the player is free to withdraw or shift his bet, as he pleases. Bets may also be made on *" coleur,"* or *" envers,"* the former winning, when the winning color is the same as that of the first card dealt; and the latter, when it is not. These ties, like all other manifestations of chance, occur with great irregularity. On some days there will scarcely be one; on others they will occur with terrible frequency. M. Blanc invented a system of insurance against these ties at thirty-one, and heavy players generally avail themselves of it. It consists, simply, in the player paying to the bank one per cent. of his bet, which being done, the bank does not take any of his stake when such tie occurs. In such a case the player pays one per cent. for the privilege of playing a game in which the chances are precisely even.

At Monte Carlo no bet of less than a louis (four dollars) is taken at the trente et quarante tables, and no bet larger than 12,000 francs ($2,400). The smallest bet allowed at roulette is five francs, and the largest 5,000 francs. On a single number, nine louis, or 180 francs, is the largest bet permitted. Roulette, compared with trente et quarante, is a very unfavorable game for the player.

Formerly, at European gaming resorts, the game was played with two zeros and thirty-six numbers; that is, two chances out of thirty-eight were reserved for the bank. With the advent of M. Blanc at Homburg a more liberal policy was inaugurated, and only one zero was employed. When M. Blanc went to Monte Carlo he made the game still more favorable to the players by taking, when the ball struck zero, only half, instead of the whole of the bets on the colors, odd or even, etc. Including the zero, the Monte Carlo roulette table has thirty-seven numbers, and the player on a single number is paid thirty-five for one. In backing two numbers with a single bet, one is banking one-

The Gambler's Last Play—From Monte Carlo to Hell.
Contains 152 Suicides at Monte Carlo.

eighteenth of the table, and is paid seventeen times his stake. In backing four numbers, " *en carré,*" as it is called, he bets on one-ninth and is paid eight for one. Accordingly, as he places his bet, the punter, even though he stakes but a single coin, can play one, two, three, four, or six numbers at once. He can also bet on the first, second or third twelve in the thirty-six numbers, or one of the three columns in which the numbers are arranged on the board, or on the colors, or odd or even, or on what is called " *manque et passe,*" the former signifying the numbers from one to eighteen, and the latter those from nineteen to thirty-six. Betting on the columns, or the dozens, against which the bank pays two to one, is a favorite game for punters, who potter about the room with a handful of five-franc pieces, and struggle all day long to win or lose a louis or two. Twenty francs is a louis, in the language of the gamester. However he may bet, the advantage is ever preserved by the table.

One of the strangest cases of getting a living that I ever heard of, was that of a man who gave lessons to would-be visitors to Monte Carlo, in the gentle art of beating the bank when they arrive there. The man poses as a professor in this line, and charges the sum of $5 for half an hour's lesson. Let me say right here that it is useless for anyone to throw their money away on a proposition of this kind, for the only sure way to beat the bank is to let it alone entirely. Is it likely that a man, if he had discovered a secret wherewith to beat the bank at Monte Carlo, would divulge the secret for a small sum when he could work the system right on the spot and so pocket the winnings for his own benefit?

The company which now controls the Casino at Monte Carlo, has provided a fund to send home gamblers who have lost their all in the gambling rooms. The granting of the viatique is constantly being carried on. The broken gambler who presents himself at a small office in the central saloon of the Casino is, if he is found to be a bona fide loser, handed the price of a second-class railway ticket to his home, whether his home be in New York, London, or Jerusalem, and enough extra money for his meals on the journey. An Englishman is usually given from $40 to $60. Each broken gambler, who receives the viatique, signs a receipt for the money handed to him, surrenders his card of admission to the Casino, and is told that he will not be allowed again to enter the gambling rooms until he has paid back the loan. It is said that the company assists losers to the extent of $40,000 a year.

Gambling is not the only method by which the visitors to Monte Carlo lose their money. Pickpockets are plenteous and carry on a large business.

While playing at the gaming tables in the Casino, the wife of a prominent member of the British colony in Paris, found suddenly that someone had opened her bag and stolen her purse, which contained several hundred dollars. In a letter to her husband she writes:

" It was about five o'clock when they entered my complaint and a description of the purse in the ledger. I returned after seven o'clock, and the clerk had to turn back three pages to find the entry.

" ' Surely,' I said, ' these are not all losses that have occurred since I was here two hours ago?'

" ' Yes, madam, they are,' he replied, ' and it's the same every day.' "

The writer thinks that losses is scarcely the right word to use. She relates the case of another Englishwoman who was robbed of $1,000 in the same way as herself. The victim actually caught a woman's hand in her bag and she held on until some detectives arrived, but the thief had already passed the notes to an accomplice, and she was allowed to go.

Where can language be found to express the awful situation that exists at Monte Carlo by the number of suicides that occur day by day. The average is said to be not less than one for each day of the year. Some mother's boy goes out into the world to " sow his wild oats," and eventually finds himself at Monte Carlo. He is in for everything that is going on, for he wishes to be considered a good fellow by his associates, and it is no difficult matter to find " professional " friends at these resorts. They lead the young man on until he is thoroughly debauched by sin and wickedness. Wine, women, and gambling,— the devil's trinity—play an important part in his ultimate downfall. He becomes so satiated with these various forms of vice, that after awhile he awakes to the consciousness that they have robbed him of all manhood, honor, and respect; of his money and reputation. A man can commence to obtain money by commencing at the bottom rung of the ladder, but a reputation is not to be so easily regained. The mother at home is thinking of the welcome she shall prepare for the home coming of her boy, and of the loving kiss she shall bestow upon him, while the boy— conscious that he has disgraced his mother, conscious that he has lost all else worth having,—seeks consolation in suicide. A few days later the newspaper prints a notice to the effect that " the son of Mrs. So and So, who has been travelling in foreign parts, has been lost and given up as dead."

QUESTIONS.

What merchant wants a gambler for a clerk?

What boss wants a gambler for a workman?

What foreman wants a gambler for an apprentice?

What family wants a gambler for a doctor?

What firm wants a gambler for a salesman?

What bank wants a gambler for a cashier?

What depositor wants a gambler for a banker?

What railway wants a gambler for a conductor?

What citizen wants a gambler to represent him in the legislature?

What boy would wish to learn so disgraceful a trade?

What woman wants a gambler for a husband?

THE RACE-TRACK: A NATIONAL VICE.

If reckless indulgence of games of chance of every description, in lottery enterprizes, in the board of trade, and in the pool-room, can be, as it is, appropriately denominated as a " national vice," that appellation belongs with especial emphasis to the gambling of the race-track. This is true, probably, mainly because of the fatal facility with which contact is there had with the evil influence that draws boys, aye, even women and girls, into its deadly toils. The race-track is governed by presumably respectable persons. It has the convincing support of the press, universally, to sustain its claims to harmlessness. Church members and people of recognized reputable position, bankers, merchants and professional men are openly seen " making their bets," in the face of .thousands of their fellow citizens. Women surrender to the glamour of its fascinations, and may be seen in numbers, any day on any grand-stand, " backing " their favorite in the race. In the face of such example as this, then, how can we expect that the youth of the land shall escape? Already they are sufficiently imbued in their personal and business ambition with the spirit of speculation that pervades the nation, and in the feverish haste to get rich suddenly are ready to turn to any resort that may seem to offer them the opportunity of making large winnings for a small investment. True, the youth may have been warned by a pious mother or a prudent father that gambling is a vice, and one of the most dangerous and pernicious of all that threaten the interests, the welfare and even the safety of society. But when the young man sees the pillar of the church, or the refined lady leader of society, who mayhap occupies the front pew in the church which he attends, openly patronizing gambling, is it any cause for wonder that he concludes the good counsel which he brought from home was merely a mistake, and that there's " no harm in it " after all? At once in the circle of that treacherous maelstrom of vice, at first imperceptibly to himself and in slow and apparently safe revolutions, he is gradually but irresistibly drawn to the fatal gulf, in which character, integrity, hope, and the best opportunities of life are remorselessly swallowed up.

Every bet that is made upon a race-course is emphatically and indisputably participation in the commonest kind of a lottery —is gambling pure and simple; and if it has been found necessary by Congress, acting upon the advice of the National Executive, to legislate against the existence of the incorporated lotteries that exist by State authority, why is it not equally the duty of Congress to declare all betting unlawful? This is not a new proposition. Under the existing laws the illegality of gambling by betting is recognized in the refusal of the courts to enforce debts or contracts incurred under a bet. If the principle were logically carried out, it would afford a safeguard to society which, as yet, moral sentiment appears to have been unable to entend. But what moral restraints, the teaching of parents and the exhortations of the clergy, have failed to achieve, may be accomplished by what this book contains: by tearing away the mask of harmless sport from the death's-head that grins behind it, and exposing, in all its hideous nakedness, not the moral wrong that there is in the vice of gambling by betting, but the personal rascality toward the individual, the plain and evident object of robbery that is involved in all the schemes of the book-maker, the pool-seller, and every other person who makes either a *profession* or a systematic *practice* of offering bets upon the results of the race-track.

The Pool-Room. This is one of the most nefarious of all the modern instruments of evil, and ought to be summarily abolished by specific law in every State in the Union. Its worst feature, perhaps—in addition to the fact that it is a skin game played to catch " suckers," as the gamblers term their latest dupes— is that it seeks out and offers opportunity to a class of citizens who could never be reached by these machinations by any other way. Clerks, students, apprentices, and such, would in all probability never have the time nor the means to squander in a trip to New York to Sheepshead Bay, to witness a horse-race. He can visit them at his noon hour or in the idle hours of his evening rest. Here he is deluded into the belief that a small investment will bring a rich return, and is easily wheedled by a " capper " into investing his small hoard in " tips " that he is assured are certain to win. Of course he loses, and to retrieve his loss will probably go to his employers' funds to get the means to continue his play. And so from bad to worse till exposure and ruin overtake him.

Pool-rooms are conducted upon the science of exactness, not only as to the promptness and accuracy of the reports upon the blackboard, but also with regard to the certainty that the pool-seller will be the only one in the room who will be a sure winner each time. The pool board displays the whole course of the race, in its smallest details. It shows when the horses are " off," which one is " in the lead;" which " second " and which " third;" how they stand at the " quarter," the " half," the " three-quarter," and their positions down to the " stretch," and within ten seconds after the " finish," will display which horse was winner, and which took second and which took third place. Previous to the race the board has reliable and definite information of the state of the track, whether " fast " or muddy; gives the name of the jockey who is to mount each horse, the weights and all information necessary to the man who governs his bets by what he considers the most reasonable chance to win.

The pool-seller works him gambling racket on what he calls the percentage system. In all pools sold by auction, he deducts a certain sum, generally five to fifteen per cent. from the amount of the pool, and pays the balance to the winner. The book-maker arranges his book with reference to the " odds " for or against; that is, the individual chances of each horse upon the information which he has available, and which if he be at all expert in the business will enable him to insure his personal success every time, except only in the case where all the patrons buy the same horse and that horse should prove the winner—a contingency that is, however, not as one to one hundred, and about as liable to happen as that the sucker who has bought on a " cinch tip " will win the pot.

Methods of the " House." Let it not be supposed, however, that the book-maker, or his confederates who stand in with him, are to be contented with a fifteen per cent. upon the money that passes through the pool book. On the contrary, he is the most expert and successful of all the gamblers who " play the races." He is generally the only one of this nefarious outfit who receives a genuine and reliable " tip." His intimate relations with the jockeys, stablemen and all the *habitués* of the training stables and racing grounds, are such that he is generally able to pick out a winner, and to discount the results of a race in advance. Thus assured he skilfully sends out his touts to give " tips " that will bring the most grist to the mill, that is to say, to industriously disseminate the belief that that horse will win, which he knows has no chance of success. Under this influence the amateur sport, and the average patron of the racing ground or pool-room, will generally plunge largely on the horse they imagine is to bring them a rich booty, while the pool-seller looks on complacently, knowing that all the money in the strong box belongs to him as surely as if the race had been already run.

The Friendly " Tip." In every pool-room, amid the conglomeration of representatives of "queer" industries always there to be found, is invariably a liberal sprinkling of " cappers " or " touts." These are the lowest and most contemptible of all the instrumentalities employed by the turf sharp, and the most dangerous because they always do their work in the guise of pretended friendship, and under the basest kind of betrayal of confidence. The lowest kind of a bunko steerer is a gentleman by comparison with this most contemptible of all the crawling things that infest this footstool. We have given some insight into the character of his operations. Let it be remembered that every tout is in the employ of the book-maker; that every man who offers another a " tip " on the race-course or at a pool-room is a " tout," beyond any peradventure, and be certain that his frank and apparently generous and off-handed advances are but in reality the means by which he intends to aid in the operation of picking your pocket. He is a liar by instinct, by choice and by occupation, and no matter how engaging his manners, or however plausible his representations, you may safely set him down as a thief, and deal with him accordingly. His very approach is an insult to the intelligence of every man whom he seeks to " play for a sucker."

Never a Local Affair. It is to be remembered that when the race meeting has closed, when the principal thieves with their robber retainers have departed for the scene of their next activity, and good people heave a sigh of relief that their boys or their clerks or their students are now no longer in danger of this temptation, their deadly influence still remains. While the races, for instance, are progressing in St. Louis, the pool-rooms, the billiard-rooms and saloons, by use of the telegraph, continue to keep alive the taint of turf gambling, to keep the temptation to our youth ever present, and to make easy to all, the deadly descent to Avernus. Here, too, the work of the skin gambler, the jackal of his tribe, is made particularly easy. Fraternities of these fragrant personalities are organized, who between the different cities keep each other "posted" on the true tips on races, and give the very latest and most reliable information as to the probabilities of each race. The dupe bets on the regular "blackboard" reports; the scoundrel upon a dead cer-. tainty. The robber rejoices in his good fortune; the victim curses his "bad luck," perhaps, but has no suspicion that he has not had an even chance for his money.

Pool-Room Habitués. If any young man, or old man for that matter, who is in the least degree fastidious upon the point of keeping decent company, will but get some one acquainted with the character of pool-room assemblies, or take the trouble to exercise judgment for himself, he will learn or perceive that which will make him take himself speedily away. Here all the proper distinctions of society are violated, and the lawyer or doctor, lost by his infatuation to self-respect, may be observed taking "pointers" from a ragged and ill-smelling stable-boy. The banker, with the cashier of his competitor, are jostling with a frowsy bootblack; the business man discusses the board with the pick-pocket; the thief and gambler is everywhere. The odor of states prison associations is upon many. The pimp, the bummer, the thug, the midnight housebreaker and the daylight robber, all mingle in the throng with the representatives of business probity and youthful innocence—with the prop and stay of one family, and with the hope and pride of another household. If it were not for the fascination that centers upon the betting board and renders decency oblivious to its shameful surroundings, no man of sense, with a spark of manhood or self-respect about him, could, for a moment endure the contamination of surroundings so degrading. The scene is one of the most repulsive that any pure mind could conceive. It is the monstrous anomaly presented of the vesture of life with warp of virtue and woof of vice.

The Lady Gambler. At the race-meet we may observe the lady of fashion in her costly equipage stopping to dispatch her coachman for a card, and to take instructions for a tip. Of course he gets the tip, for he knows where to go for it. He and the tout are pals, and after the lady shall have lost every one of her eager and confident ventures and leaves the ground with pocket-book light and disappointment in her heart, we may get a glimpse at the decorous coachee as he smiles softly to himself, and thinks upon the liberal portion of his mistress' money he will have to divide with the tout in the evening,. Ladies who visit the race-track to bet are carefully " spotted;" their servants are suborned, and they become the very easiest and silliest victims that fall to the lot of the " fancy."

The Confidential Stake-Holder. A common swindle in the crowd at the pool-seller's stand at the track is the eager and excited young man who is victimized by a brace of sharpers. They have watched him and sized him up; they recognize when he is ripe enough to pick and then dexterously perform the operation of gathering him in. " Bet two to one on Susie G," cries Mr. Verdant Green, after a short argument with his elbow neighbor. " I'll take you," retorts the other, counting out his bills, " we'll put the money into the hands of this gentleman here." Benevolent-looking rascal, who has been abstractedly looking the other way, is appealed to and consents to be the depositary of the wagers. The race is on; excitement becomes intense; everybody is straining eyes upon the flying horses. Not so the confidential stake-holder and his friend. They have gone from the gaze of Mr. Verdant Green—" though lost to sight, to memory dear." If they could be found ten minutes later they might be discovered in the act of dividing an easily earned " swag."

Skin Games Outside the Track. One of the very worst features that attend race meetings is the unavoidable presence, at every point of proximity to the race-track, and lining every approach and avenue to the central scene, of all the known skin games of which the reader of this book will have been afforded ample knowledge elsewhere. Here assemble the three-card monte swindler, the shell-game shark, the wheel of fortune fakir, and in short every conceivable representative of the smaller forms of swindling by means of the practice of gambling. They cannot, it is true, get into the enclosure. Race-track representatives draw the line of its virtue there. True they are not a whit worse than their brethren inside, who play for higher game. Both are merely plundering honest people by means of gambling schemes. It is the case of the pot saying to the kettle, " Keep off; I fear you may besmut me." But the shell game man and his confreres do not hanker to be within the sacred high fence. They can catch their kind of suckers just as well outside, as they come and go; and many a confiding innocent beside, who has not enough money to buy a seat on the grand stand, nor to make a bet on the race, has yet sufficient to lose by the turn of the wheel. They are not particular, bless you, these smaller knaves. They do not want the earth. So long as they get all the sucker has got, even though it be a little, they are content:

Ways that are Dark and Tricks that are not Vain. In no other enterprise is it more frequently demonstrated that " the race is not always to the swift." It is a not uncommon practice for owners of a horse by confederacy with book-makers, and other necessary aids, to groom a horse to win a heavy stake upon a dead certainty. First the horse and his capabilities are discovered. Then he is ridden in one or two races to lose. He becomes regarded as a permanent tail-ender. His appearance on the blackboard is greeted with derision. Reports are circulated that the horse is " sick," particularly just before the event for which he is being held back. He makes his appearance when the time has come. Nobody will bet on him. The wildest sort of odds against him are cheerfully offered, and as quietly gathered in by the confederates of the owner and pool-seller. He takes the field and comes in an easy winner in such a handsome manner that old sports who were not in the combine, recognize, with words not loud but deep, as they go down into their pockets to settle, that they have been " sold again." In this as in all other ways the average bettor or amateur gambler stands no show. He has no chance, though he may think he has. He is simply food for sharks.

The Jockey. As the " king maker " to the claimant to the thrones of the days of old, so the jockey to the horse race, and to the high hopes which rest upon the particular animal in his charge. The jockey is generally the kind of person who would be a stable-boy, a bootblack or a street sweeper, if he were not a jockey. Being a jockey, he is clothed in purple and fine linen, and gets his $10,000 or $12,000 per year—which would pay salaries for two ministers of the gospel of the very first water, or at least four superintendents of schools. Is the jockey paid this magnificent salary for being a jockey? Not at all; nor is he paid for being honest. It is for being honest to his employer in carrying out his wishes in regard to the horse, as it may happen to be more profitable to the owner to win or lose. Do jockeys ever sell a race? Probably: sometimes in obedience to the orders of the owner, and occasionally on his own account. In the latter event it is generally his last race; but he can afford to retire to an opulent private life, for his reward is exceedingly liberal. Who shall tell when the jockey is riding honestly or dishonestly? He alone knows the minutest shade of the temper and capacity of the horse. Half a nose may lose the race when he has seemed to have done his best. And yet he might have won by a neck had he so elected. The plain amateur, everyday sport who is slated to be swindled in any case, as well as the anxious owner, the vendor of pools, and the maker of books, are all at the mercy of the discretion of the jockey. Hence the frills upon his raiment; hence a salary so large that it is concluded that life can offer him no other temptations. In very many instances, indeed, the jockey is the instrument through whom

the thousands of dupes are sold, the owner sometimes directing the robbery, and on other occasions being included in the list of goods delivered. The high-salaried jockey is a part of an evil system. Take away the gambling feature from horse racing, and let us have an honest sport, and the jockey would be glad indeed to ride " square " for a reasonable wage. And there will be no honest competitions of speed on the race-track until the immoral, rascally and thieving element of betting on the result, or gambling, as you may be pleased to term it, has been abolished, either by legal enactment, by public opinion, or by repudiation on the part of the people who now patronize it—in which latter case, the victims refusing to come to the fold to be sheared as they do now, the evil would die for want of pockets to pick.

The Gambling Mania. Speaking of the universality of this gambling mania, a story goes that some years ago a St. Louis wholesale merchant's cashier came to him one day and said:

"I should like to get away this morning, sir; my sister is to be married to-day."

"Certainly, certainly," said the good-natured merchant.

Presently came the book-keeper, with a rueful countenance, and said:

"I'm feeling very unwell, sir, and if you could spare me, I'd like to be excused for to-day."

The amiable merchant cheerfully gave the requested permission. Shortly after the errand boy appeared.

"Please sir, my grandmother died last night, and she's to be buried this afternoon. Please may I go home?"

"To be sure, my boy," said the merchant. "Sorry for your mother; here's a quarter for you."

"Well," soliloquized the merchant, "since they're all gone, I might as well shut up shop. I guess I'll call and see the doctor to-day."

At the doctor's he got word that the physician had just been called away to visit a patient in the country, so he concluded to do some business with his lawyer. At the latter's office he discovered that the man of law had gone to file a paper in the probate court.

"Well, if I can't see anybody," said he to himself, "I might just as well go over to the races a while."

As he approached the grand stand he observed astride the roof a small animate object, which closer inspection proved to him was his office boy, who was thus attending his grandmother's funeral. In front of the stand stood the doctor holding a roll of bills in one hand, and shouting for bets on his favorite horse. Up on the stand he observed the lawyer wildly swinging his hat and hallooing like a maniac. Passing around the corner of the stand he came upon his sick clerk and the one who was marrying his sister, each with a schooner of lager in his hand and in an evidently hilarious condition.

"Well," mused he, "King David was a good judge of human nature when he said, 'All men are liars.'"

*   *   *   *   *

We must have an honest human race before we can have an honest horse race.

The POOR MANS CLUB

"The picture above shows a popular POOR MAN'S CLUB in a thriving Illinois town.

"It is the best patronized and by far the most profitable place in the neighborhood.

"Its principal feature is the bar, the same as in ordinary saloons, but it is a real CLUB for the poor man because it enables him to pass an hour or an evening just as pleasantly as the rich man can do it in HIS club.

"It is a place where a man can drop in any time, and find something that will amuse and interest him as long as he cares to stay.

"Patrons of this club don't feel they have to take a drink every few minutes—and the proprietor doesn't care whether they do or not. There are plenty of other things to do—and they pay the house just as well.

"Patrons can try their luck on various games of chance.

"They can 'take a whirl at the wheel.'

"They can exercise by punching the bag.

"They can test their strength and prowess in various ways.

"They can see the latest pictures and hear the latest vocal and instrumental hits from the plays and operas.

"They can buy gum, candy, chocolate, etc., to take home to the kids, or for their own consumption.

"These attractions get the club the steady patronage of all the social men in the community, bringing in many who would not ordinarily patronize a saloon, and greatly increasing the business of the bar—yet the running expense is not a cent more than when the place was an ordinary saloon.

"It is a case of 'Everything coming in and nothing going out,' simply because the proprietor of this club has learned "THE ART OF MAKING MONEY AUTOMATICALLY."

*　　*　　*　　*　　*　　*

The above cut and description of "The Poor Man's Club," are sent out by a firm of manufacturers, as an introduction to their slot machines, some of which are illustrated in these pages; and which, in my opinion, constitute gambling devices.

If they are recommended to the keepers of saloons, billiard and pool rooms, bowling alleys, cigar stores, etc., as great money makers, it necessarily follows that those who are foolish or ignorant enough to go up against them, must lose their money easily.

I met a young man one day who told me that he had been a constant player on these machines, and had lost several hundred dollars, in consequence of which he was unable to complete his education by going to college as he had intended; but he received an "education" that will follow him through life, and which has taught him the lesson that "he could not beat the other fellow at his own game."

A minister of the gospel once asked me if it were not possible to put the slot machines which pay out money out of business, because he was anxious that they should be if it were at all possible, for his boy had such an inclination for them that he could hardly keep him away from them. I told him they were against the law and we then made arrangements to have them confiscated.

While giving my demonstrations of crooked gambling devices in Cleveland some time ago, a federal government official came to me and asked me how to put the slot machines out of business which were in operation on the boats on the lake. I gave him all the particulars I could about the machines, and what course to take in getting rid of them. To-day they are not allowed to operate on the boats, having been ordered out by the authority of the federal government.

I oppose these slot machines as gambling devices on the principle that "to gamble, is to play for money or other stakes." Some of these machines pay out rewards in coin, and some of them in checks, which are redeemable in trade to the amount marked on the checks.

Let the reader study carefully the description of the following machine. If this is not gambling then I should like to know what is. It is here reproduced exactly as it is advertised by the manufacturers:

"It Rattles the Bones"

And rattles the coin into your till

It is "On The Level"

THE HOTTEST PROPOSITION YET

Eight inches square

SIX SLOTS.

One 25c   Two 10c   Three 5c

Shoot 25c on the field, pays 50c

Shoot 10c on 7 or 11,   pays 40c

Shoot 10c on field,   pays 25c

Shoot 5c on 7 or 11,   pays 20c

Shoot 5c on over 7,   pays 10c

Shoot 5c on under 7,   pays 10c

They can't resist it.

Good for $50.00 a day.

Now I have never known any gambling that was "on the level" in all the years that I followed the profession. If a "friendly" game of cards is being played there is generally some one among the number of players who will try to do a little cheating on his own account, but should they be professional players, then there seems to be no end to the number of schemes devised with which to cheat the unsuspecting victim.

On the machine illustrated above, six persons can play at one time. In the " poor man's club " the saloon keeper does not care whether the customers take whisky or not, for " there are plenty of other things to do—and they pay the house just as well." This machine is one of them. If a man comes in with his weekly wages and commences to play on this machine, he would indeed find it a " hot proposition," for it would not take many minutes to burn a hole into his pockets. He would be very " lucky " if he could get home with enough money in his pockets with which to pay his board bill. The mechanism of these machines are very much on the same principle, and it is possible for the proprietor to " fix " the machinery and so change the percentage, whenever he deems it necessary to do so. In fact, all you have to do, is to " shoot " your money into the slot, and there is always a place ready to receive it.

Here is a machine made expressly for this purpose, and is known as

THE MANILA.

This is supposed to be " a game of skill, pure and simple, but so fascinating that it will hold the crowd like no other machine yet placed on the market has ever done."

To operate this machine the player puts a nickel into the pistol and shoots it at one of the four slots shown in the farther end of the glass covered tube. If the aim is correct, he pulls the button in front of the machine corresponding to the slot into which coin was shot and the machine automatically delivers a prize, good in trade for the amount indicated thereon.

The coin very rarely goes into the slot. It might get there by accident. Skill really plays a very little part in its operation. In some stores where it is operated the proprietor will give an extraordinary cheap cigar for every nickel played, but the majority give nothing. Then again, should the player be successful in shooting the nickels into the slots, then the rewards are of different value, and this in itself constitutes gambling, for he receives more than an equivalent.

Boys and girls are initiated into the arts of gambling by the use of these slot machines. I have seen their eagerness to get a

penny with which to play on one of these machines. They are
not old enough to know evil connected with gambling, and they

would probably not understand it if they were told that it was
gambling. It seems just fun for them to drop a penny in the slot
and watch its operation until it falls into one of the grooves provided for it, and which denotes the amount of the reward.

The most popular slot machine for children is shown in the
accompanying cut, and is known as

THE LITTLE DREAM.

The manufacturer's description is better than any I could
give, and so for that reason I leave it to the reader to judge for
himself, and is as follows:

"It is no idle dream. It's always busy. It's never interfered with. You get a lot for a little when you buy it and the same when you operate it.

"Absolutely lawful, entitles player to at least a piece of gum with every cent played, or a five-cent package when played with nickels.

"Gives bigger prizes when coins go in certain compartments, and that's what makes them play it.

"Players are after big prizes and usually don't take the gum they win.

"Good for operation because every coin played in and every cash prize paid out are accurately registered.

"Will take in from $12 to $20 per week, with net profits of from $6 to $12.

"First class gum is furnished by us at $4 per 1,000.

"For operation in stores and where game machines are not permitted it cannot be beaten."

In one raid where about ninety keepers of saloons, cigar stands, fruit stores, etc., were arrested for operating slot machines as gambling devices, the machines being confiscated and made into a bonfire, several of these machines were brought in, and in every case where they were charged with operating this particular kind of machine, a plea of guilty was entered.

A special note is made of the fact that the gum is not usually taken, even if won, for players are after the big prizes. I do not call this a legitimate gum vending machine by any means. I think the average person who really wants gum would rather buy it in the ordinary way than "take a chance" on this machine.

HY-LO CARD MACHINE.

"The greatest draw poker machine ever built. Fill their hands and your cash box.

"The Hy-Lo is entirely different from all other draw poker machines.

"Player has option of taking his chance on one spin, or may draw to fill by paying an extra coin for each card drawn.

"Machine has six slots—Coin placed in slot at right allows all reels to spin when handle is depressed. To fill hand, player

must place additional coin in individual slot over each reel he wishes to spin.

"Player has only one chance to fill, but may 'draw' as many cards as he wishes by playing a coin on each. If first spin shows aces on reels 1, 3 and 5, player may try for full house or four of a kind by dropping coins in slots 2 and 4 and depressing handle again, when only reels 2 and 4 will spin.

"This feature makes the play fast and furious, and puts the Hy-Lo entirely out of the class of the machines that allow the player an unlimited number of draws.

"All coins played in show in plain sight under their respective slots.

"Slot which actuates all reels locks automatically, while other slots are being used in drawing.

"Cards line up perfectly, and have finest spin of any card machine made.

"One lever operates all reels, both on first play and 'draw.'

"Fine for operators, because it gets quick, steady play and can't be tampered with. Many players will try for four aces to fill a hand. Machine gets one to four extra coins every play, and this is why it takes in six to twelve times as much money as any other card machine made."

These machines are usually to be found resting on a pedestal, and sometimes on the counter. The description given above ought to be sufficient to show that this is one of the greatest robbers on the market; and the man who, after knowing how they are operated, goes deliberately and places a machine of this description on his premises for the sole purpose of fleecing the public, I say he ought to be branded as a common thief and placed in the penitentiary; and I would send the person, who supplies him with the machine, to keep him company.

THE JOCKEY.

This is a card machine showing poker hands, but the player cannot "fill his hand" as in the Hy-Lo.

"The Jockey is a five-reel machine and all reels are interchangeable.

"It is quickly adjusted to operate with a nickel or penny, by simply removing a slide.

"Special reward cards are furnished, so that machine may be operated with either nickels or pennies.

"Three poker hands are shown on the Jockey. Three can play and it is possible for three to win. The hands are numbered 1-2-3 to correspond with the three coin slots, which are distinguished from each other by being numbered in the same manner. The last coins played are exposed and they remain in sight until the next play. One person can play one, two, or three hands at a time, or three persons can play at one time."

The cut on the right shows the appearance of the machine when mounted on a cabinet.

There are numerous kinds of card machines, and while they

are to be condemned as gambling devices, they should also be condemned as tending to educate the public to the nature and value of poker hands. Many a young fellow who has never been

addicted to playing cards, learns for the first time what poker means. He looks at the machine and wonders what the combinations of the cards mean. The card at the head of the machine specifies that certain rewards are given if certain poker hands appear. He accordingly asks the attendant or some one who may happen to be around, and is thus initiated into the gentle art of poker. This will probably lead him on to a desire to play the game of poker, and eventually, from one stage to another, until he becomes an inveterate gambler.

THE COMMERCIAL.

This machine is said to be one of the latest products, and that 10,000 of this particular kind are in operation in the State of California alone. I have not yet been to California, but I trust many copies of this book will reach there and will be read by many good citizens of that state, and that they will be moved to action to see that every one of these machines are put out of business. Let the women, who have the vote in California, do their part in ousting these machines, and thus remove another temptation from their husbands, brothers and sons.

One of the first things about this machine that strikes the eye is the announcement of " free cigars " at the head of the reward card. This is very misleading. In the first place, the player may drop in the nickel and receive nothing in return. He may drop in several nickels and yet not receive anything back. Then again, he may get a winning hand and receive from 1 to 100 cigars. Supposing he wins; the operator does not stand to lose anything, because the machine works on a system and the percentage is so " fixed " that the cigars which are doled out as rewards, is a very small consideration compared with the amount of money that is dropped into the machine.

OWL AND JUDGE TWINS.

Ten slots are provided on these machines. Ten can play at one time, but only two can win, providing any winning numbers should turn up. The combination of the two machines stimulates the players to compete with each other, thus making big money for the machines.

THE LITTLE GEM.

"A perfect card machine and then some.

"Will take in more than its cost in one day in a good location.

"Records every coin played in and tells business done at end of day.

"Red flag shows through glass in back of machine; disappears when machine is tampered with. Cheating absolutely prevented.

"Coin detector always shows last coin played in.

"Safety chute takes only one coin at a time, and throws out all wrong coins.

"Mirror reflector enables proprietor to see the hand from back of counter. Mechanism is easily accessible by opening door in back of case.

"Every seventh nickel drops in a separate cash drawer, contents of which may be offered as additional prizes for drawing special hands. This Jack Pot feature makes a big hit."

The reader will notice in the above description that everything is so arranged to protect the interests of the operator. A special provision is also made for every seventh nickel to go into a separate drawer. If the operator only rents this machine on commission from agent or dealer, then he is usually kept in ignorance of the operation of the seventh nickel, that being reserved for the dealer. In Detroit, a machine is manufactured that has a secret pocket for every fifth nickel played. This machine is usually put into a saloon or store on a commission basis. When this secret pocket gets full, it invariably puts the machine out of working order. The operator, not knowing the cause, sends to the firm which supplied the machine, and a man is sent to put the machine in order again. Of course he does not leave this money with the operator. It is here shown that the operator who robs the public with this particular machine, is in turn robbed by the agent or company.

ROULETTE.

"The most wonderful automatic game machine ever constructed. A genuine roulette game that is absolutely on the

square. Gives every player a fair chance for his money; and gives a fair percentage to the house. More exciting than any other game invented. Pays all rewards automatically. No attendant required."

This is a seven-way machine, and is made for nickels and

quarters. There are 80 spaces on the dial and are divided as follows:

1 " 00 " paying $2.

2 " 0 " paying $1 each.

3 double stars, paying 75c each.

5 single stars, paying 50c each.

20 yellow crescents, paying 25c each.

Balance red and black, 25c each.

The above rewards are given when nickels are played. When quarters are played rewards vary from 50 cents to $10. This is an attractive machine, and is therefore all the more dan-

gerous. Where it is at all possible to obtain such big rewards, the " suckers " will keep on playing with the hope of securing them. It looks attractive to see $10 offered for 25 cents, but while it may be " offered," the proprietor will often see to it that it will be impossible for any one to get it. It is a very common practice for the operators of coin slot machines to " plug " the big prizes. Where there are seven slots for money to be played into the machine, two or three of the tubes representing the highest rewards will be " plugged." Should the machine not be doing the amount of business desired by the operator, he will then release the pay-out tubes for awhile, with the hope of drawing more business.

" Pays automatically, through tube.

" Slots lock when coins are played in, preventing more than one player playing the same color at one time.

" Slug detector shows last three coins played on each color.

" Color register shows which color was played last.

" Mechanism in plain view from top of machine which is made of glass and perfectly flat.

" Ball is always in sight of player and it can lodge on any color."

Another form of roulette slot machine is known as the

LITTLE MONTE CARLO.

This is a combination machine, and operates with either nickels or pennies. Read the description carefully, and it will not be necessary for me to explain the advantages that the operator has against those who go up against it.

"Has two slot-plates. Five-slot plate permits five to play at once, but only one can win.

"Wheel has twenty-five pockets and shows five colors. Winning number is designated by pocket ball drops in.

"When one-slot plate is used, player gets cigar for each coin played, and has a chance to get from one to four more if ball drops in any one of five pockets.

"Machine has two balls and six different reward cards permitting all kinds of combinations and greatly increasing play.

"Two outside slots can be closed, leaving center one open, and the Monte Carlo is then not a chance machine. Cigars are given with each play."

It will easily be seen that any way the machine is operated, there is the element of chance, although it is denied when the one-slot plate is used. If it is possible to get from one to four cigars by using this plate, then the element of chance is there and it makes the machine nothing but a gambling device.

THE LITTLE BROWNIE.

This machine is made for nickels to be played on, and pays out cash prizes from 10 cents to $1. The colors automatically register, and remain in view above dial until next play. A slug detector is provided, which shows the last three nickels played on each color.

A favorite method of beating slot machines has been to play slugs, the size and thickness of nickels. This has now been partially stopped by means of the slug detector. It is said to be a crime to use slugs, but not a crime to run the machine. The reader can draw his own conclusions.

Most Marvelous MoneyMaker

THE LIBERTY BELL.

"The most marvelous card machine ever manufactured. Four machines in one.

"First, can be operated with a five cent coin or check, and will pay rewards automatically in five-cent checks.

"Second, can be operated with five-cent coins exclusively, and will pay rewards automatically in five-cent coins exclusively.

"Third, can be operated with five-cent checks exclusively, and will pay its rewards automatically in five-cent checks exclusively.

"Fourth, can be operated as a plain trade card machine by simply closing up the pay-out tube.

"Can be adjusted to meet all requirements in your town. You can change it at will from one style of machine to another. In the twinkling of an eye it becomes a trade stimulator, a money machine or a check machine."

♠ ♠ ♠	**Wins $1.00 In Trade**
KING KING KING or KING KING ♠	**Wins 80 c In Trade**
QUEEN QUEEN QUEEN or QUEEN QUEEN ♠	**Wins 60 c In Trade**
JACK JACK JACK or JACK JACK ♠	**Wins 40 c In Trade**
☊ ☊ ✡ or ☊ ☊ KING	**Wins 20 c In Trade**
☊ ☊	**Wins 10 c In Trade**

N B.—Rewards are only paid when spots or signals are shown on Reels in exact position as printed on reward cards. Reverse positions of same do not pay anything

Liberty Bell Reward Card.

THE TOTEM GUM VENDER.

The Totem like the O. K. is a dividend-paying gum vender. The fortune feature is also retained. But for those who object to reels, on the Totem a dial with three revolving arrows is sub-

stituted. This dial is divided into sixteen wide spaces. It is attractively painted in four bright colors and enclosed by glass. As these arrows rotate they indicate the customer's fortune, the clue to the combination of mysterious symbols being given on the card at top of the machine.

This machine possesses the same window feature as the O. K., which announces beforehand, exactly what the player is going to receive. When a dividend falls due the fact is further emphasized by the ringing of an automatic bell.

Now comes the trick. " The dividends are given voluntarily by the dealer *out of his own profits,* to secure the steady trade of his customers. Notice is given when such a dividend is to be paid and *the patron is free to accept or decline.''* In other words, the machine itself indicates when a dividend is to be paid, but the patron reserves to himself the right as to whether he shall play another nickel to obtain it or not. Are the patrons more generous than the dealers? It creates a peculiar situation, and is nothing more nor less than " whipping the devil round the stump."

THE NEW AUTOMATIC GUM VENDER.

This machine has been put on the market with a view of overcoming legal objection, and for that purpose an arrangement for vending gum was made. In some localities gum is vended when nickels are played, although it is possible to get rewards in value from ten cents to one dollar. While some of the machines profess to give gum, there is no such arrangement on them, and the player does not get the gum unless he asks for it at the counter. This new device has an arrangement whereby gum is delivered on each play when nickels are used, but it also has another arrangement whereby the gum is returned automatically back to the machine if the player does not take it out. This is conclusive that it is not expected that players really want the gum, and in practice it proves they do not. The gum can be purchased at sixty cents per hundred packets, thus giving the operator $4.40 profit on the gum, providing it is all taken out of the machine each time the machine is played. The better argument against these machines is to be found in the literature sent out by the slot machine company, of which some extracts will be given.

" The new automatic gum vender is sold and usually operated as a plain five-cent gum vender automatically delivering a package of gum on every nickel. Some idea of its possibilities is obtainable when you learn that it *can be operated in more than 20 different ways.* For instance in opening up a location it is often advisable to run it as a straight gum machine. *Under no circumstances* can this be objected to and the resulting profits are large enough to satisfy most men. Later on, if business must be stimulated a little, by making a few very slight changes in the machine, the co-operative trade check pay-out features can be added, or, if this is prohibited the pay-out tube can again be plugged and small reward or premium cards, each good for a certain amount in trade (percentage regulated to suit yourself) can be enclosed in a few of the gum packages, answering the purpose admirably.

"The many other ways in which this machine can legitimately, yet profitably be operated will be explained in detail on request. The main point, however, that makes it so valuable to operators is, that *regardless of conditions,* it can positively *always,* as a plain gum vendor, be operated, with the full consent of the authorities, *on a good paying basis,* anywhere."

It will be noticed in the foregoing that they are very cautious in presenting the qualifications of this particular machine, for while they make it possible to operate these machines in several ways they put it out as a simple gum vender. Then they say that the authorities cannot object to that. Of course not; if the machine vends gum only, when operated, and no possible chance of any rewards being given, then the greatest moralist on earth would not object. The next paragraph will make their position quite clear.

"Our —— New Gum Vender is constructed as a legitimate machine and is so made as to fit the present day requirements of operators throughout the country. We have attempted to, and we believe that we have built a machine that complies with the laws of the different states in this country as well as the laws of foreign countries. Our attorneys, who are in our opinion, the best constitutional lawyers in the country, have advised us that our machines are legitimate machines and no valid law can be passed which prohibits their operation. Should, therefore, there be any statute or ordinance in your vicinity which prohibits their use, we will cheerfully place our attorneys at your disposal, free of cost to yourself, to test the constitutionality of said law."

Talk is cheap. The company knows full well that the services of their attorneys would never be needed to protect the operator in exhibiting a simple gum vending machine. Let us see what else they have to say.

"We have been informed that in some localities operators have used these machines by giving coins, checks or premiums in addition to the regular merchandise vended." (The regular merchandise being gum.) "While these machines have been so operated in many cities in the United States, we of course are not obligated to guarantee their operation when used in this manner." (Understand clearly, the machine is so made that it can be operated in the foregoing manner.) "We suggest that if you desire to use same in this manner, that you consult some good attorney, or frankly state the proposition to your authorities."

"By simply readjusting a few screws, this machine in five minutes' time, can, if desirable, readily be converted into a profit-sharing, trade stimulator with trade check pay-out and play back. When this feature is prohibited, the new automatic can always and continuously be operated *at a profit* as a plain gum vender.

"When adjusted with trade stimulating feature, the New Automatic like the Bell can be played either with nickels or checks. The coins going straight to money box, the checks to pay-out tube, the overflow of checks by a special device, going to a separate compartment of the money drawer. Note, however, that *the machine vends gum only when nickels are played.*"

It will be seen from the above statement that although provision is made in the machine for trade checks to be used (each trade check representing five cents in value), yet no gum will be delivered when checks are played.

As a special inducement to prospective purchasers, they are urged to omit nothing in reading the circular, and if every detail is not clear to read the description again. "*Read between the lines.*"

NEW GUM VENDER WITH THE PREMIUM FORTUNE TELLING FEATURE.

"The grocery man's plan of giving away premiums can be used most advantageously to boost the sale of gum.

"In adopting this plan the dealer will first decide what proportion of his profits he can afford to set aside for the purpose.

"Then, to add the premium feature to the new gum vender, it is only necessary for the proprietor to insert in gum packages, some of the premium fortune cards. These premium cards will usually be of a different color from the plain fortune cards so that the attendant may know instantly when a premium is won.

"In this connection it should be noted that these premium cards read that player 'should' receive certain articles, not that he 'will.' The proprietor, after player has read aloud his card, has therefore the option of literally making his fortune 'come

true' by presenting his patron with the merchandise indicated,
or may 'pass it up' if he so desires.   As liberality is usually
rewarded by increased trade, and also that the merchandise thus
given is splendid advertising both for your store and the machine, the majority of dealers will probably find it to their interest to give away the premiums.

"These premiums may consist of merchandise specially purchased or the wares ordinarily sold over the counter, or BOTH.
And the value of the premiums may either be uniform or range
in cost from 5c to $1 each."

The following wordings
appear on some of the premium
cards used in this machine:
"Fortune favors you.   You
should to-day receive two good
smokes."   "Friends will help
you.   One should soon treat
you to a good meal."   "Your
lucky star is in the ascendant.
Someone should to-day present
you with a handsome watch."
While this seeks to evade the
letter of the law, in my opinion,
it does not evade the spirit of it.

O. K. GUM VENDER.

A new feature in connec-
tion with this machine is that it
tells what the player will receive on the next play, before
he deposits the coin.   "The
dropping of the coin and receipt of gum constitutes the
entire transaction."   Now then;
supposing ten trade checks are
thrown out after the coin has
been   dropped,   the   handle
pulled, and the wheels revolved,
what does that constitute?   Re-
ceiving the gum in return for the nickel constitutes the legal

transaction, that is, from the manufacturers' standpoint; and again, if checks are returned as rewards for the nickel played, then from their standpoint, it is an illegal transaction, because, to use their own language, "We emphasize the fact that the machine is shipped only as a plain GUM VENDER," and "It is not a gaming device any more than a pool table is a gambling device UNLESS it is used as such." Therefore it must be classed as a gambling device, for though it does indicate what the player shall receive on the next play, the element of chance is not entirely eliminated. The manufacturers know this, and that is why they will not undertake the responsibility of "guaranteeing the machine" when it is used other than as a plain gum vender only.

In July, 1912, Forest Whitmer of the Derby saloon, Canton, Ohio, was charged in the local police court with operating a slot machine as a gambling device, contrary to the laws of the State of Ohio. The O. K. Gum Vender was the machine in question. The assistant city solicitor, acting police prosecutor, prosecuted the case before Police Judge Quinn (my namesake, but no relation to me).

Attorneys for the Southern Gum and Tobacco Company, of Akron, Ohio, and a local attorney, defended the case. Briefs were prepared on both sides, that of the State being as follows:

IN THE CRIMINAL COURT OF THE CITY OF CANTON, OHIO.

STATE OF OHIO, } ss. :
STARK COUNTY. }

THE STATE OF OHIO,
Plaintiff,
vs.   *State's Brief.*
FOREST WHITMER,
Defendant.

I. OBJECT OF GAMBLING STATUTES.

Section 13066 was enacted by the State Legislature, under the police powers of the State. At Common Law, gaming was not held unlawful. States for the purpose of eliminating and retarding the growth of the gambling spirit among its citizens, enacted laws prohibiting the exhibition and use of gambling devices. This object, we submit, should be kept constantly in mind by the court in construing statutes prohibiting the exhibition of gambling devices.

II. THE OHIO STATUTE.

This prosecution is brought under Section 13066 G. C. Defendant admits that the machine in question was exhibited and operated in defendant's place of business in Canton, Ohio, with the defendant's knowledge. The one question, therefore, that arises in this case is the following: Is the machine marked " Exhibit A," a gambling device? The Supreme Court, Appellate Division, 4th Department, 99 N. Y. Supplement, page 1097, in commenting on what constitutes a gambling device, says: " There was no rebate or reduction, but obviously the scheme was to entice trade by stimulating the gambling spirit. The player had no knowledge of the arrangement of the mental discs and played in the hope of securing one or more of these, calling for a larger sum, and knew that no loss could accrue to him in any event. The proprietor expected to make up for the few checks in excess of the actual value of the nickel in the increased trade, and a consequent profit inuring to him." Later in the same case the court says: " The chief element of gambling is the chance or uncertainty of the hazard. The chance may be in winning at all, or in the amount to be won or lost. In using the present machine, we may assume that the player cannot lose. By far the greater majority of the checks called in trade for the precise sum deposited in the slot. If every ticket represented five cents, the machine would not be patronized. The bait or inducement is that the player may get one of the checks for a sum in excess of the nickel he ventures, and that is the vice of the scheme. If he wins more than he pays, the proprietor must lose on that discharge of the ticket. To constitute gambling, it is not important who may be the loser." Later in the opinion the following appears: " The inventor of the present machine has attempted to obviate the criticism to which other slot machines have been subjected, by cunningly returning to the player operating the machine a check or ticket which secures to him in cigars or liquor the amount of his stake. *Like most inventors, to adhere to the letter of the law, while violating its spirit, he cannot succeed.* The present device attractively ministers to the gambling humor, the same as other slot machines of substantially similar design. Unless it did this, it would not entice the customer. . . . It is the hazard, the chance of winning more than the sum returned which draws people to the machine, and that element was the conspicuous one retained in its mechanism, and it is that which brings it within the condemnation of the statute forbidding gambling in a place where liquor is sold.".

The defendant contends that since the dial on the machine marked " Exhibit A," at the close of one operation of the machine indicates just what the machine will eject at the next operation, that the machine in question, therefore is not a gambling device. We submit that this effects, if anything, *not the substance,* but the form; and that this invention is, as was said. by the New York Court, but an effort on the part of the *inventor through a subterfuge to conform to the letter of the statute while violating the spirit, and hence cannot succeed.* Wherein we inquire, does the machine marked " Exhibit A," cultivate and develop, any less, the gambling spirit—and, that we think, must be admitted to be the aim and purpose of our statute—than did the original slot machine?

The exhibitor of the machine marked " Exhibit A," in effect says to the player, " If you place in the aperture of the machine a nickel, when the dial shows the word ' Gum,' you will receive a package of gum, and also being in possession of the machine, a chance to receive as high as twenty five-cent trade checks by placing in the machine *another nickel."* This is where the gambling feature enters into the transaction. The new machine marked " Exhibit A," is identical with the old machine with the exception that the player plays *one operation in advance* of that played by him with the old machine. We do not believe that the court in consideration of all these things, especially in the light of the character of the package of gum ejected by the machine, and which is before your Honor in evidence, can hold that the machine marked " Exhibit A," does *successfully evade either the spirit or the letter of the Ohio Statute prohibiting the exhibition of gambling devices.*

III.   CITATIONS.

Heman vs. Ohio, 9 O. S. 274.

99 Maine 486.

99 N. Y. Supplement, page 1097.

20 L. R. A. (N. S.) 239.

24. Century Digest, paragraph 198.

Respectfully submitted,

FRANK N. SWEITZER,

Ass't City Solicitor.

After due consideration Judge Quinn ruled as follows:

" The question before the court is whether or not the O. K. vender is a gambling device," said Judge Quinn.   " It is not necessary for the state to introduce evidence to show that the persons who might have operated this machine had in mind the intention of playing for chances to be submitted in the future. The defendant is not being charged with having engaged in gambling on a particular day, but he is charged with having exhibited for the purpose of gaining money and other property of value. a gambling device.

" When the metallic trade checks. are played in the machine without the machine ejecting any gum, then certainly no one would contend that the player is doing anything but playing for a future chance to get more than the value of the trade check for either another trade check or five cents.   This is evident, because the machine will not pay for trade checks anything but trade checks, and it is only when the machine pays trade checks that anything in addition to the package of gum is ejected.

" There can be no doubt that trade checks being good for five cents in trade are things of value and property which would come under the definition of 'other property.' If the machine in the case at bar were a legitimate gum vender, it seems strange to the court that unless the purchaser immediately takes his gum from the shelf upon which it is ejected, he will lose the chance to get even the pack of gum for a nickel unless he goes to the proprietor and induces him to give him a pack of gum.

"According to the defense the purpose of the machine is to act as a gum vender, and certainly it would not be a useful gum vender if the purchaser of gum had to go back to the counter in the end to get his five-cent purchase. The very fact that this machine is so constructed that it will take back the package of gum it ejects, unless the purchaser takes his gum before playing again, makes it evident that the machine is founded upon a scheme of trickery and is a confession that it is not a mechanism for the purpose of vending gum."

The court stated that the packages of gum appeared to be very inferior to the ordinary five-cent package of gum in size as well as quality.

"The court considers the size of the package of gum only in-so-far as it throws light upon the probability that purchasers would be apt to play the machine for the sake of the chewing gum, without the added inducement that the machine holds out something in addition to the gum at some future play," said the judge.

The judge said that he also found that if the player did not immediately take the gum when it was ejected it would be swept back into the machine. He concluded with the statement that the machine was a "further improvement of the slot machine which gave five cents in trade with a chance not indicated beforehand of getting something in addition on each play. The present machine is more cunningly contrived, but depends upon the same gambling spirit for its business.

"Therefore, the court is strongly of the opinion that the defendant is guilty as charged in the affidavit of violating the laws of the State of Ohio."

THE NATIONAL.

This machine differs in all others in that while it shows what the player will get on the next play, it does not deliver gum like the automatic gum venders. Many times the player gets nothing whatever in return for the money played in. If the player got an equivalent on each play, then it would be impossible for the machine to give more than an equivalent on any play.

The following description is sent out: " The greatest card machine ever built because it is not a game of chance. Because it shows what you will receive before you play. Because it throws out a ticket numbered consecutively with the amount printed on, automatically prints a fac simile of hand shown, tells your fortune, shows last coin played in and the case is constructed on the order of a cash register."

This machine is said to be able to run in any town where " the lid is on, " even in " Old Puritanical New England." It seems to me that it would be better if the laws all over the country were a little more Puritanical. It is the duty of every state to safeguard the moral interest of the community. If a certain thing is right, then let it continue; but if it is wrong, then I say the best thing to do is to crush it out, even if sledge hammers have to be used. I believe we should obey the Scriptural injunction: " Fight the devil and he will flee from you."

BEN FRANKLIN.

This machine is one of the earlier makes of gum vending machines, and is made to be played by dropping a penny in the slot and pressing the lever, when the reels are made to revolve.

It delivers a piece of gum on each coin played, and if any of the combinations, mentioned on the reward card at the head of the machine, appear, then the player will receive the reward.

To name this machine after Benjamin Franklin is an insult to his memory. Franklin was ever on the side of honesty and truth. The following is a part of his prayers: "That I may be averse to craft and overreaching, abhor extortion, and every kind of weakness and wickedness. That I may have constant regard to honor and probity; that I may possess an innocent and good conscience, and at length become truly virtuous, magnanimous and helpful to my fellow men—Help me, O God!"

Can the manufacturers, agents, etc., who handle these machines pray in a like manner, and with as much sincerity?

THE DEWEY.

This machine has six slots, and is made for either nickels or quarters, with or without musical attachment. The cut here shows the musical attachment added.

There are one hundred spaces on an eighteen-inch dial.

Nickel machine pays rewards from 10c to $2.

Quarter machines pay bigger amounts and make bigger profits for the house.

It has a non-repeating device which prevents two successive wins on same color.

Color flags automatically regulated, machine cannot pay on wrong color.

On some of the Dewey machines the Jack Pot feature is added, and is always in full sight of the player. It pays out on the blue. This is a great inducement to the players to continue the play in order to get the Jack Pot.

The Jack Pot constantly accumulates, until it looks to the player like a whole handful of nickels.

The Jack Pot takes the place of the $2 reward on the regular Dewey.

LITTLE BIG SIX

This machine is provided with six slots, and pays five for one on any color.

Straight percentage play. Always one sure win out of six plays.

Can't repeat on any color. Dial revolves at a different speed each play.

Six different National flags arranged in thirty-six spaces on dial. Corresponding flags under slots.

Slug detector shows last three coins played on each color.

Flag color plate shows last play.

Clogging prevented by device which automatically vibrates tubes each play.

Pay-out is guaranteed accurate.

20th CENTURY.

Two different machines of this design are made, viz., eight slots for nickels, quarters and trade checks; five slots for half dollars or dollars. It will thus be seen that both the " pikers " and " high rollers " can be accommodated with a machine to suit their pocket books. In either case there is an excellent chance of the contents being reduced.

The machines pay as follows: On 5c play, 10c to $5; on 25c play, 50c to $25; on 50c play, $1 to $10; on $1 play, $2 to $20.

" Heavy play means heavy profits."

The new dial has 130 spaces, half of them inverted, allowing all colors to show large.

Disputes avoided by device making it impossible to play two nickels in same slot at same time. Handle is locked until all coins are played in.

THE OWL.

This machine is similar in construction to the Dewey and other kindred makes, is provided with five slots for nickels, quarters or trade checks. The rewards paid are as follows:

Automatic bell announces amount won; rings once when machine pays 10c on red or black; rings twice for 25c on yellow; three times for 50c on white; four times for $1 on green.

The man is " green " who will go up against these machines after reading these pages. The machines are there to get his money, and they will get it.

THE UMPIRE.

This device is similar in construction to the "Check Boy," and is one of the latest placed on the market. It is a five-slot baseball machine for penny or nickel play. Any number of players therefore, from one to five, may play simultaneously, or one man may play all the five colors himself. But *one color, however, can win on each play.*

The rewards are paid out automatically in single trade checks. The pay-out tube is at the bottom end on the right hand side of the machine.

Adjusted for penny play, the Umpire automatically pays out rewards of respectively five, ten, twenty and thirty cents in single checks, redeemable only in trade.

The revolving reel is subdivided in fifty spaces, twenty-five reward-paying colors, and twenty-five non-paying blacks. The layout of the penny machine consists of nine reds or singles, paying five cents in trade; nine greens or doubles paying five cents in trade; five browns or triples paying ten cents in trade; two blues or home runs paying twenty cents in trade; one Umpire or " game won " paying thirty cents. Rewards are paid *only* on the above colors.

This machine is considered to be a gold mine to the man who operates it.

REWARD PAYING PUNCHING BAG.

" This machine is made to operate with either nickels or pennies and when a coin is dropped in the slot, the action releases the bag, so that it may be pulled down in position (see cut) to receive the blow. When struck, the bag hits the hinged underside of the upper projecting portion of the machine, causing the same to raise, which action registers the weight of the blow on the dial in pounds. Upon reacting, the bag automatically returns to its first position and is immediately locked there, ready for the next play. The player gets one punch for each coin played in.

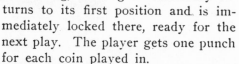

" Magazine holds 200 brass checks. One of these is paid out when player strikes bag just hard enough to drive pointer around to one of the winning points on the dial as shown by reward card.

" If operated with pennies, the value of each check is 5c in trade ; if with nickels, each check is worth 25c in trade.

" An extra prize to boost the game may be arranged by putting one or two 25c checks in pay-out tube if machine is operated with pennies ; if operated with nickels the extra prize should be worth a dollar in trade."

It is claimed for this machine that it cannot be classed as gambling, as the winning of the rewards depends upon the skill of the player. This is not true. The following will explain: " Machines leave factory arranged to pay on even hundreds from 200 to 1,100 ; but can be made to pay on units of tens from 10 to 1,100 if desired ; or the machine may be regulated to pay only one good prize on one number." This clearly shows that the player has very little chance of securing a reward or prize, and that skill has nothing at all to do with it.

THE SILVER CUP.

This is a double-dial automatic machine. Is a combination trade check or money machine. In some localities where "everything goes" this machine is operated on the money basis, that is to say, it pays out rewards in coin in the same manner as the large floor machines. Other localities, while permitting their use, insist that trade checks be used for rewards. They contend

that it only constitutes gambling when the actual cash is played for. A little common sense would convince them there is no difference in principle between the cash and the trade checks being given out as rewards. The only difference, if any, lies in the extra profit that accrues to the owner of the machine when trade checks are used, as he is able to make a profit on his goods given out in trade.

Should there be any move on the part of the authorities at

any time in opposition to these machines, then a simple device is constructed in the form of a special gum sign which can be attached if " necessity requires it." That means that it becomes a gum vender, from the point of view of the owner, and he expects thus to escape the officers of the law.

From one to five persons may play the machine at the same time, or one person may play all the slots at the same time. Rewards vary from ten cents to two dollars.

ROYAL JUMBO: OR, KING FRAUD.

This machine is made for either pennies, nickels, dimes or quarters. Of course the rewards vary considerably according to what the machine is made up for. Large numbers of these machines are in use all over the country, but it is quite time the State Legislatures took action to put them out of business, for they obtain money under false pretense.

Laws are in vogue that fasten themselves on the man who deliberately obtains money under false representation from another man, and those same laws should be applicable to every form of misrepresentation which causes a man to be fleeced of his money. Admitting that it is unlawful to gamble, that is no reason why machines should be allowed to operate that deliberately induce men to put up their money with a view of trying to win a big prize when it is impossible for him to do so.

Three illustrations are here shown, representing this particular machine. The first illustration shows the machine as it looks to the player. The second one shows the wheels which revolve inside when the coin has been placed in the machine and the lever pressed. The third shows the cards in the exact order as they appear on the wheels.

As I write this I have the actual machinery in front of me. This machine is made for nickels, and the rewards on the card read as follows:

DROP NICKEL IN THE SLOT.

Rewards in 5 cent Cigars.

Royal Flush (Ace, King, Queen, Jack and Ten
of either Suit)........................100 Cigars
Straight Flush (all of One Suit in Rotation, as
3-4-5-6-7) 50   "
Four of a Kind............................ 30   "
Full Hand (Three of One Kind and Two of
Another) 20   "
Flush (All of One Suit, Regardless of Rota-
tion) 10   "
Straight (All in Rotation, Regardless of any
Suit) 8   "
Three of a Kind.......................... 5   "
Two Pair 3   "
One Pair (Tens or Better)...... .... 1 Cigar

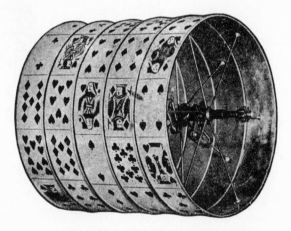

Now in looking carefully at the five rows of cards on the opposite page the reader will notice that it is impossible to get

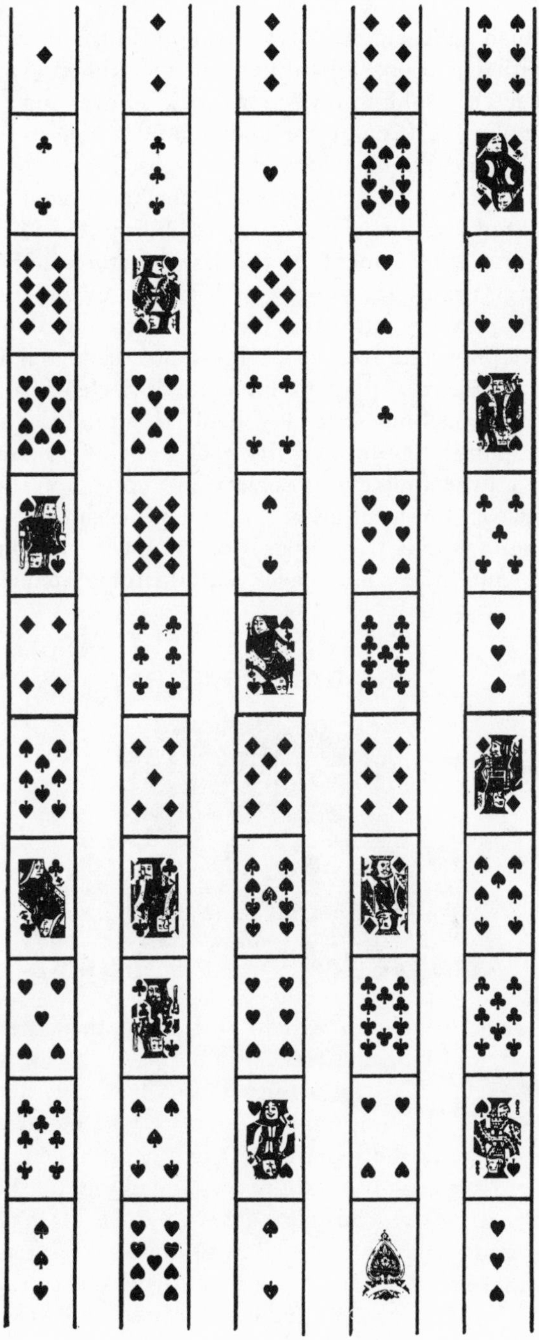

a Royal Flush (100 cigars) or a Straight Flush in rotation (50 cigars) ; neither is it possible to get four of a kind above nine. In any case it is very seldom that four of a kind ever turn up.

This makes it fraud pure and simple when it records rewards for certain hands which it is impossible to obtain. The percentage in favor of the owner of the machine is so strong that he will not readily refrain from exhibiting it, and it will take the most rigid enforcement of the law to stop their operation.

The large prizes are offered with a view of inducing players to continue playing with the hope of securing one of them. They might play against one a thousand years and never succeed. Of course the players have no knowledge of the true nature of the machine, but this book is intended to open the eyes of the public to the rascality that is being practiced.

Again I urge that every society promoted for the uplift of humanity work for legislation that shall be sufficiently strong as to not only prevent the operation of these machines, but to make it a penitentiary offence to manufacture them.

" NO-GAMING " SIGN.

Another scheme with which to defraud the authorities has been devised, and is in the form of a sign which can be attached when necessary. The following is the language used by the manufacturer: " This sign is made entirely of metal with raised letters and is handsomely plated. It can be attached or detached in a moment's time—it is simply clamped on to the coin detector. In many places this sign TAKES OFF MUCH OF THE ' CURSE ' and machines are allowed to be operated in places where without it operation would be entirely out of the question. We know of operators who have submitted this sign to Chiefs of Police, Mayors and Judges, with the result that in many instances the machines were allowed to run."

This wording appears on sign:

THIS IS NOT A GAMING DEVICE.

Any person desiring to gamble must not put any money in this machine. As a consideration for the use of this music machine and the music furnished, it is expressly agreed that all of the nickels which come out of the cup below, must and shall be played back into the machine; thereby giving more music.

It is obvious from the above that whatever the sign may say, it is hardly to be expected that a group of men will continue to play a machine by putting in their nickels if music is the only thing that can be gotten out of it. "Music is that elevated science, which affects the passion by sound. There are but few who have not felt its charms and acknowledged its expression to be intelligible to the heart. It is a language of delightful sensation far more intelligible than words can express." No doubt the addition of music to the slot machines is intended to create a passion for throwing away nickels and dimes, etc., by dropping them into the machines, but it is very seldom that the music charms them back again.

THE YANKEE.

This machine is one of the greatest schemes of chance ever placed on the market, and is also one of the most dangerous. Just imagine a young boy who is " out for a good time," jingling the little pocket money in his hand given him by his parents before he started out. He sees one of these machines and the first thing he notices is the amount of coin shown in the five pockets of the machine. Immediately it calls forth a vision of immense possibility in his mind should he be successful in obtaining the amount of coin that is contained in only one of the pockets of the machine. He makes enquiries as to how it works and is told that if he will place a nickel in the slot at the top, pull the lever and shoot the coin across into the prize target at the opposite left hand side, and it does not lodge there, it may fall into

one of the five pockets located at the bottom of the pin board. In this event the coin will lodge at top of pocket and will remain in sight until the handle is pressed, when the winnings will be delivered to him.

This sounds good to the young boy. He tries this machine to see what it will do for him. After a few nickels have been played he becomes discouraged, but he sees some one else come up to play the machine and soon they are competing with each other as to who shall first secure a prize. Before he realizes just what this may mean to him his little pocket has dwindled away and he can play no further. What shall he do? What shall he tell his parents what became of his pocket money? Finally he hits upon a plan, and resolves to tell his parents that some one grabbed his pocket book and he could not run fast enough to catch him, so he had to walk all the way home.

The owners of these machines can regulate the percentage so easily that the " rake-off " can be fixed ten to seventy-five per cent.

GAME CARDS.

Legitimate business is being more and more replaced by what is known as "trade stimulator." The slot machines have been placed in this category, and now "game cards" and "punch boards" are also included. The excuse given is that the American public is of a speculative turn of mind, and that they would rather have a little fun by taking a chance on some of these games than make their purchases in the ordinary way. Assuming that this was absolutely true (which of course it is not), then the idea of the brotherhood of man being recognized by the people of America, is out of the question, for the principle involved is such that instead of "doing unto others as they should be done by," they are trying to do each other. The man who exhibits the "game card" with the expectation that men will take a chance on it, is inwardly and outwardly desiring their money, in return for which he hopes to give little or nothing. Those who play these games have a similar thought in their minds, so far as the hope of gain is concerned, but when they put down a nickel or a dime for a chance they hope they will be "lucky" enough to secure a large prize and get away with it. They also are inwardly and outwardly desiring to get the better of the other fellow.

So far as these games are concerned there is not an atom of skill connected with them in any way. The cards are made in various ways, but the system of play is the same. The one shown in the illustration is known as "Everybody's Game," and contains 255 poker hands. Five cents is the price of a chance. When the seal is removed a poker hand is revealed, and in order to get something back in return for the five cents paid, the hand must correspond with one of the following, which also gives the amount won, and which is distributed in trade:

Fours ....80 cents in trade.
Full House ....50 cents in trade.
Straight ....40 cents in trade.
Three of a kind ....20 cents in trade.
Two Pair ....10 cents in trade.
Jacks or Better .... 5 cents in trade.

Should none of the above hands be drawn the player gets nothing.

Everybody's Game

TRADE CARD

ALL PRIZES PAID IN TRADE

Fours - - - -	80 cents in trade
Full House - - -	50 cents in trade
Straight - - -	40 cents in trade
Three of a Kind - -	20 cents in trade
Two Pair - - -	10 cents in trade
Jacks or Better - -	5 cents in trade

5 Cts. a Chance

Pick-Out Card

I have seen groups of boys and young men in pool-rooms and cigar stores on Sunday around the counters playing these games. It does not take very long for the owner to use up one of these cards, and the profits vary, according to the card used, from $2.20 to $7.00, aside from the profits made on the goods distributed in trade.

Sometimes the cards have the name of a horse or a fish underneath the seal. Other cards have numbers, certain numbers winning candy, and one number, corresponding with a number under a seal (which is not removed until all the numbers have been played), gains a special prize. As each seal is removed the player writes his name or initials in the space from which he removed the seal, and if he should have drawn the winning number he is entitled to the prize. It sometimes happens that the winning prize is never delivered to the party to whom it rightly belongs, and for several reasons. It may be that a traveller has been the successful one but he never inquires any more about it; a casual visitor to the store, or a person who is very indifferent as to whether he wins or not, might be the successful one; then the proprietor will take the prize for himself and none of the players get it.

Another form of card has a display of fancy case pipes. One I have before me just now contains 300 seals which sell at ten cents. The dealer puts up six pipes valued at fifty cents each, and twelve pipes valued at twenty-five cents each, making a total value of six dollars. He pays one dollar for the board and possibly three dollars for a capital prize to be given to the winner of the "lucky" number. This makes an outlay of ten dollars at retail value. The sale of 300 seals at ten cents nets him thirty dollars, thus making the profit on the whole transaction of twenty dollars. This ought to be sufficient to satisfy most men.

Then there is a card made which contains a display of merchandise, but the player does not know what he has to pay for his chance until he has removed the seal. It may be a name or a number that will be found under the seal, which will represent the amount to be paid, varying from ten to fifty cents, and even then he may not be successful in obtaining anything in return for his money.

PUNCH BOARDS.

The punch board consists of a board about half an inch in

thickness pierced with a number of holes. The one shown in the illustration contains 600. In each of the holes is concealed a small piece of paper on which is printed a number. The usual price for a chance on the board is ten cents. The player takes a small peg and places it over one of the white spots, presses it into the hole, which action causes the paper with the number on to come out at the back of the board.

A number of prizes are given with the board, and on this particular make something is given with every play. The majority of boards are not nearly as generous as this one, for while a few prizes may be offered, the chances are that 590 times out of 600 nothing at all is given.

The reader will notice a circle at the top of the illustration which denotes that a hidden number is placed there. One of the numbers punched out of the board should correspond with the number hidden there. Sometimes the proprietor will so arrange it that none of his customers get the grand premium, but will take it himself and sell it outright in the same manner that he sells other articles in his store. Other premiums are given.

It is claimed for these boards that they are perfectly legitimate because they give something with every play, and are therefore "trade stimulators" and not gambling implements. The very fact of the board containing a prize larger in value than the amount paid for the chance constitutes it gambling for the player would not generally play on the board unless there was some inducement to gain more than he paid.

It is surprising to see the number of merchants who exhibit these game cards and punch boards. What business has a reputable dry goods merchant or a druggist to lend their aid in instilling into the minds of the young people the principles of gambling? A mother once told me that she wished they could be put out of business for her boys were losing all their money on these games.

An agent showed me a letter he received from one of the manufacturers in which it urged him in introducing the punch boards to make an appeal to the self-interest of the merchant. That is the truth of the whole situation. Greed is the predominating factor in the mind of the average merchant to-day. Show him where he can make a few extra dollars easily, or without working for them, and he will grab at it. Elders, deacons and church workers are not exempt from this fault. I know many

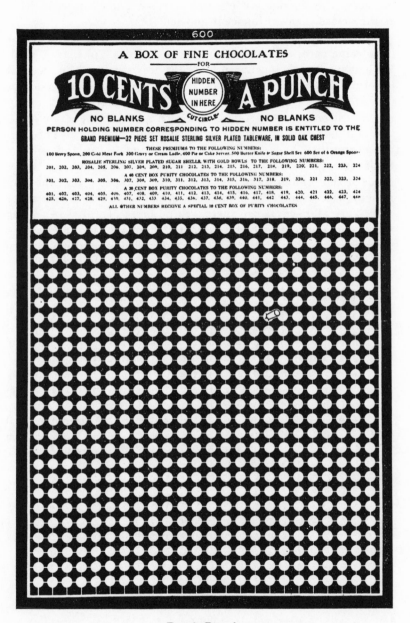

Punch Board.

of them who do not scruple to put these games on exhibition as they class them as innocent amusements.

On one occasion I went into a store and saw a boy playing on a game card, or what is commonly called a " pick-out " card. He had spent eighty cents in five-cent draws, and all he received in return was five cents in trade. Unfortunately the losses do not deter the boys from playing for they reason that after so many reverses it must surely soon take a turn for the better.

It would be well for the citizens of this country to get after the authorities and see that these implements are put out of business. They are a thousand per cent worse than the poker room or the regular gambling house, for in those places the play is somewhat limited to numbers; while in towns where these games are allowed to run there will be hundreds of stores using them, and it necessarily follows that there will be hundreds of persons who will play them. Thousands of boys and young men would never know anything about the arts of gambling if it were not for these games.

How can we expect the ministers of the gospel and teachers in our public schools to exert a moral influence over our boys if such games are to be allowed to run without any interference? No other means can be calculated to make this country a nation of gamblers more quickly than the games here represented.

Let every institution for the betterment of morals and every parent join forces in crushing out this viper that is destroying the true principle of manhood; and now that the women are securing the vote in many parts of the country, it will be well for them to take up this matter in the most earnest manner possible, and so take away this vile temptation.

THE GAMBLER'S CHILD.

You ask me why so oft, father,
    The tears roll down my cheek,
And think it strange that I should own
    A grief I dare not speak;
But oh, my soul is very sad,
    My brain is almost wild;
It breaks my heart to think that I
    Am called a gambler's child.

My playmates shun me now, father,
    Or pass me by with scorn,
Because my dress is ragged, and
    My shoes are old and torn;

And if I heed them not, " There goes
 The gambler's girl," they cry;
Oh then how much I wish that God
 Would only let me die.

You used to love me once, father,
 And we had bread to eat;
Mamma and I were warmly clad,
 And life seemed very sweet;
You never spoke unkindly then,
 Or dealt the angry blow;
O father, dear, 'tis sad to think
 That gambling changed you so.

Do not be angry now, father,
 Because I tell you this,
But let me feel upon my brow
 Once more thy loving kiss;
And promise me your heart no more
 With gambling be defiled,
That from a life of want and woe
 Thou'lt save thy weeping child.

DON'T.

The late John W. Gates, famous the world over as " Bet-You-a-Million " Gates, the best advertised " gamblin' man " in America, on December 15, 1909, astounded the seventh annual conference of the gulf division of the Methodist church, at Port Arthur, Tex., with the following spectacular " Don'ts ":

Don't gamble.

Don't play cards.

Don't bet on horse races.

Don't speculate in wheat.

Don't speculate on the stock exchange.

Don't throw dice.

Don't shirk honest labor.

Don't be a gambler; once a gambler, always one.

The ministers agreed these " don'ts " were all right, coming as they did from a man whose heavy betting on horse races aroused the Jockey Club of New York to warn him to modify his wagers; whose spectacular gambling at " draw poker " and bridge are famed in song and poetry; who matched pennies for $1,000 a throw, who cornered corn and bucked Standard Oil and United States Steel " off the boards " in the stock exchange.

CHICAGO.

The year 1911 saw the greatest upheaval in the police department of the city that was ever known. Two commissions held active investigations into the vice conditions of the city, viz., the Chicago Vice Commission, under the presidency of Dean Walter D. Sumner, the other being under the City Civil Service Commission. Both of these commissions deserve great credit for the work done in revealing to the public the true conditions as they actually existed, and for the action taken to remedy the same.

The vice commission probed into the very heart of the vice districts, not for the purpose of prosecuting those connected with vice, but to discover the causes and recommend an ultimate remedy. The civil service commission requested certain information from the vice commission, but Dean Sumner did not see his way clear to furnish all they asked for, and gave his reasons, in part, as follows: " It was clearly understood that the material secured from this sociological study and deliberation was not for prosecuting purposes. Had any other understanding obtained it is questioned if any member of the present commission would have acted in the capacity as a member of the commission. The commission was specifically appointed to discover causes and recommend a remedy. This was done. By way of furnishing exact facts as to existing conditions, the report contains statements of actual cases of violations and evasions of various laws. The statements of these cases were made not for the purpose of laying cases before the proper authorities for the institution of prosecutions, but for the general purpose of showing weak points in the present method of administering and enforcing laws affecting vice. The laws and machinery to execute and enforce them were in existence long before the commission was thought of. The vice commission was not appointed to do the work of prosecuting officers, grand juries, state or city commissions, or other inquisitorial bodies, but to do its own work in its own way, and, among other things, to report its conclusions as to why the conditions were as bad as they are."

The above explanation is sufficient to show the nature and extent of the work outlined for the vice commission. Mayor Harrison acted in the best interest of the public when he stood at the back of the commission.

In the course of investigation much evidence had come to hand regarding the gambling situation in Chicago. The real fight commenced when the civil service commission undertook to investigate the police department. Among the first to be brought in were the police officials who were on duty around Comisky baseball park on Labor Day. As a result of this investigation Lieut. William W. Walsh was found guilty of neglect

Courtesy Chicago Tribune.

of duty and inefficiency. The verdict is said to have been reached on the evidence of photographs depicting gambling scenes at the park and the testimony of a few newspaper men and citizens. Against this was the testimony of nearly one hundred policemen who, after taking oaths, solemnly insisted they " saw no gambling." Lieut. Walsh admitted that gambling took place, but did not hold his men to blame for not seeing the games because of the great crowd of people which filled the streets near the park and the almost continuous blockade of street cars.

Assistant Chief of Police Herman F. Schuettler testified before the commission that he believed gambling existed in Chicago. He also asserted that occasional gambling raids were tipped off by the police and that gambling can be suppressed if the police make an honest effort to drive it out. He had previously been in charge of the gambling squad, for two previous periods, during which time gambling had been practically eliminated. He also stated he believed Mont Tennes was still in the gambling business.

Schuettler gave his experiences of the two periods when he had charge of the gambling squad. He stated that his first squad closed out Washington park, drove out lotteries and raided all sorts of gambling houses, making a total of 4,850 arrests; that 200 operators were indicted, 300 telephones torn out, and $35,000 fines assessed against the gamblers. During the second period that he had charge of the gambling squad he was not so successful in suppressing gambling as he was frequently interfered with, and that the men whom he thought were doing good work would be ordered away from him. When asked for the reasons why they were ordered away from him, he said that sometimes they were accused of grafting; that two men who had never pulled a gambling house in their lives had been accused of grafting.

It was alleged that on the return of Schuettler from the civil service commission enquiry, that he had a hot interview with Chief McWeeny. It ended by McWeeny giving his subordinate orders to suppress gambling and offered him all the men he wanted. The testimony of Schuettler before the commission was flatly contradictory to that of McWeeny. McWeeny had contended that there was no gambling; Schuettler had said that there was and that an honest effort on the part of the police could suppress it. He was now given an opportunity to prove his assertions and make good. He was to be held responsible for any gambling that took place in the city.

It was 4:05 o'clock in the afternoon when the assistant chief left his superior officer's office. The chief had given his O. K. to a list of twenty men for the gambling squad. At 4:20 o'clock a visitor entered the assistant chief's office. Schuettler was at the telephone. "Tear them out," he was roaring through the transmitter. "Get every telephone and every racing sheet." He explained to the visitor that it was the first raid made by his squad, and went on further to say, "One of my men just reported they caught a couple of dozen fellows and wanted to know about tearing out the telephones. Yes, it looks like I guessed right when I told the commission that there still is

gambling and Mont Tennes is doing business.   The boys say
Ed. Tennes, Mont's brother, is one of the men under arrest."

Within fifteen minutes after the raid every gambler and
book-maker doing business in the city was flashed the news,
" Schuettler's on the job."

The gambling place raided was over Billy Mangler's saloon
and restaurant at 21 North La Salle Street.   It was said that in
the earlier part of the afternoon over a hundred men had visited
the place.   About fifteen men got away by means of the fire escape and the back stairway.

Schuettler continued to keep his squad busy.   Mayor Harri-

Courtesy Chicago Tribune.

son gave him every encouragement to go ahead and clean up
the city and get rid of the gambling fraternity.

Detective Sloyer found a gambling telephone in operation
at the Welch cigar store, 4007 West Lake Street, and confiscated
it.   A search showed no gambling evidence and no arrests were
made.   The telephone bell rang.   " I'll make this bet," Sloyer remarked and answered the phone.   He listened to a man who
wanted to make a racing bet and then pulled out the instrument.   " It's being used for gambling purposes," the detective
said in answer to protests.

It appeared that in some instances the gambling squad
brought information to Schuettler that gambling houses were
being guarded by policemen.

The raid into Chinatown resulted in eight gambling places being raided, 158 inmates and operators arrested, and $388 in money confiscated. It was claimed that of the 6,000 Chinese in the city, that each leave of an average $1.50 a week in the gambling houses, or almost $500,000 a year, also that the " joints " were so openly operated that they bore gambling house signs in Chinese on the doorways, and lamps were left in the hallways at night to guide strangers to subterranean gambling rooms.

Inspector John Wheeler testified before the commission that he knew of the existence of the Chinese gambling places, but declared the inability of his detectives to understand the language and nature of their games prevented convictions. Fantan and bungloo are the favorite Chinese games.

It appeared during the investigation that McWeeny had a peculiar view of his own as to what constituted gambling. On the 23rd of September an order was issued to the effect that all forms of gambling in cigar stores and saloons were to be stopped. The officers immediately began to see that the law was enforced. What was the result? The report as appeared in the " Chicago Tribune," September 27th, will explain matters.

GAMBLING AS SEEN BY M'WEENY (AND OTHERS).

Gamble. To play or game for money or other stake—Webster's Unabridged Dictionary.

*   *   *   *   *   *   *   *   *

Gaming. Whoever shall play for money or other valuable thing at any game of cards, dice, checks, or at billiards or with any other article, instrument, or thing whatsoever which may be used for the purpose of playing or betting upon, or winning or losing money, or any other thing or article of value, or shall bet on any game others may be playing shall be fined not exceeding $100 and not less than $10.—Illinois Revised Statutes.

*   *   *   *   *   *

Sept. 26, 1911.

To Inspectors. Relative to the order issued the 23d instant concerning dice shaking in cigar stores, saloons, etc., you are advised that this order had reference to games where the dice shaking degenerated into a form of gambling for money and was not intended to prohibit games where the customer received an equivalent in merchandise in stock and for the sale on the premises and which are operated merely for the purpose of stimulating trade, provided that the amount to be played for does not exceed 25 cents.—John McWeeny, General Superintendent.

*   *   *   *   *   *

"The Chief finds that dice throwing for drinks and cigars with a 25 cent limit is a perfectly innocent game. Any 'hiking' of this modest stake is to be considered as gambling."

"I see all the dice games are running again," said a reporter to Chief McWeeny late in the afternoon. "Have you changed your order about stopping them?"

"Yes," was the reply after a moment's pause. "They went too far in enforcing it. It wasn't meant for the games except where there was gambling going on."

"You mean that you will permit the '13' and '23' games for cigars and drinks to go on?"

"Yes, there's no harm in those. Why, I've had a lot of kicks because they were stopped. Why, one man who lives in a hotel told me that he came down this morning and said to the bartender that he would shake him for his morning's morning, and the bartender said there was nothing doing. He had a kick coming."

"Then all these games will be allowed to run?"

"Why, there's no harm in it if a man wants to shake for a cigar or drink; and there's no harm in it if he wants to take a few checks and put them in his pocket and go in and get a drink or a cigar now and then."

"And you changed your order to stop these games?"

"Yes, I modified it. I issued it because we heard that there was some gambling in connection with these games. It's all right where they don't cash the checks in afterward."

"What's the difference between a man gambling against another man and a man gambling against 'the house?' Isn't one gambling just as much as the other?"

"O, anything's a gamble you take a chance on. You might make a date with one girl and she'd turn you down. You're taking a chance."

"Then you think that playing for checks for cigars and drinks is not gambling?"

"No, that isn't gambling."

Here we have the case where a chief of police issues an order on his own private opinion instead of applying the law as laid down for him in the Statute Book. It is the general opinion

Courtesy Chicago Tribune.

that the police are appointed to enforce the laws as they exist, and if the laws do not suit their own individual opinions, and they are not willing to enforce the laws, then they should get out, of the office as quickly as possible. There is certainly no injustice done to anyone in enforcing the laws against gambling. The quotation from the Illinois Revised Statutes very closely defines what is meant by gambling, and it would be well for other states to do likewise.

The late Professor David Swing once said of Gambling, " It is difficult to measure this vice, but it is so great as to merit from all civilized States immediate destruction. Like the opium habit, it must be checked by law. When the police will not enforce an existing law, they cease to be police, because the word ' police ' implies the care of a city, the study of its welfare. It is a bad condition of wool-growing when wolves are employed to guard sheep."

The civil service commission, on evidence obtained, suspended several police officers of various grades. This had the effect of inspiring the remainder to active service.

Charges of graft in connection with protection of vice was freely alleged.

Henry Brolaski, a reformed gambler, who sometimes works in connection with the American Civic Reform League, was on the stand for three hours and related his version of " underground Chicago." He testified, under oath, of paying $40,000 for protection for a gambling business which was stopped by a government fraud order. He also swore that he had furnished McWeeny with innumerable reports on vice conditions since the chief took office. He stated that his connection with two high police officials had been reached through Ben R. Hyman and " Tom " Costello, two formerly powerful figures in the gaming " trust " of the city. He described Hyman as a confidential man of the chief, and Costello a corresponding relation to Inspector Hunt.

The following monthly scale of " protection prices " according to Hyman's report, as read by Brolaski, were in force: Saloons open all night $50; All night saloon with music $75; Crap games $50; Poker games $25; Resorts selling liquor $100; Apartments, liquor selling $15. Ald, Coughlin and Frielman were stated to be the agents for Egandale whisky and compelled all dives to use their brand, and that all cigarettes and silk kimonas used by inmates of the resorts had to be purchased from the levee trust.

Chief McWeeny, after Brolaski had testified, said much of the testimony of the former gambler was false.

Louis Levine, alleged west side resort keeper, named from the witness stand as chief beneficiary of vice tribute levied on west side resort keepers and gamblers, Barney Grogan, Eighteenth ward " boss." He said the rates paid were as follows:

That he paid $400 to " Barney " Grogan to be allowed to operate his resort at 123 North Sangamon Street.

That he paid $250 to Grogan for Percival Steele, attorney for Harry Brolaski, and head of the Affiliated Civic League.

That a flat rate of $200 a month was paid by gambling houses to " Patsy " King, Grogan's gambling collector.

That $40 a month was paid by gambling houses to Detectives McShane and McSwiggen, confidential men of Inspector Dorman.

That gambling houses which ran more than one sort of game other than book-making had to pay 20 per cent of the extra game profits to Grogan's collector.

That Inspector Dorman and Capt. Plunkett (who resigned under fire) were the police " bosses " with whom Grogan divided the vice tribute.

Levine's testimony not only shook the police department and the politicians but brought forth a statement from Mayor Harrison. Every ounce of pressure possible was brought to bear upon the mayor to check the police investigation.

" I want to say that nothing can stop this investigation," the mayor said. " It's going to the bottom—no matter whom it hits. This was started for a purpose—for the purpose of finding out whether the members of the department are in collusion with vicious interests. The investigation will be finished. * * * *
It has been suggested this investigation was started to get certain men out of the department. This is not true, for all the men that have been mentioned could have been eliminated in other ways, as every captain and inspector with the exception of three could be retired if that was all that could be desired. It was also suggested that this investigation was for the purpose of reorganizing the department along new lines and the elimination of all police inspectors has been mentioned in this regard. The inspectors could be eliminated easily by not making a budget appropriation for their salaries. The purpose of this investigation is to find out the guilty men, if there are any,

and to put the fear of God into the hearts of others who have not fallen so that they will remember this investigation of the year 1911."

Levine when asked if he had ever seen money paid over by the gamblers answered that he had.

The civil service investigation will long be remembered by the citizens of Chicago for the fearless manner in which the members of the commission carried on their work; for the clean-up of the police force; for causing the break-up of the gambling trust and other forms of vice; for the number of gamblers who were compelled by circumstances to seek a livelihood in a more honest manner; for the exposure of the graft system that prevailed; and for the noble stand taken by the mayor of the city.

When will the heads of the executive power in our cities understand that the people are committed to their care in a very real way? When will they take the opportunity afforded them of protecting the citizens from the gamblers who prey upon the public, stand on the street corners, and congratulate themselves on the protection afforded them by the police? If the mayor of a city will not enforce the laws then he is a dishonest man and even ceases to be a law-abiding citizen himself, for he refuses to recognize the laws he had sworn on oath to enforce. I venture to say that a large percentage of the mayors of cities in this country could be impeached for malfeasance and nonfeasance in office if the truth of their administrations were brought to light. Let us hope for the time to come when politics and politicians will cease to be corrupted with graft, and seek only to serve the common good of the people.

THE POCKET DROP CASE.

This machine is the latest form of drop case out. It is made specially for those who wish to make the "quiet play." As the size is only 4½ by 3½ inches, it can be easily carried in the

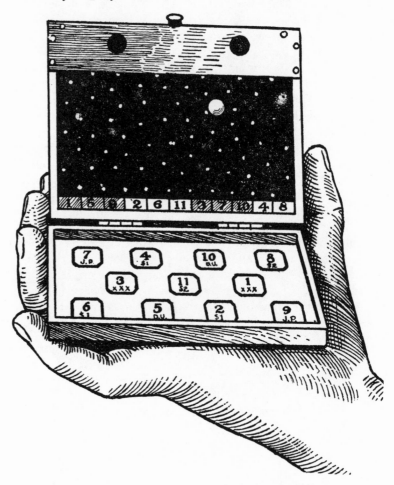

coat pocket and brought out for display when a convenient opportunity occurs.

It has all the arrangements designed for getting the victim's money just the same as the larger machines. The operator has the same control, and can make it come blank or prize, or "represent" at will. It looks innocent enough, but is not nearly as innocent as some of the young boys who are induced to venture their nickels and dimes upon it. It may *look* like a toy—but it is *not* a toy.

THE CHICAGO COUNTRY STORE WHEEL.

This is advertised as a "Miniature Department Store," and the most unique merchandise vender ever invented. Also that it will not only *attract* the crowds but *hold* them.

The spaces shown in the cut are intended to be filled by the merchant with assorted articles which often vary in value from a collar button to a nickel watch. There are 190 spaces, ten of which are for special prizes. These special prizes are usually of much greater value than the amount paid for a chance, which is usually ten cents.

To the right is a celluloid indicator which tells the prize won on every roll. Suppose twenty patrons have paid ten cents each for a roll at one time, it means that all of them will receive the same kind of article as a prize. Were there no possible chance of receiving a larger prize in excess of the value paid for a chance, there would be very little business done on a machine of this description, for the patron can purchase the same articles in a greater quantity for the same amount of money.

If the proprietors gave anything like value for value received on these machines, they could not afford to pay $50.00 for a machine in order to dispose of their goods. This alone speaks for itself.

CARD DICE.

Here is something new and declared to be a decided novelty. The above cut represents a set of card dice, which contains a full deck of fifty-two cards on each set of five dice. All kinds of games are played with these dice, but are usually played as poker dice, each player shaking three throws to beat his opponent.

AMERICAN HAZARD.

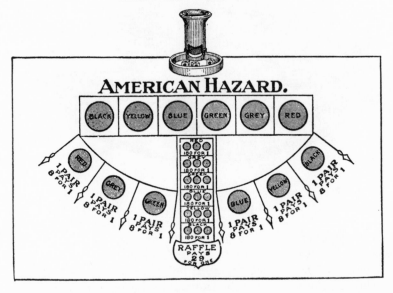

This is the latest *Club Room Creation* and guaranteed to get a play anywhere. The manufacturers claim that dice users have been looking for something new so this is offered them.

The game is operated with three cubes, each containing six different colors on them, and intended to be thrown from a special dice shaker, as shown in the cut, although this is not necessary.

The outfit consists of a very handsome layout, three cubes and a dice shaker.

This game has "A HANDSOME PER CENT IN FAVOR OF THE HOUSE." Reader, draw your own inference.

THE ROULETTE "BIG SIX" TRADE MACHINE AND PADDLE WHEEL, WITH LAYOUT.

This machine can be used as a trade stimulator, or can be run for nickels, dimes or dollars. It is claimed that this is the latest and greatest of them all and has all the others beat.

It is an entirely new departure and an unlimited number can play it at one time. "Nothing to get out of order. All can

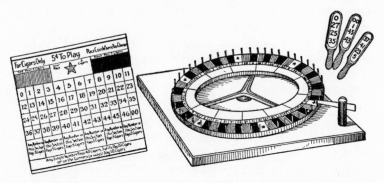

understand the game at a glance. This machine can be operated anywhere, as trade machines are never molested. *Remember this is no slot machine, but will bring you in more money than any five slot machines could."*

"The illustration serves to show, in a miniature way, what the printed matter on the face of the regular machine really is, the actual size being 11¾ inches in diameter. It is finely balanced and runs on a pivot, and on which is the round colored design between the spaces are brass pins dividing the colors and spaces. A celluloid indicator runs between the pins and indicates the stopping place of the wheel."

Twelve paddles, each containing four numbers, are the necessary adjunct.

THE GOLD BRICK FRAUD: TRUE STORIES FROM LIFE

By One of the Gang.

In exposing this stupendous confidence game, the author believes that the authentic stories herein told will prove the most effective method of showing up the tricks of the professional swindler, especially as they are given from a reliable source. Fiction has played its part in the past, and the author has been much amused by some of the accounts given. While no names will be mentioned in the relating of these incidents, the author wishes to inform the reader that all the participants were well known to him. Although many years have passed since the events actually occurred, yet even of late years stories of gold brick swindling have come to light.

Of all the devices which the fertile brain of the confidence operator has originated, it may be questioned whether any is more ingenious in conception or has reaped a richer harvest for the scoundrels who have operated it than has the " gold brick swindle."

The wise as well as the unwise are liable to bite at the bait of the gold brick swindler and get caught. To play the gold brick scheme successfully, the co-operation of at least three confederates is essential, of whom two must be gifted with some dramatic power. Some little cash is also required, it being necessary to procure a sample of filings of refined gold, one or two gold nuggets, and a " brick," or bar, of some thirty pounds in weight, composed of brass and copper, costing about twenty-five cents per pound.

The three confederates are known respectively as the " miner," the " trailer," and the " Indian."

The next important step is the selection of a " victim." He must be a man whose resources are such as to enable him to produce, at short notice, a considerable amount in ready cash. It is not considered wise to waste time with a man who would have to ask accommodation at his bank, inasmuch as such action on his part might result in the institution and prosecution of numberless inconvenient inquiries by the bank officials.

The victim having been carefully selected and located, the next step is to excite his cupidity.

One of the confederates, attired as a miner from Mexico or the far West, calls upon the party chosen at the latter's residence. Every detail of his appearance is attended to with the utmost care, from the seemingly sun-browned face, the apparent result of years of honest toil in the open air, to the well-worn, patched trousers carelessly tucked in the large, coarse, dusty boots. A battered cowboy's sombrero is negligently perched upon the

head, and around his waist is drawn a buckskin money belt. Having gained the presence of his prospective dupe, the pretended miner from the rude camps of the " Rockies " presents a paper on which is written, in sprawling characters, the victim's name. For the purpose of illustration, any name will answer; let us suppose it to be Mr. Thomas Jones. After the miner has handed this paper to Tom Jones he simulates acute disappointment at discovering that he is not the Tom Jones for whom he has been looking. He draws out an old red cotton handkerchief and wipes his eyes, as he sinks. apparently exhausted, into a chair. Naturally the sight of so quaint-looking an individual awakens the interest of Mr. Jones, and his simulated fatigue and grief arouse his curiosity, if not his sympathy, and he asks the cause of his distress. " No, no," the sharper answers, " You're not the Tom Jones I knows; and we's come so far, and the Indian's so sick he can't tote the gold no furder. And Tom Jones he was to give us the paper money." And here the miner permits his feelings to get the mastery of him again, and he bows his head in deepest sorrow. Mr. Jones would be either more or less than human if, after this, he did not seek for further information. " What Indian? What gold? What paper money?" are among the questions which rise to his lips. The miner hesitates for a moment, and if there are any other persons in the room requests that they withdraw. Then he says to Mr. Jones, with the air of one imparting a great secret: " You looks honest, and I'll tell you. We'se got lots o' gold, me and the Indian; and we'se looking for Tom Jones, cause he's got lots o' paper money, piles o' paper money locked up in an iron box. And now I can't find him. I could make him and all his children rich." " Where did you get the gold?" asks the now deeply interested Mr. Jones. " We'se tooken it out o' the mine, way down in Mexico." " Where is it?" pursues Mr. Jones. " The Indian, he's got it," replies the miner. " And where is the Indian?" " Oh," answers the miner, " he's down to the big camp, back over there (pointing) with the house built over the water (a bridge). He's sick, and couldn't come no furder."

At this stage it occurs to Mr. Jones that he has been strangely unmindful of the duties of hospitality, and asks his wife to prepare some refreshment for his guest. While this is being done, the host seeks further conversation by asking the stranger his name. " Well," the miner says, " they call me Dan in the mines." On his wife's return with the refreshments, Mr. Jones introduces the miner to her as Mr. Dan. The coffee is poured and Mr. Dan insists upon Mr. Jones taking a swallow of his coffee first, for one of his friends was given sleepy water (chloroform) once, and he lost all his money.

The miner takes from his pocket a small button of gold and hands it to Mrs. Jones, and says, " Mrs. Jones, take this for a present from me and my Indian friend." " Thank you," replies Mrs. Jones; " Is your coffee sweet enough?" While this is taking place, the " sucker," who has by this time become very urbane, tells the stranger that perhaps he is a brother to the Mr. Jones he is looking for; that his brother went out West some years ago and has not been heard from since. He also impresses the fact upon the miner that he is an honest man and rich, that he owns lands, stocks and property of various description, also piles of paper money, lots of it in the iron box at the bank, and therefore it is unnecessary for the miner to look further for the other Jones, as he can do business with him. To this proposal, however, the miner refuses to assent. He wants to see " his " Mr. Jones, and he expresses his intention of going on to the next town, where he professes to believe that he can find tidings of the whereabouts of that mysterious individual. Before he takes his departure he promises, in compliance with the oft-repeated request of his host, that in case he fails to find the man of whom he is in quest he will return.

The miner now takes from his belt a nugget of gold, hands it to the interested dupe, requesting him to take it to the medicine store (drug store) and have some smoky water (acid) poured on it, then go to the watchmaker's (jeweler's) and sell it for what it is worth, bring back the proceeds and pay himself for his trouble. This shrewd move of the confidence man serves a double purpose: it convinces the victim that the miner actually has the gold, and at the same time leads him to suppose that he is dealing with a man wholly inexperienced in the ways of the world. The miner bids Mr. Jones and his family good-bye, and goes on his journey to locate " his " Tom Jones.

After a few days the swindler returns, attired as before. He has failed to find his Tom Jones, but has learned where he is. He looks up with tearful eyes into the face of Mr. Jones, asking him to please write a letter for him. About this time Mrs. Jones suggests that Mr. Dan have a good dinner, after which Mr. Jones would write the letter for him. "No," says the miner, " I can't eat till I know the letter is gone on the railway." Of course Mr. Jones assents, and the epistle is indited to the mythical personage, something after the following manner, dictated by the miner:

" Dear Friend, Mr. Tom Jones:—I hope you are well, and me and the Indian has come on with the first lot of gold." (Here the miner looks around the room as if he feared some one would hear this valuable secret and asks his victim if he will keep the secret. Mr. Jones, who is anxious to know the great secret which is to follow, readily promises that he will. The miner, however, insists upon shaking hands to bind the bargain). " We'se got all the rest hid away, and there's ten millions worth of it. Now Tom, you come right off with the paper money, 'cause the Indian he's sick, and me and him wants to go back to the mines to get more."

The thought of ten million dollars' worth of gold in the hands of an ignorant old miner and an untutored child of the forest excites the cupidity of Mr. Jones to a high degree. He believes that his superior knowledge of the world and his familiarity with business customs and forms would render it comparatively easy for him to make himself the owner of the lion's share of an immense fortune, and mentally belittles the other Tom Jones.

The letter having been completed, the miner is asked to give the address. He promptly answers, " Canada." " Canada," repeats Mr. Jones, " Why man, Canada has hundreds of towns and cities." " What city? I don't know any city but Canada," replies the miner, and instantly begins to bemoan his hard lot at having come so far to no purpose, and the Indian being so sick.

Mr. Jones believes that this is his opportunity, and assures his new friend that he will get the paper money for the gold, and after much persuasion prevails upon the miner to reveal the whereabouts of the Indian who has in his custody so much of the precious metal.

The result of this interchange of confidence is that the swindler and the " sucker " start together for the town where the Indian is supposed to be. (Often the Indian and the trailer are on the same train.) A point at a distance of from one to two hundred miles is usually chosen in which to locate the mysterious personage. Mr. Jones insists that the Indian must return with them to his home, bringing the gold with him. The miner tells him that the Indian is too sick to come any furder. On the way to the station the miner makes a cunning play by handing Mr. Jones a nugget of gold, telling him to buy the tickets, well knowing the ticket seller would not take the gold nugget, and that Mr. Jones would have to pay for the tickets out of his own pocket and hand him the gold back.

On arriving at their destination, the other two confederates (who have been apprised of the hour of their arrival) are there at the railway station, and carefully note the signal given by the

miner.   If the latter raises his hat, they know that everything
is proceeding satisfactorily.   If he shakes the lapel of his coat,
they understand that " the jig is up," and that they had better
" take quick steps and long ones."

Immediately upon receiving the pre-arranged signal at the
station, the first confidence man and his victim now repair to the
spot in the woods, where the Indian had previously gone to get

" Mr. Jones gets a glimpse of the glittering, but spurious metal."

himself in readiness to receive his visitors.   On reaching the locality the " brick " is exhumed from its hiding place, and Mr.
Jones gets a glimpse of the glittering, but spurious, metal.

If the latter should go to a drug store and purchase a bottle
of acid, with which the supposed gold may be tested, the services
of the third confidence man (the trailer) are called into requisi-
tion, but he himself is kept carefully in the background, as his
duty is to keep his eye continually on the victim.   When the

dupe procures the necessary acid, the trailer buys a precise dupli-
cate of the bottle. The contents of this latter bottle, however,
are poured out and replaced by water.

When the victim returns to the spot where he has left the
Indian and the supposed miner, the latter has already received
from his confederate the bottle of water, identical in size, appearance and label with that which the dupe has in his pocket.
Mr. Jones tells the miner he has a bottle of acid and would like
to test the metal. The miner says, "Well, I'se glad; but just
let me take it and show it to the Indian, so he will know it's
smoke water (acid) and not sleep water (chloroform)." This
ingenious request is satisfactory to Mr. Jones, who hands the
bottle of acid to the miner. On his way to the Indian he changes
bottles. On his return he hands to Mr. Jones the bottle of water
which is poured over the metal with no effect. The face of Mr.
Jones is illumined with results, and he says, " Mr. Dan, your
kindness to me in this transaction shall be reciprocated by my
punctuality in giving you the paper money for this gold, as I
have promised. I will go now to the bank and get you the
paper money, $5,000." " No, no," says the miner, " I wants to
satisfy you more fully," and proceeds to hand Mr. Jones an augur
and a brace, requesting him to bore into the " brick " and take
the shavings to a watchmaker to prove the value of it. As soon
as Mr. Jones bores a fair sample of shavings, the sharper places
them in a piece of paper torn from that in which the brick had
been wrapped, and ostensibly hands them to Mr. Jones; but
in reality he gives Mr. Jones genuine gold shavings he has previously arranged in a package similar in appearance.

Mr. Jones hurries to the jeweler. The test shows gold of
from 18 to 20 karat fineness, and Mr. Jones is now quite ready
to make the purchase. He goes to his bank, draws his money,
and returns to the Indian and the miner. The bar is weighed
and its value is computed. Mr. Jones then asks how the money
is to be divided. " Why," replies sharper number one, " into
three piles; one for you, one for me and one for the Indian."
This arrangement is eminently satisfactory to the " sucker," who
has probably already attempted to defraud his companions by
means of a false computation, and who now thinks that he sees
his way clear to make a purchase of pure gold at about two-
thirds of its value, pays the money to the miner who takes it to
the Indian some thirty or forty yards off in the brush. Return-

ing to Mr. Jones, he gives him a hearty handshake and bids him good-bye.

In a couple of days Mr. Jones is the recipient of a letter as follows: " Mr. Tom Jones, Dear old Friend Tom:—We have just dined sumptuously at your expense on spring chicken, cream gravy, humming-bird pie with celery sauce, and a cup of pure Jave and Mocha with whipped cream thrown in. You have been a good soft sucker. If you tell that you have been caught in the old ' gold brick scheme ' you will be the laughing stock of the town, and the people will say, ' Did you ever hear of old Tom Jones being caught? Well, it's good for him for he has robbed lots of people.' Tom, get a cake of ice and lay it on your head. Goodbye. (Signed)   Gold Brick Swindlers."

It sometimes happens, in working the gold brick swindle, that the swindlers find a merchant who is willing to aid them on a percentage basis. Two men who had been partners together in the chattel mortgage business, one of whom had become president of a bank, the other having gone into the grocery business, were leading features in another swindle by the same party. The president of the bank still remained in the chattel mortgage business. The merchant becomes the confident of the miner, and gives him valuable information about his former partner, for which he is to receive ten per cent. of the amount the banker chose to invest.

Having laid all his plans with the utmost care, the miner proceeds with his acquaintance with the banker, and in due course of time has the satisfaction of selling him four bricks for which he is to receive the sum of $10,000. While in the woods the banker asks the miner if he has any more bricks at the same price. " Yes," says the miner, " We'se got four more just the same size in Kansas City you can have for paper money." " Bring them to me," says the banker, " I will pay you the paper money when you bring them." The miner asks him if he will give him a paper to show that he would pay him the money as soon as he came with the gold. The banker takes from his pocket a check book and writes a check for $10,000 to be paid on the delivery of the bricks. The miner gives the merchant his ten per cent., and hurries away to have four more bricks made to deliver to the banker, leaving the trailer behind to watch the banker.

In a few days the miner returns and calls upon the merchant, telling him that he was prepared to deliver the four bricks. " No, no," says the merchant, " Don't do it; he will catch us all and send us to prison for life. If you won't go to the bank with the other four bricks I will give you back the $1,000 for I haven't slept an hour at a time since you gave me that money." (Conscience makes cowards of us all.)

The miner not being at all satisfied with the attitude of the merchant, goes to the hotel, puts on a new frock coat and silk hat, walks into the bank, gets a $500 bill changed and satisfies himself that the banker has not tumbled to his being swindled.

The three confederates were stopping at separate hotels. They had a quiet meeting place where they came together and agreed that the proper course was for the miner to go back to the merchant and tell him the situation was shaky, and that if he would return the $1,000 he would leave town. The visit of the miner to the merchant is successful. The miner and the Indian go to a small town seventy miles away, leaving the trailer to watch the banker. The banker receives a letter begging him " to come with the paper money as the Indian is sick and not able to come furder, that he is worn out and could not get to his town." Early in the morning the trailer watches the bank. About ten o'clock the banker arrives in his carriage, goes into the bank and stays about an hour, and on coming out walks to a trunk shop, and buys two valises. He takes the noon train as the miner requested him to do. On the arrival of the train at its destination, the trailer signals to the miner that the banker was all right (buying the valises was proof enough), so the miner meets the banker with a hearty handshake, and they start off together to meet the Indian about a mile away. The banker, in his eagerness to get the gold, does not even go to the trouble of testing them, but quickly counts out the money in $500 bills and receives back the check he had given. He makes the Indian a present of $100 extra, takes the next train home, and places the four bricks in the vault with the four others.

Some six weeks later the banker saw in his daily paper in great headlines, the following: " Another ' sucker ' caught for $6,000 on the old gold brick fraud." The banker went out quietly and brought in the jeweler to his bank to test the bricks with acid, the test proving them not to be gold, as they smoked like a tar-kiln. He bore his trouble silently for he well knew his past record in business was bad, for he was evading the usury law and had taken furniture, even babies' cradles, from poor people to satisfy his claims, and men were at this time interested in furnishing a chattel mortgage man with money which was being loaned at six per cent. per month on personal property. The merchant was correct when he said he did not believe the banker would squeal on account of his past business record.

The gold brick men knew the situation of the merchant, and sent the Indian along to play the detective to the merchant, thereby succeeding in scaring him out of $1,000. The merchant finally becoming disgusted with the state of affairs, sold out his business and left for parts unknown, never to return.

The principle upon which a great majority of men act, is,

"Had taken furniture, even babies' cradles."

how much they can get, not how much they can give. Get all they can and keep it all. In other words legalized robbery. Some men speak several languages, but gold speaks them all fluently. Sousa's, Godfrey's and Gilmore's bands are not in it. The jingling of gold is "sweet music." John Wesley once said, "Get all you can, save all you can, give all you can."

This same trio of swindlers played a certain man for the sum of $10,000, believing him to be a wealthy cattle dealer. He was a great believer in palmistry and fortune telling, and had subscribed liberally to the support of spiritualism. The gold brick men opened a place and inserted the following advertisement in three consecutive issues of the local daily paper: "SATYAT NAST PARODHARMAT. (There is no religion higher than

17

truth.)   Ramasmami, the greatest mind reader and palmist known, is at ———, for a few days only.   Past, present and future, health, love, marriage, divorce, inheritance, prospects and results of business transactions made known in strict confidence." A copy of the paper with the palmist's advertisement marked, was sent to the prospective victim.   Eighty-three "suckers" called at the place of business and were fleeced out of $135.

On the afternoon of the third day the victim came in, paid his five dollars and presented his left hand for a reading.   The palmist told him he was a very industrious man, that he was dealing in some kind of animals but was going to change his business very soon, and, in fact, had already almost completed the arrangements, and if he went through with it he would become a very rich man.   The cattle man says, " I am quite satisfied."   " No," says the palmist, " the life line in your left hand which runs from the wrist to the middle finger, also the line of glory with the line of power all point to your right hand as holding the key to the secret of your success or failure, and to tell you for certain the outcome of your prospects (the palmist could tell just as much by reading his foot) I must read your right hand."   " How much will it cost?" asks the victim.   " Ten dollars," replies the palmist.   " Here's your money."   The palmist proceeding says, "The right hand shows heavy money transactions, gold, gold and piles of it, which will make you, your wife and three children independent."   " That will do," says the victim, " I am satisfied you know your business when you tell a perfect stranger he has a wife and three children ; it is marvelous."   The " sucker " hurries home to meet the miner, whom he is expecting.   The miner, who has been away looking for his friend, returns after four days not having succeeded in "finding " him.   He asks the " sucker " to write him a letter.   " No," says the dupe, " I will give you paper money for all your gold." While the trailer was playing the palmist, the victim had been to a drug store and purchased a bottle of acid, and the sharpers never knew from which drug store.   The farmer convinced the miner that he himself was the right man to do business with, that he was compelled to be honest in his dealings on account of his children, that his duty and aim in life was to so live as to not reflect discredit upon those three little darlings he has to support.

The miner, accompanied by the victim, starts on the journey

to meet the Indian. Stopping at an hotel for the night, they both occupied one room in which there were two beds. The miner took his bed and made it up on the floor miner fashion. While the farmer was sleeping, the miner crawled to his bed, took the bottle of acid from the " sucker's " coat pocket, emptied out the contents (and in so doing burned his hand very badly), filled the bottle with water and placed it back into the " sucker's " pocket. In the morning the farmer discovers that the miner has his hand wrapped in a red cotton handkerchief, and asks him what is the matter with it. " Oh," says the miner, " it is a breaking-out miners have, caused from digging in the mines."

The visit to the Indian having been made, the victim pays over the sum of $3,000 in return for the spurious metal. He had borrowed this money from his wife, which had been left to their children by her father and she had been appointed administratrix or executor for the children, and she had given security, making those who had gone security responsible to the children for the money when they reached the age of maturity.

A short time after the deal had been completed, the wife discovered that something was wrong with her husband and tried to relieve him of his despondency. The wife would ask him every day about the cattle. She finally went to a detective and asked him to find out what was the trouble that preyed upon her husband's mind. The farmer told the detective that he had been swindled out of all his money on the gold brick game, that he had lied to his wife to get it, which hurt him worse than losing the money; that he had deceived a good wife who had been a good mother to his children.

When the wife learned the facts in the case she applied for a divorce. This action of the wife's so upset the husband that he was taken seriously ill to the hospital, and came near dying of a broken heart.

When the gold brick men heard of this happening, one of them went to see him at the hospital. The interview between the gold brick man and the farmer was a long one, in which the latter told all about how the money was obtained and the consequent result. The sharper told him that it was certain that the men who had swindled him would be caught and sent to prison, and the money restored to him. " No, do not do that," said the victim, " for it would not do me any good to send the men to prison who were smart enough to beat me."

The sharper went out and bought a basket of fruit, and on his return offered it to the sick man. He thanked the sharper and said that he would much prefer that his wife and children have it. They both cried. A single glance in the sick man's face showed the great agony he was undergoing. As the sharper bade him good-bye, he told him that in a few days he would hear good news. To say that this information cheered him is but a timely expression. Here conscience, yes, an enlightened conscience, regulated by the inspiration of a higher power, and not by the mighty dollar, showed itself upon the heart and face of the man who had caused so much sorrow.

The sharper met his confederates and reported the above facts to them saying, " Boys, we have robbed three beautiful children of their bread, broken the hearts of their mother and father, and caused a fair home to be broken up, and their name dishonored. Something must be done to make amends, or the black waters will flood our own door." One of them answered, " You should have been a preacher." " Yes," replied the sharper, " We dug the pit for this man and his wife's feet to slip into, and if we don't make good and return this money, there will be a pit open to us that our feet cannot escape."

The three companions in crime took a journey about two hundred miles off, went to an express office, obtained a money order for the sum of $3,100, and sent it in an envelope to the wife with the following letter:—" Mrs. ———, Dear Madam: No doubt you will be surprised and as we hope agreeably so, when you receive this package with contents from the three gold brick men who swindled your husband out of $3,000. We return to you the money, with interest, and wish we were able to bring your husband back to you and your three children. This act has invalued consequences to us, which we believe to be more painful than to you and yours. To return to you this money is our only source of consolation. It says in the Bible somewhere, " Vengeance is Mine, I will repay, saith the Lord." There is no other remedy to quiet our conscience. We all hope that the sense of your husband's past folly, which you both have felt so keenly, may be forgotten and you again be reunited and live happily with your husband and children. Forgive us, and your husband also, is the desire of three gold brick men. Take your husband back." Upon receipt of this letter she went to the hospital for her husband and took him back home with her.

The authorities caused an investigation to be made, resulting in a fight on the fortune teller and the palmist. It was the palmist who first read the hand and then buncoed the client with a large glass globe which rested upon a table in the parlor with four tubes attached, running down through the table legs under the floor, along the wall and up to the attic, where another man is hidden. This man speaks through the tube, and represents to be the spirit of the dead friends of those who called for information from the spirit world. In one instance an aged lady, whose son while on the top of a box car passing under a bridge was struck on the head and instantly killed, called upon the palmist for information. She was induced to part with her son's watch and $17.00 in cash. This caused many members of the fraternity to leave St. Louis for new fields and seek fresh victims to skin.

One man who sold furniture on easy payments (made hard) advertised $300.00 worth for $5.00 per month. He was induced to purchase a brick for $6,000.00. The trailer who assisted in disposing of the brick, purchased furniture from him on the easy payment plan, had paid over $200, and failing to make another payment when due the furniture was taken from his home during his absence, thus leaving his wife and three children without a chair to sit upon or a bed to rest upon. The trailer said he had lost many thousands of dollars at gambling, but the $2,000.00 he received as his share from the money received from the easy payment man made him feel easy and even on all his hard luck gambling. The following letter was sent to the easy payment man: "Mr. ———, Dear Sir:—We advise you to keep cool; we have only taken a small percentage of the money you have robbed your customers out of by means of the easy payment plan (made hard). You can give the gold brick men spades and beat them, for they only skin the rich and the 'skinners,' while you rob poor men, women and children. Take your medicine you old robber and keep quiet." He kept quiet.

From earliest ages the *love* of money has dominated the actions of men. The Apostle Paul says, "The love of money is the root of all evil." This probably accounts for the gold brick schemes being worked so extensively throughout the world, causing its victims to commit suicide with poison, and often the sound of a pistol rings out the sad news of another gold brick victim sending himself before the court of Eternal Justice,

there to be tried by the great Judge of all.   In this Court there
can be no false entry, no fine for contempt of Court, no bribing
the jury, no dickering with the Judge, no forfeiting of bonds, no
fleeing from justice, no immunity for turning King's evidence,
no attorney to plead your cause.

One of the greatest confidence men known, after making
hundreds of thousands of dollars, died a pauper.   His friends
bought a cheap coffin wherein to place his remains, sprinkled it
with a few flowers, and as the coarse bloated wretches from
whom every vestige of manhood had long since departed,
filed up for a farewell look upon the face of their old friend
Bill, their baneful breath seemed to wither the flowers.   Perhaps
a bunch of night-shades twisted with thorns would have been
more appropriate for the occasion.   One of the gamblers said
"stop the box."   "What for," asked another who had been with
Bill in some of his schemes.   "I will bet $500.00 to $50.00 old
Bill is not in the box," was the reply.   Another gambler said,
" double the bet and I'll take half of it."   One old white-haired
sinner shivering with cold, with tears streaming down his
wrinkled face said, " boys, there goes my best friend; I have
known Bill many years.   His money has many times kept him
from jail, but the devil has got him now, and all the money in
the universe cannot keep him out of hell, and we will all go the
same way if we do not change our lives.   I shall begin a new
life from this moment."   He kept his word, and when he died
a respectable funeral was given him.

An honest old farmer who had a grocery store tried his
luck in the wheat market and met with several reverses.   He
borrowed money and made an assignment to his wife.   The
general opinion was that he had a lot of money laid aside.
Two gold brick men, hearing of this, drove out to his farm
and at a chosen spot buried a chunk of brass, and at the same
time making a chart showing the lay of the land and so treated
as to give it the appearance of antiquity.   All preparations having been carefully made the confidence men wrote him a letter
wanting to buy his· farm.   The farmer wrote back that his
wife owned the farm but would sell it.   The sharpers drove to
the farm, looked it over and remained over night.   The next
day they divulged what was meant to be a great secret.   They
pointed out to the farmer the location on the chart where the
supposed gold was to be found, and he had therefore no diffi-

culty in finding the spot. With a shovel and pick the treasure
was found. The glittering appearance made the farmer smile,
and every instinct of cupidity was aroused within his anxious
mind. One of the sharpers proposed to buy the other two out,
and after making the proposition walked off to give the other
sharper and the farmer an opportunity to talk the matter over.
The brick was weighed and the value was computed at $6,000.00.
This being equally divided amounted to over $2,000.00 each.
The farmer and one of the sharpers bought the interest of the
other sharper for $2,000.00. The farmer went into the family
room and brought out $1,000.00 in cash and paid it over to the
sharper. The other sharper drew a check for the same amount.
The farmer agreed to remain at home until one of the sharpers
should return to accompany him to Washington City, where
they would then go to the U. S. Mint to get paper money for
their brass. The journey was never accomplished, for the
reason that the sharpers divided the farmer's money, and wrote
him the following letter: "Dear Mr. S———: You old robber.
You failed in business, made your property over to your wife
when you had plenty of money, and thus swindled your cred-
itors. We advise you to take your medicine. You can now
understand how those you have swindled feel. Skin your friends
out of more cash and we will plant another chunk of brass on
your wife's farm. Wishing you a Merry Christmas and a Happy
New Year. From your friends, Gold Brick Swindlers."

The case above mentioned was of a man whom the neigh-
bors believed was an honest man. The Golden Rule is not only
brushed aside by gold brick swindlers, but in every line of business there is too much craft (graft) and deceit. The way
business is carried on in this age would make gold brick swindlers and gamblers blush with shame of their ignorance of the
methods practised when compared with such frauds resorted
to by those who are believed to be dealing square with the
public. " Shall I count them pure with the wicked balances, and
with the wicked bag of deceitful weights?"—Micah vi. 2. This
is caused by the two equal evils, viz.: the pernicious activity of
the vicious and the pernicious inactivity of the virtuous. The
inherent villainy of such transactions by men who are passing
as honest men recoil in disgust, if not in horror. The author
knows that men of unblemished reputation occupying high
positions in social, professional or commercial circles, some fill-

ing posts of responsible trust in public life have taken money which constituted their agreed proportion of the money obtained by fraud from the wretched dupe,—their friend.

Three men by the name of Creek, Lavin and Curtis, were the only party ever known to carry a genuine gold brick with them, and which was valued at $12,000.00. Another set of gold brick men learned of this, and they forthwith manufactured a "sucker" who bought the pure gold brick from the Creek party for $3,000.00. Creek and his party had also a brass brick exactly

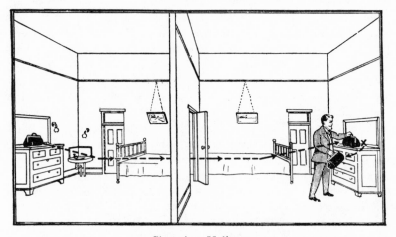

Changing Valises.

the same size as the gold one; this was used as a ringer. They had two valises of the same size and color. The sharper who had bought the genuine gold brick from the Creek party took it with him to the hotel. The Creek trailer went to the same hotel with his brass brick and engaged a room. The two sharpers entered into a conversation. The "sucker" sharper asked the Creek trailer what was the best train for him to go home on. The Creek trailer said, "I will go down and find out for you." While he was gone the "sucker" sharper took the genuine gold brick from his own room and placed it in the room of the Creek trailer, exchanging it for the brass brick. When the Creek trailer returned he told the "sucker" sharper that he had better go himself to make certain of the best train, as he could not obtain satisfactory information, but that if he intended to go to Chicago he hoped to be allowed to accompany him. The "sucker" sharper then excused himself and went to the station. During his absence the Creek trailer rushed into his room, took the valise he thought contained the brass brick into the "sucker" sharper's room, exchanged the valises, and took back to his own room what he believed to be the genuine gold brick, but what was in reality the brass one. He then took advantage of the earliest opportunity to leave the hotel, taking the brass brick along with him. The "sucker" sharper therefore was left with the genuine gold brick, having made a profit of $9,000.00. He never returned again to his own party. The loss caused quite a disturbance in the Creek, Lavin and Curtis camp, as they suspicioned their trailer with standing in with the "sucker" sharper. But this was not true.

This did not, however, deter Creek, Lavin and Curtis to abandon the business, for they had another gold brick manufactured, costing $20,000.00. They were successful in selling it to a real estate man, who was known to be a skinner, for $6,000.00. The trailer followed him several hundred miles before he got a chance to exchange valises. The trailer managed to engage him in conversation in the sleeper on the train, and invited him into the dining-car to take lunch with him. Arriving at the lunch table the trailer excused himself to go back to the sleeper to get some choice cigars. Here he took the opportunity to exchange the valises and then hurried back to the dining-car, throwing down some cigars, saying, "Try one of these I brought from Mexico." The man was not aware at the time that the Mexican cigars had cost him over $6,000.00. The trailer got off at the next station with the $20,000.00 gold brick, while the victim traveled on to his destination with the $9.00 brass brick.

Retribution is sure to follow close to the heels of the evil doer, and the case of Creek, Lavin and Curtis was not an exception. They played the biggest stake ever played with the gold brick scheme, by robbing an Englishman at Tuscola, Florida, for $50,000.00. The first play they made netted them $10,000.00, and on the second play they secured $40,000.00. In getting away with the money, they ventured in a canoe, capsized, and men, money and all were lost. They were never heard of again.

The last case I will narrate is that of a man who was known as a "fence," that is, a receiver of stolen goods. Detectives had long failed in any attempt to catch him. When a crook would bring in a watch or other article of stolen jewelry, he would ask, "How much do you want for this, six or fifty dollars? If I want it at that can I have it?" "Yes," would be the answer. He would then excuse himself and go to the back room, place the article into the crucible, melt it, and return to his customer with the money. He had been in court many times but had been discharged for lack of evidence. He finally sold out his store and went into the auction business. In this line of business he skinned the public so openly that the authorities imposed a heavy license fee on him and his kind. But this only succeeded in putting the smaller fry out of business. He never employed less than three "cappers," and when an article was to be bid for, he would start the bidding himself and the "cappers" would follow suit. As soon as the price was bid that he wished to obtain for the article, he would knock it down to the person bidding. One day our friend the "Miner" went in with his miner suit on, and bought a shaving razor and strop. When the packet was brought him he said to the clerk, "Will you let me go behind your place and bring out some gold?" "Certainly," replied the clerk. The miner took from his belt a lump of gold worth $26.00, and said to the clerk, "Take it out of that." The clerk called the governor, and the governor and miner went to a jewelry store, had it tested and weighed, and received $22.00 for it. The jeweler made $4.00 on the transaction. On the way back to the auction shop the governor asked the miner if he had any more like that. "Yes," said the miner, "we's rich." "Who is we's, have you some one with you?" "Yes; my Indian friend who is very sick, and I tell you he has lots of gold." "Have you got it with you?" asked the auctioneer. "No, but we's got it near here, but we came after a friend to help us get paper money for our gold." "What is the matter with me?" asked the auctioneer. "Is you honest, can you get the paper money?" asked the miner in return. "Yes, I can get a wagon load; see my big shop? and I have thousands of paper money in the bank." "Well," said the miner, "will you be here in your shop in three days?" "Yes," replied the auctioneer, "but I want to have a talk with you; come with me and we will have a drink." "No," objected the miner, "I don't drink; it ruined my father and brother. The men who sell it might give me sleepy water." "Well, come, we will have lunch," said the auctioneer. While at lunch the auctioneer gave the miner his home address, and asked him to take supper there with him. After supper, the miner asked if he could have a room to himself for a few minutes. This request was readily granted. When the miner came out he handed a lump of gold valued at $8.00 to the auctioneer's wife, saying, "take this from me and my poor sick Indian friend." When the miner left he asked the auctioneer to take care of his shaving outfit, as he was going to try to find his friend, who would give him paper money for his gold. The miner returned to the residence of the auctioneer on the second day much disheartened because he had not been successful in finding his friend. The auctioneer and miner started for Kansas City the next day. A test of the gold was made and the auctioneer bought three bricks, paying $8,000.00 for them.

The trailer had gone on the same train and taken a suit of clothes for the miner. A letter reached the home of the auctioneer almost as soon as himself. It was as follows:—" Dear Sir: Go and soak your head. A man who has skinned as many as you have and gets caught by an ignorant old miner, should sneak off and hide. Hurry up and skin the people in the auction business and we will let you have three more bricks at the same price. Believe us your friends, Gold Brick Men."

Only about ten per cent who are caught on the gold brick scheme make their losses known to the public. They are restrained by a sense of shame to unfold the full depths of their ignorance, knowing they will command no sympathy from those who know them, as the game is usually played upon men who justly bear the reputation of skinners, greedy, credulous, covetous, shrewd and cunning manipulators. The most essential thing is to know that the proposed victims have the cash in the bank, as it is unwise to play for men who may find it necessary to ask accommodation at the bank, inasmuch as it might result in the institution and prosecution of numberless questions by the bank officials. The way the sharpers obtain information of moneyed men is through business men who are promised a percentage of the dishonest gains should the fraud be successfully consummated by the gold brick swindlers. They care little about what people think or say regarding their hope for a future world, but will quickly assert themselves when present possessions are in any degree endangered.

Friendships are more easily broken through matters of

money than anything else; the most sensitive part of most men is their pocket-book. This question is not local but international.

CONSCIENCE! CONSCIENCE!! CONSCIENCE!!!

It is true some men seem to have no conscience, beyond some educated habit, and they will, I fear, learn too late that God is the Supreme Judge, and Justice hath her balance.

To speak of earthquakes, cyclones, tornadoes, floods, shooting, stealing, lying, swearing, drinking, gambling, sheriffs, jails, electric chairs, the scaffold and the hangman, wars and rumors of wars, etc., are nothing to be compared with the stinging reproach of conscience. It never lies; it is judge, jury and witness. The verdict is always right; no hung jury, no false swearing, no alibi. There is but one remedy that will quiet it, and that is to be just in the sight of God and our fellow men.

CHINA.

By way of dealing with the gambling evil in the province of Canton, the Chinese Government has adopted summary measures, such as Western folk can with difficulty understand. Mr. Sherwood Eddy, who was in Canton during the week when the edict of suppression came into force, writes: "Although three-fourths of the revenue of the entire Canton province came from gambling dens, the new viceroy perceived that it was ruining the people. He issued a proclamation stating that gambling had gone through his people like fire and flood. He substituted other taxes to meet the needs of the province, and on March 29, the first day of the third moon in the Chinese calendar, all gambling-houses were closed and their signs removed! A hundred thousand people assembled on the bund to watch the great procession, to celebrate with rejoicing this bold innovation, and to create sentiment in favor of the prohibition of gambling. Floats carried on the shoulders of men represented in picturesque drama the ravaging effects of gambling. The figures of twelve great dragons were carried, some of which took 20 men to bear. It was a picturesque sight, and took over two hours to pass.—*London Christian.*

NEW YORK: THE PARADISE OF GAMBLERS.

It has been claimed that New York, the great American metropolis, is the very paradise of gamblers. This assertion will not be disputed by members of the fraternity. The carping critics declare that there is scarcely a street without its gambling resort, all private, of course, yet the location of which is well known to those who indulge in that excitement.

The favorite game played in the city is faro, and the stakes vary according to the class to which the house caters. In some of the lowest hells a stake of five cents is not despised. In recent years roulette has also become quite popular. The majority of roulette tables, however, is to be found in the clubs of the aristocrats, and many a man has fallen from that high (?) estate by means of the roulette.

In the cheap eating houses that abound in or near Broadway, from Spring Street north to Tenth Street, are to be found the shabby-genteel men who bear unmistakable evidence in their speech, manner and appearance, of long continued, and generally disastrous "fighting with the tiger." These are the *canaille* of gamblers, who hang precariously on the edge of a terrible fascination, and manage to supply the necessities of life in a cheap way, from chance success in small bets and by a few dollars picked up by guiding more profitable customers to the houses where they are known. Strictly speaking, there are more "cappers" than gamblers. Their right to the proud title of "sporting men" is stoutly denied them by their more prosperous and reputable brethren of the green cloth. They are usually the most improvident and unscrupulous beings in existence. Every house has several of these forlorn attachés, who play when they have money, and introduce a desirable stranger when they can; who are constant in their attendance upon the banquets that are daily spread in these houses, but are thus obliged to take the chances as to lodgings, and raiment. When they have worn threadbare the hospitality of the gaming house keeper (as sometimes happens), they subsist—God and themselves alone know how.

The aspect of another class of gamblers who are to be found on any fine afternoon decorating Broadway with the splendor of their apparel, is far different from those just mentioned, for they are unexcelled in elegance of attire. If you meet in Broadway a man who lounges listlessly onward as though he had no well-defined object in life, and whose garments are cut in the latest style and of the finest material, you may assure yourself that he is a gambler in good luck, provided his silk hat is in the highest possible state of polish and his watch chain unusually massive. Gamblers of this type are usually men of intelligence far above the average, and among the hundreds of men eminent in science, literature and art who flock to the high-toned hells of New York, it is no easy task to find greater brilliancy of wit, higher polish of deportment, or more geniality of manner than are exhibited by the dealers at first-class metropolitan gaming houses.

In the Bowery may be found professionals of a very different class; brazen-faced men, with bristly mustaches and hair closely cropped like a convict, with apparel obstrusively gaudy and loaded with jewelry apparently of gold and precious stones. These are men to be avoided as the sharks which their appearance and their every act proclaim them to be. They are the proprietors of, or "steerers" for the third-rate dens, where a " square " game is never played, even by accident. Honest labor they abhor and despise. Any man, they say, can make a living by work, but it requires a smart man to get it without. In view of their uncouth, repulsive appearance and address it is surprising they are as successful as they are in enticing strangers into the wretched holes where they can be fleeced.

These strangers, thus inveigled, come under the name of " occasional players," and are the vivification of all gambling, whether guided by the better class of ropers into gilded resorts, or by these vampires into the lower cribs. So long as one sporting man may win from or loses to another, no apparent harm is done to the community at large, but no good is done the gamblers. It is not singular, that the novice is so apt to try his luck when he has once been induced to enter the gambling house.

The gambling house is made yet more alluring by its surroundings. Nowhere has sumptuous elegance been attained in such perfection as in the first-class gambling saloons of New York. Generally each has a suite of rooms, the largest of which is devoted to faro, with perhaps a roulette wheel in one corner, while others are sacred to short card games, and one is always exclusively used as a banqueting hall. All are furnished without regard to cost, but there is never anything in any one of them to offend the most fastidious taste, although there may be sometimes a grim humor in some of the decorations, as is the case in one house where a magnificent oil painting of a tiger is suspended from the wall immediately over the table, so that none of the players can look up without meeting the glaring eye of the beast, which is held to be the presiding deity of the game. Take that away and the visitor would imagine himself in the private parlors of a gentleman whose great wealth was fortu-

Wall Street.   (1) The Fray.

nately equalled by his refined taste. This delusion would be strengthened by a seat at the banquet, where the viands are of all possible varieties, and the best quality, and are served with a finished elegance in the plate and all table appointments, including the waiters, which are not exceeded even in the most select private houses. Liquors of an excellent quality are usually served. No sight is rarer in a first-class gaming house than to see a man maudlin drunk. An intoxicated man is never allowed to profane the place. If he appears in the person of a valuable patron, he is quietly led away, to be put to bed in some remote room; but if he comes as an unknown casual he is put into the street with little ceremony but without violence.

These statements, however, apply only to the first-class and most prosperous establishments. The places next in order ape them in everything, but are far below them in all. A second-class house has sometimes more glitter than its rival, but it is easy to see that it is pinchbeck grandeur. The refined taste in decorating and furnishing is also lacking. The suppers and liquors, however, most plainly proclaim the lower caste of the place. While the variety of both is abundant, the first are execrably cooked and served, and the quality of the latter would not be strange to the most experienced patron of the ordinary Bowery saloons, which are proverbial for furnishing every kind of beverage except good.

But if the second grade houses are bad in this respect, there are some below them which are much worse. If a man can digest the so-called "game suppers," and survive any considerable drinking of the liquids which are offered as pure whiskey and brandy in the lowest classes of faro houses, he ought to be able to insure his life on the most favorable terms, and the appointment of these houses are in keeping with their entertainment. They are repulsively suggestive of squalor and unprosperous vice; and if by any chance a gentleman enters, he leaves at once, to lose his money under more elegant, or at least cleaner, auspices.

Periodical raids are made—for more purposes than one. The raid which made John Daly move, and which produced so great a stringency in the chip market for the time being, started at No. 1 Ann Street. It is rarely that an eye-witness describes, from the inside, an official descent on a gambling house. There are generally too many personal reasons for silence. Here is a description by a player at the time of that famous raid. It might also serve as a good description of almost any raid on New York games:

"I had just 'coppered' $5.00 on the queen to the intense disgust of a half dozen fellows who were playing her to win, when the negro who kept door came bounding upstairs, three steps at a time, fairly pale in the face, and whispered to the proprietor: ' Boss, there's some men at the door that won't go away, and say they'll break the door down if I don't let 'em in.'

" 'Quick!' answered the proprietor, 'open the door and ask 'em to step right up.' The words were not out of his mouth before he had slipped the bank roll into the safe, gathered all visible chips of the banks, and asked all the players to gather up theirs, stuck the chips into the safe and locked the safe door, saying, 'Boys, put your chips in your pockets and come around this afternoon and I'll cash 'em for you.' In a flash all evidence of present gaming were wiped out. There were only a couple of tables, a dozen or so players, the proprietor, smiling blandly, and—a policeman in sight.

"In less time than it takes to tell all this the still shivering door-keeper had ushered in three 'plain clothes' men from head-quarters. At the same time the police officer, in full uniform, who was already in the room—and who had been playing with the rest of us, mind you—edged towards the door so as to seem to have come in with and after the raiding officers. He was the worst frightened man in the crowd. But, with quite remarkable presence of mind, considering the strain on him, the officer in uniform stepped promptly back in the foreground, with a pitying smile on his face, and seizing the beard of the proprietor of the game, said to the raiding officers, who looked as if they wondered where he had come from: ' Gentlemen, this Mr. Bud Kirby '—

" 'And sorry I am, gentlemen,' ' Bud ' interrupted, with a bow and a smile, 'to make your acquaintance under such un-favorable circumstances! What will you have to drink?'

"You could have knocked me down with a feather. 'This then,' thought I, as all hands stepped up to the sideboard and took a friendly drink; 'this then, is one of those terrible raids we read so much about!'

" The players, fortunately for me, were not molested in the least. They melted away into the early morning gloom, it was then about two o'clock, and the officers who carted away the cards, the faro layouts and the roulette wheel, melted away to headquarters and made their report, and that afternoon we all went back and Kirby cashed our chips—of course he knew just about how many were out—and everything was lovely. No officer thought of touching the safe which contained the 'roll,' the only thing of any great value about the establishment, and nobody suffered any great loss or discomfort. But there wasn't any more dealing there for a great many months. And maybe the officer in uniform, who was playing there in blissful ignorance that a raid was to be made, didn't catch it from Kirby for not giving him warning!"

What does protection cost a gambler? About the time of the afore-mentioned raid, a New York business man—whose
18

name may be put down as Allan Allriver, being not altogether
unlike the same—was approached on Twenty-eighth street by
a professional gambler of his acquaintance who had paraded
Broadway and hung about the corners until he was almost on
his uppers. "Look here, Mr. Allriver," said the gambler, "Let's
you and I open a gambling house. I know of a good ranch
on this very street that we can rent cheap, and if you'll furnish
the roll and let me run the game we'll both make a barrel of
money."

"That's all right," answered Allriver, "but what's to prevent
us from being pulled the very first night?"

"I've inquired into that," replied the gambler, "and am
assured on high authority that we will be guaranteed police
protection for exactly $25.00 a week. The usual price is from
$25.00 up to $100.00; we are getting off cheap."

Mr. Allriver is still thinking about this offer and the remarkable statement with it. There is thought for food in it for
the taxpayers. But the charge that police officials are bribed
by gamblers is—as the old English Judge said about the charge
of assault on women—"most easy to make and most difficult
to disprove." It has the advantage, however, of being even
more difficult to prove.

Suppose a police captain or lieutenant were paid $25.00 a
week by the proprietor of a gambling house for protection or
advance notice of raids, no papers, or writing, or receipt, or
voucher of any kind will pass between them. The proprietor
and the police officer will not meet, nor will they be seen or
known to communicate with others in any way except through
trusted intermediaries. Through them, one representing the
"sports" and the other the "boss cops," the agreement will be
made and the money will be paid. They may meet each other
and slide a "wad" from fist to fist as they shake hands on Broadway of a fine afternoon, or they may do their business over a
friendly glass of beer at a Sixth Avenue saloon table about
2 a. m. If either of these agents tries to "squeal," his principal promptly denounces and disavows all knowledge of him.
Then who is believed, the poor, unknown, characterless "go-
between" or the "reputable business man" and "faithful police
official?"

The elaborate system of bolts, bars, chains, double-doors,
and the like, which confronts one—either stranger in search of

sport, or officer in search of prey—at the entrance of an established gambling house is not intended as a direct barrier to
the admission of those in authority.   Unauthorized raiders
are of course kept out by this means.   But no proprietor
of a gambling house in New York would dare to maintain
that system of defense in the face of known police or detective authority.   It would "get the force on him" forever.
When an opening is demanded "in the name of the law,"
the bolts are shot back, the chains loosened, and the big
nail-studded doors unlocked.   But all this undoing, and un-
loosening and unfastening takes so much time that the proprietor has had an opportunity before the police get into the "hell"
itself to put away that which he wishes to conceal, and to put it
away so securely that all the police in town couldn't find it unless they tore down the walls and pulled up the flooring.   It
is quite useless to say that the players, if they choose, may
also utilize this interval by escaping over the roof or down the
back stairs.   That some of the New York gambling houses are,
or have been, directly connected with Police Headquarters by
means of a private wire, or at least with the nearest station
house from which a raid would be most likely to be made, is
firmly believed by some sporting men.   But how prove it?   Certain it is that there are no "slicker" citizens nor more artful
dodgers, than are the professional gamblers.

Numerous pool-rooms have also existed in the city of New
York.   A man named Allen owned the largest number ever
known for one individual to own at one time.   When the
Anti-gambling bill was before the State Legislature, at the
time when Governor Hughes held the reins of office, it is said
that he disbursed about $560,000 in buying up members of the
Legislature.   He gave $10,000 to one of the members to spend
in his interest, that interest of course being to defeat the measure, but he learned that instead of using it in the manner directed, he placed it in his own pocket and for his own use.   Allen
then invited the member to meet him at a hotel, whereupon he
drew a pistol and compelled the dishonest member to hand back
the $10,000.

The bill was designed to break up the great gambling trust.
The day before the bill came before the house Mr. Belmont,
the great race-horse man died.   When the bill was presented
the vote stood 25 to 25.   As one of the members had died a new

one was to be elected. Governor Hughes went out on the
stump and helped to elect the new member, who was known to
be favorable to the bill. This aroused the ire of the opposition
to the measure, and they consequently tried to kidnap the new
member and so prevent him from casting his vote. This they
did not succeed in accomplishing as he was sick at the time,
but two doctors accompanied him in a carriage to the Legisla-

Wall Street.   (2) The Struggle for Humanity.

tive Hall; where he cast his vote for the bill, thus causing it to
pass by the majority of one.

This broke the back of the race-track trust, taking from
them many thousands of dollars. The reader will understand
more clearly the effect it had upon the sporting fraternity when
some interesting figures concerning Coney Island race-track are
given. One hundred and fifty bookmakers paid $125 per day
for the privilege of making books; from 60,000 to 125,000 people visited the race-track each day, each paying one dollar ad-

mission fee; from 10,000 to 20,000 people were admitted to the grand stand at $2.00 each.

What was known as the Dowling law, which allowed pools to be sold inside of the fence, had no penalty attached to it; but if a person was found selling pools outside the track enclosure, he was considered worse than a robber and was locked up in jail and fined.

William Randolph Hearst headed a deputation of about 150 ministers and representative business men, who went to Albany in the interest of the Anti-gambling bill. This move caused much public sentiment and aroused many to action.

Shortly after the passing of the bill Allen was afflicted with a deadly disease. I made several efforts to interview him, and finally succeeded on the fourteenth effort. I inquired into his spiritual condition, and he consented for me to pray with him. He invited me to call and see him again. I talked and prayed with him and finally he expressed himself of having found the Light and that he would live a Christian life henceforth.

On the occasion of my next visit I was accompanied by the Rev. Robert Bagnell, D. D., and Police Commissioner Morse. After a season of prayer Mr. Allen began telling us of graft money, and pointing his finger at Mr. Morse, said, "I have spent thousands of dollars with the police officials of New York City, but there is the only man I could not buy." What a high honor conferred upon Mr. Morse by a man who was in a critical condition and not expected to live, and not knowing when the Great Judge should call him into His Presence.

Unfortunately, the penalties imposed upon gamblers are not nearly sufficient. This is one reason why the fraternity does such a thriving business and treats the law with impunity. If the penalty for attempting to beat a man out of his money was made a penitentiary offense there would be less crime in this respect. I will give but one instance.

When William Travis Jerome was prosecuting attorney for New York City, it was reported that young Hostettor, of Pittsburgh, lost half a million dollars in Dick Canfield's gambling house. It was also alleged that young Vanderbilt was wanted in the case, but that he kept out of the way of Mr. Jerome until he was excused from the case by the statute of limitation. It was also stated that young Hostettor died soon after losing his money. It so cut him up that it broke his heart. Dick Canfield was brought into court and fined $1,000 for this transaction, the amount of the fine no doubt being the limit the law exacted. Canfield would probably not mind another $1,000 fine if it brought him another half a million dollars into his coffers. Let the gambler once understand that fines will not obtain any longer but that the penalty will be a term in prison with hard labor, and I venture to predict that there will be less gambling practised, little or no graft, and certain there will be no killing caused through this demoralizing vice.

One of the most sensational murders ever committed in the city of New York was on July 16, 1912, when Herman Rosenthal, a noted gambler, was shot to death in the glare of the lights of the Hotel Metropole. His murderers came to the scene and escaped in a high-powered automobile, which easily out-distanced the taxicabs pressed into service by the police.

It is said that Rosenthal was recognized as the agent of certain influential politicians; that he had "talked too much," and had therefore been ordered out of town by his patron a few days previous.

One of the four shots fired at him struck him on the bridge of the nose, crashing into the brain. As he was talking with a man on Forty-third Street, a big touring car drove up and three men alighted from it. The first man out fired the first shot which caused Rosenthal's death. In a less space of time than it takes to tell, the occupants of the car resumed their places and they went speeding on their way. Several prominent gamblers were soon on the scene.

It was rumored that Rosenthal had received warning that he had been marked for death, and that his wife had tried to influence him to leave town.

It was charged that the police were "sore" because Rosenthal had declared that Lieut. Becker, one of their number, had "cut in" on his gambling house and demanded a 20 per cent rake-off. They also condemned Rosenthal for his declaration that organized protection was again the rule in the police department. The gamblers had turned against Rosenthal because he had "squealed."

Rosenthal, following the raiding of his gambling house by the police about a week before he met his death, charged police officers had "oppressed" him. He said Police Inspector Hayes, Capt. William Daly and Lieut. Becker had demanded tribute from him for allowing him to run his place. He also declared "men higher up" received tribute from hundreds of New York gamblers in return for "protection."

Rosenthal's charges aroused the heads of the police department. Commissioner Waldo and District Attorney Whitman cut short their vacations to investigate. They placed no credence in the gambler's story. It was the general impression that Rosenthal would be quickly sat upon as a "cheap squealer."

Waldo at once issued a statement to the effect that Rosenthal's charges were utterly false. "The lid has never been on so tightly as now," Waldo declared in a letter to Whitman. Waldo, however, asked a thorough investigation by Whitman of Rosenthal's allegations.

It is now a matter of history how thoroughly Whitman carried out the investigation. This crime being committed in the most outrageous manner possible, it was whispered among many good people that Whitman would not be successful in bringing the murderer to account. It was also the general impression that it would soon blow over and nothing more be heard of it. But they reckoned without their man. If it were possible to elect only half the number of District Attorneys in this country that possessed the same amount of courage and tenacity of purpose that Whitman showed at this time and until the close of the trial when Lieut. Charles Becker was convicted of being the chief instigator of the awful crime, I venture to say, there would be less general talk of graft, less crime, more efficient service rendered by the elected officials and police department, and more confidence would be placed in the administrations.

It is unnecessary to burden the reader with the details that occupied the attention of the authorities preliminary to the trial, except to extend credit to them for the successful method in which they worked. At one time it looked as though the link which would fasten the crime upon the real perpetrator was broken, when Jack Zelig, one of the "gun-men," who had given evidence, and was to be one of the chief witnesses for the prosecution, was murdered. At his funeral "gun-men" were present to prevent anyone securing photographs of the scene. Were the police entirely powerless at this time, or must we come to the conclusion that the metropolis of the United States of America was at the mercy of a band of cut-throats and murderers? Far better to have an open war with our natural enemies than to have our citizens fear and dread to walk the streets of New York on account of the probability of being molested, and perhaps murdered.

The *Cleveland Plain Dealer,* October 14, 1912, editorially says:

"To the country the most amazing and shocking feature of the revelations which have come out of the metropolis since the murder of the gambler, Rosenthal, who ' squealed,' is not the rottenness uncovered. It is not the police corruption charged and apparently proved. Those shameful conditions were fairly well understood. They have not seemed out of keeping with what has been known about New York. But the country has learned in astonishment of the existence of gangs of actual and potential murderers, familiar to the underworld and feared as men who could be hired for the butchery of any one hated by persons in authority or those with plenty of money to pay for the assassination of their enemies.

"It has not been generally known that the largest city of the country tolerated the presence of bands of cut-throats who killed for a price, or to placate some public official as cruel and brutal as he was false to his trust. The nation has never been taught to believe that the police were powerless, even under Tammany, to beat down and crush all violent and bloody lawlessness.

"The need of reform in the chief center of population, wealth, commerce and industry in the New World is evidently greater than the most pessimistic Americans have supposed. It goes farther down toward the savagery which it was thought had at least been made less bold and bestial on Manhattan Island than it is in the wildest towns of the newest states and the crudest mining camps."

Several investigations were started with a view of learning the real truth concerning graft and crime existing in the city. The Board of Aldermen were authorized by Mayor Gaynor to investigate; a special grand jury was brought together by the orders of Governor Dix; Police Commissioner Waldo had an investigating committee; the citizens also formed a committee to investigate vice conditions.

Jack Rose, one of the gun-men, and who testified that he was a collector for Becker, stated that the amount of graft annually amounted to $2,400,000.

Allan Robinson, Chairman of the Citizens' Committee ~~

pointed at the big mass meeting to protest against police conditions, sent a letter to Mayor Gaynor shortly after the meeting, tendering him the assistance of the committee for the bettering of civic conditions. The Mayor was not invited to participate in the mass meeting, an omission that was commented upon at the time. The Mayor took his time about replying to Mr. Robinson's letter. The reply made public reads as follows:

Office of the Mayor, City of New York.

Aug. 24, 1912.

Dear Sir: I am very glad indeed, to receive your letter. Up to the present time I have received no assistance, but rather opposition and embarrassment, in the reorganization of the Police Department, which has been gradually going on ever since I became Mayor. I suppose your committee knows that the way to stop graft in the Police Department with gamblers and the like is to reduce contact with the sources of graft down to the least possible—to one contact if possible. If you allow the Inspector and Captain all along the line to deal with matter you cannot possibly avoid graft. I trust you will get a list of the Captains and Inspectors and study their personalities carefully. I shall always be glad to have your assistance. Of course, I notice that the Mayor was not invited to the public meeting, and from the tone of it I felt that it was not organized to assist the Mayor. I trust that it will turn out that I was mistaken. Everyone in this city knows how hard I have worked since I have been Mayor, to eliminate graft from all the departments. I hope I shall now be supported from all quarters.

Sincerely yours,

W. J. GAYNOR, Mayor.

The following article on the subject of graft appeared in the *New York Times,* August 1, 1912:

$3,095,000 GRAFT COLLECTED IN 1900.

The statement of Jack Rose that an annual tribute of $2,400,-000 has been exacted by the police from gamblers and others for "protection" is not considered extravagant by those familiar with conditions in the underworld. As a matter of fact, the amount stated is nearly $700,000 a year less than was collected some twelve years ago. In an exposé of the gambling situation in New York in *The Times* of March 9, 1900, it was shown that $3,095,-000 was the yearly tribute of keepers of gambling houses and other resorts to the police and other powers of the City Government for "protection."

The public at the time was simply dumbfounded by the array of facts and figures published by *The Times*. This enormous amount of money, it was shown, was handled by what was known among the gamblers as the "Gambling Commission," composed of a commissioner at the head of one of the city departments, two State Senators, and the dictator of the poolroom syndicate, who was before the Mazet Committee, and who was allied with Tammany Hall.

The frequent assertion that men "high in the councils of Tammany Hall" had been receiving money from the gambling combine led to the appointment of a committee of five, of which Lewis Nixon was Chairman, to investigate the truth of the charges. In his official report Mr. Nixon said:

"There is an organization of men, known as the 'combine,' that is organized for systematic blackmail, and they cloak their workings by pretending to be paying Tammany Hall the money they collect for the protection they are supposed to furnish in its name.

"The men who wish to open places know whom to see, and having found that certain men who act in defiance of the 'combine's' orders are given short shrift, are naturally inclined to believe that these men do collect this money on account of Tammany Hall, and that if matters reach a climax this organization will protect them. This accounts for the almost defiant attitude of the gamblers."

The investigation and report of Mr. Nixon's committee followed the exposure made in *The Times* of March 9, 1900, when the functions of the "Gambling Commission" and its methods of conducting a levy on gamblers for protection were related in detail. *The Times* said at the time:

"This so-called commission meets weekly in the apartments of one of its members, not far from Forty-seventh Street and Broadway. The money is not only apportioned at these conferences, but licenses to run gambling houses are virtually issued there.

"Not a gambling house is running in this city to-day that is not known to this board, and not a place is running that does not pay its tax to this board. Its system is as complete as any branch of the City Government. There are no leaks, and no unauthorized place can run for twenty-four hours without either putting up or shutting up.

"The requisite for opening a gambling house, large or small, and this includes poolrooms, is to go to the Captain of the precinct. The request to be allowed to open is accompanied by the 'initiation' or 'introduction' fee of $300, and the Captain tells the applicant that his case will be acted on in time.

"A week later the applicant is notified of his fate. If he cannot open, his fee is returned to him, though cases of this kind are rare. The matter has in the meantime been reported to the

Gambling Commission as the Board of Governors passes upon the application of a man for club membership.

The Tribute Then Exacted.

"If the application is passed, it is not accepted without an investigation, tending for the most part to find out the ability of the would-be member to pay his dues promptly and whether he is a person who is to be relied upon. The Captain of the precinct is responsible for that part of the matter. For his work therein he is allowed to retain the initiation fee.

"From that time on little that comes from the gaming crib sticks to the Captain's fingers. There are regularly organized collectors, among them ward men and Inspectors, and there is not much leakage before the money finally lands in the Gambling Commission's hands.

"The amount that lands there is made up as follows:

Poolrooms, 400, $300 each per month, or per year	$1,440,000
Crap games, 500, $150 each per month, or per year	900,000
Gambling houses, 200, $150 each per month, or per year	360,000
Gambling houses, large, 20, $1,000 each per month, or per year	240,000
Envelope games, 50, $50 each per month, or per year	30,000
Policy, per year	125,000
Total	$3,095,000

The revelations made by *The Times* came as the result of a complaint on the part of the gamblers, who contended that the Gambling Commission, in its desire to make all it could in as short a time as possible, was licensing gambling houses indiscriminately, and that the business was to a large extent being ruined through too much competition." The article further stated:

"A gambler who knows every ramification of the 'protection' business said that there were in the greater city more than 2,000 illegal 'joints' which pay for non-molestation. Every one of these was required to put up an initiation fee of $300 before it could open. This part of the plunder went to the Police Captain and his henchmen, so that in the last three years over $600,000 had been paid to this part of the protection combination."

Later, when Lewis Nixon, speaking for the investigating committee, stated that he had the names of fifteen men in the gambling combine to present to the District Attorney, John D. Crimmins made the following comment:

"There are probably fifty men in the Democratic Club who could tell you all about the gambling combine. When *The Times* printed the article some time ago about the gambling commission, I made inquiries and learned that the statements made in *The Times* were the truth. The system of levying blackmail was in that article fully exposed. I heard from a man who is authority on such matters that the information printed by your paper was correct."

Drawing a line between what Tammany Hall did as an organization and leaders of Tammany did as individuals, Mr. Nixon concluded that men who were leaders in the Tammany Society, though not as high up as Richard Croker, might have received money from the gambling combine.

Wall Street.   (3) The Dollar Wins.

Referring to the statement about Mr. Croker, Mr. Crimmins had this to say:

"If you go to certain disgruntled men—men who have a grievance, and there are many of them—you will learn all about the levying of blackmail, and the percentages which certain forms of law-breaking pay for protection. Tammany Hall is a big political machine. On election day it has crowds of workers. Of course this large sum is not turned into the hands of the politicians at one time. It is collected and held for use on election day. There are many people who can tell about such matters. These matters are discussed by certain politicians at their clubs, and it ought to be a simple matter to get the truth about blackmail and where the money comes from."

In a speech delivered at Durland's Riding Academy, October 28, 1905, William Randolph Hearst said:

"If you elect Murphy and McCarren and McClellan for four years, you surrender unconditionally to as brutal a lot of private speculators and public plunderers as ever banded together to rob and outrage the helpless people.

"Why, this city would be pillaged as captured towns have been ravaged in war, as Troy was sacked and looted when the Greeks induced the Trojans to admit the wooden horse. The selfish speculators, the corrupt bosses, the impudent puppets care nothing for popular indignation."

The *New York Journal,* September 20, 1907, in referring to the above speech said:

"The days of Tweed no longer register the low-water mark of municipal corruption. The days of McClellan will go down in history surpassing in outrageous graft and political piracy anything that has ever been known before.

"Have the American people or the people of New York lost all their spirit of independence, their sense of justice, their ideas of morality?"

While we deplore the horrible murder of Rosenthal, we must trust that good will come out of evil, and that righteousness and truth shall be the great prevailing forces from henceforth.

The *London Daily Mail,* of August 16, 1908, reported the following:

" General Bingham, ex-Commissioner of Police, in a magazine article estimates that £20,000,000 of ' graft ' and blackmail is paid in New York yearly.

" After reviewing some of the evil conditions incident to Tammany rule, he declares that the power of Tammany could be destroyed in ten years or less by a ' strong, honest, fearless Police Commissioner, supported by the police magistrates of ability and integrity and a mayor big enough to conduct his office without fear or favor.'

"He asserts that one lawyer prominent in Tammany Hall represents nearly all the expert pickpockets in New York, another the gambling-houses, and two or three the liquor law violators. General Bingham estimates that 1,500 to 2,000 of the police—about one-fifth of the force—'are unscrupulous "grafters," whose hands are always out for easy money.'

" He says that he might have made £200,000 a year, and relates an offer of £2,000 a month to let one gambling-house remain open. ' I was offered £1,000 in cash and £100 a month merely to be seen shaking hands with the proprietor of one Upper Broadway café.' "

There is too much shaking hands and too much familiarity between the officers of the law and the law violators. Mayor Gaynor asserts that the way to stop graft "is to reduce contact with the sources of graft down to the least possible—to one contact if possible." This contains a lot of truth, but while it may lessen the amount of graft money exacted, it gives no absolute assurance that there will be no graft.

One method that may be used with effect to successfully overcome this special crime—for it is a crime for an officer of the law (whose salary is paid by the taxpayers) to exact graft money so that law violators may continue to violate the law, is to do away with the fine and in its place substitute a term in the penitentiary, and make the term positive, by placing the word "shall" instead of "may," when imprisonment is part of the penalty.

If the statute declared that the judge *shall* sentence the prisoner to six months in prison, in the place of *may,* there would be less gambling and other forms of crime committed.

Should the above recommendation not have the desired effect, then I suggest that all State Legislatures enact laws providing for the confiscation of all buildings used for gambling purposes, and the proceeds devoted to hospitals or some other kind of charitable institution or for educational purposes.

The eyes of the nation will be upon New York for years to come. Let the good citizens awake and do all in their power to assist the officers of the law in enforcing law and order, and stand by them in all cases of emergency. It is not the rank and file who get the graft, but a few officers who use their position and knowledge to exact the graft in order to swell their own bank accounts.

THE MIGHTY DOLLAR.

When a man's sole object is to make money and worship it instead of his God, it becomes a curse to him and all those about him, and in this case he had better flee from it as from the most accursed blood-sucking vampire that ever up-  rose from the cav- erns of old Satan's headquarters. The il- lustration of the hands g r a s p i n g for the mighty dollar will con- vey the importance of its mighty power. The hands do not all belong to Jews; w h e n it comes to loving money we are mostly all Jews. This applies to all who add anything to the pressure upon the al- ready over-taxed and under-fed men and wo- men of the afflicted human race. Bread for the stomach in this life as well as for the spiritual soul in the next, is what is wanted.

On the American dollar are these words: "In God we trust." Woe to the nation when this ceases to be a fact. The inscription on the illustration is "In THIS GOD we trust." This is applicable to many thousands of our citizens to-day. When Theodore Roosevelt had the inscription taken off the dol- lar there was a general outburst of indignation against it. The inscription was replaced, but it gave the nation cause for serious thought. I believe Mr. Roosevelt was sincere in his action.

Our prisons are full of men whose first step in crime was the eagerness to make money without working for it. Millions of dollars have been embezzled and lost through rash speculations on the stock exchange. Money is the mark of limitation. We live in a world where work is paid for with money, and to possess it should mean to work for it.

The green cloth gamblers rob men of their money, while the produce gamblers rob them of their bread and impose famine upon people who are surrounded with plenty. The produce gamblers give the lie to the facts, places the main edibles and coal out of the reach of thousands, and would corner the air if they could in order to add a few more dollars to their millions; they care nothing as to how the poor live, or whether they live at all, but see that their own tables are well stocked with the best that the land can produce.

Where are these men's consciences? It may be that they give them opiates to partially quiet them while they wrestle in the pit through the day with bulls and bears; but their consciences get them alone at night and makes a settlement.

Wall Street should be changed to Wolf Street. It could not be better located. At the head is a graveyard, at the foot a river. The pet lambs, after they have been fleeced of their wool, can jump in the river and drown themselves, and the graveyard is handy.

When all the pride, cruelty and ambition of a man is only measured in dollars, he is not much use to the community in which he lives.

Years ago, in a southwest Georgia county, an old couple, with an only son, lived in a rude cabin in the woods. It is related that the old man was a miser, and drove his son from home to make his living in the world at a very tender age. Years passed and the boy was given up by his parents as dead.

One stormy night a tall man with beard knocked at the door of the little cabin and asked for shelter. It was grudgingly given him by the old couple, but when the stranger showed them a bag of gold which he carried in his valise they were overjoyed. That night, as the guest lay sleeping, the old man crept to his side. There was a glitter of a keen blade in the darkness, and then——

When morning came the old woman looked on the dead man's face and screamed with terror.

" God have mercy on us! " she cried. " We have killed our boy, our son that was lost! "

TO THE DOLLAR.

Mighty Dollar! our acknowledged governor, preserver and benefactor. It matters not how we live, thou canst erect a magnificent monument over our graves, with a living epitaph to perpetuate our memory. Thou canst secure feed lawyers, a bribed judge or jury to set us free. What an exuberance of joy swells every bosom when thou art upon the gridiron; thou art the joy of youth and the solace of old age; thou canst adorn the rich and feed the poor. All nations adore thee; thou art loved by civilized and savage alike, with unfeigned and unfailing affection. O, precious Dollar! be with us, we beseech thee, attended by an inexpressible number of thy ministering angels, made in thine own image, whose gladdening light will illumine the penury and want with heavenly radiance, which does cause the awakened soul to break forth in acclamations of joy. Mighty Dollar! thy

Brains and no Money.

I must go to prison.

Money and no Brains.

This man's money keeps him out of prison.

19

shining face bespeaks thy wondrous power.   Our pockets be
thy resting place.   We need thee every hour.
I leave it to the reader to interpret the above.

THE DOLLAR DOES THE BUSINESS EVERY TIME.

This world is full of wonder and every day we see
  Some strange and curious sights on every hand;
No matter where we go we always find it so,
  That money is the ruler in the land.
There's a man that's poor and lowly, with a brave and honest heart,
  Who'd scorn to wrong his neighbor of a dime;
By the wealthy he is slighted, there's none to take his part,
  For the dollar does the business every time.

CHORUS—
  Then we should not forget to remember with regret,
    That poverty is often called a crime;
  For the man with wealth and fame holds a high and honored name,
    For the dollar does the business every time.

There's the high-toned paying teller, who in luxury does roll,
  With other people's money at his hand,
When he finds himself in trouble of a pile he takes control,
  And for his health goes to a foreign land.
But should he be arrested, his friends secure him bail,
  And in court he is acquitted of the crime;
For the judge he fails to see, or the jury can't agree,
  For the dollar does the business every time.

And in our courts of justice where honor should abound
  And equal rights be given one and all,
The man with lots of money is very often found
  To excel the one whose bank account is small.
He can work the judge and jury in a scientific way,
  The verdict is "not guilty of the crime;"
But the poor man goes to prison, while the wealthy walks away,
  For the dollar does the business every time.

Our corporation president who lives in lordly style,
  With a salary of thousands every year,
Takes a quiet trip to Europe, and with him quite a pile
  Of dollars from the bank, does disappear.
Sometimes he goes to prison by the order of the court,
  And gets an easy sentence for the crime;
But his friends to him will stick, he is pardoned very quick,
  For the dollar does the business every time.

It's just the same old story, you very often hear,
  And the truth of it you never can deny,
That the man that's got the millions can every time appear
  As a man of honor in the public eye.
For money is the master that governs one and all,
  We struggle for a dollar or a dime;
And no matter how inclined, we're always sure to find,
  That the dollar does the business every time.

ARRAIGNMENT OF GAMBLING IN ITS MORAL
ASPECTS (ABRIDGED).

By Rev. Robert McIntyre, Bishop M. E. Church.

" Did you ever see the autograph of the President? " said
Warden B., of the I. State Penitentiary. He had been a member
of my congregation for years, and at his request I had visited
the prison to preach to the convicts. The wagon which brought
me from the station carried the mail bag, and, while looking
over his letters, he held up a large official envelope with the
above question.

" No," I answered, taking my eyes from the intelligent convict who sat in striped clothing writing at a desk, and whose
shaven and shame-flushed face was persistently turned from me.
" I would like to see his signature, as my vote helped to put
him in the White House."

" There it is," said the warden, handing me the document,
which I soon discovered to be a pardon for a certain youth,
who had served three years of a six years' sentence for theft
from the Post Office Department.

" Why is this pardon given, warden?" " Well," said he,
" this young man is of good family, and has dependent on him
a widowed mother, a wife and child. He became the dupe of
gamblers who fleeced him, and then the Devil, I reckon, suggested that he might recoup his loss by stealing from the Government, and in an evil hour he fell, was detected, convicted,
and with other United States men sent here. I remember the
day he came; how heart-broken he stood in the corridor till
the sheriff gave me the papers, unloosed his shackles, and turned
the gang over to me. They were coupled in irons on the cars,
and John was paired with a hardened felon who had done time
before, as had most of the lot. They glanced defiantly around
at the officers with a braggart insolence as the iron gates clanged
on them, but he paled and trembled, tears silently flowing down
his face to the stone floor. I followed to the bath-house, where
they are washed. shaved, cropped and dressed in stripes. At
the registry, when asked his age, name, etc., with great effort

he managed to answer, but when asked his father's name, a vision of the dead seemed to rise before him. Overwhelmed with shame he tried thrice with choking utterance to tell the name, and then faltered it with such a moan of agony that even the clerk, used to such scenes, felt his hand tremble as he wrote it down. You know our rules require the reading of all letters before they reach the prisoners. The chaplin, at my request, read those sent to him. We found such woe, such evidence of his former honor, such testimony to his previous good character, that friends became interested in him. I helped him, thinking it a case for Executive clemency. The President, who is a merciful man, looked into the case, pondered it a month, and sends this pardon."

"Now," I said when the sad story was ended, " warden, I want to ask a favor. Let me present this pardon to him in person. I understand that it makes him free from this hour; I wish to study the human face in the moment when the revelation that he is free dawns on his mind. May I do this?"

"Certainly," was the answer, and striking a silver bell, a " trusty " appeared. He said, " Tom, bring John R. to my office at once."

While waiting, I said, " Does he expect a pardon?"

" No," was the answer, " he knows nothing of the efforts to set him free. It will be a total surprise to him."

In a few moments the trusty returned with the man he was sent to summon. The jail garb did not wholly hide his handsome form, nor the cropped hair entirely vulgarize the intellectual countenance which fell as he saw strangers looking at him. He seemed to wonder why' he was ordered up before the warden; there was shame, sorrow, helplessness in his face as I rose, with the paper in my hand and walked toward him.

" John," said the warden, " this gentleman has a few words to say to you."

The convict braced himself up for the interview, and I said, " Your name is John R., I believe." " Yes," he replied, steadily.

" I have here," I went on, " a paper addressed to you, signed by the President of the United States. It is a pardon. You are a free man, John."

The look of assumed courage in his eyes changed to one of infinite pathos, then softened pitiously as his soul swooned with joy that was almost too much. I saw him sway as if to fall, but caught him, and leaning on my shoulder, he said, "Free! free! O God, is it true? When can I go home?" "This very moment," said I. He looked wistfully out the great door where the sentry stood, and asked, "Can I go out there now?"

"Yes," I said, "come, I will go with you," and arm in arm we walked down the great stone stair, passed the guards into the street and across to a fence beyond. He stopped a pace or two away, looked at the emerald hills, the river flowing by, the children passing, the firmament above, and as the happy tears drenched his face, said: "O, sir, I am the happiest man alive. When does the train start east?" "At three," I said. "I will see you safely started."

"Won't my wife and baby Jess be glad to-morrow, and mother, how she will smile; I am eager to be off." I took him in and soon saw him fitted with the civilian's clothes and provided with the railway ticket to his destination, and with the $10 the State gives every released convict.

How proudly he walked by my side to the station, and as the bell clanged, he held my hand and said, "You talk to hundreds of young men; sir, tell them this, tell it with burning eloquence, tell it with pleading tears, beware of gaming, shun gamblers as lepers. Cards are accursed of God, and pass-ports to perdition. Will you tell them this?" And as the train moved off I said, "I will."

To this end I write a chapter in this book, that by earnest warning or brotherly appeal, I may help to pluck young men out of the hands of this giant enemy of our race, and perhaps halt some who are already hurrying down this pathway to dishonor. Standing here at the very gates of these polluted temples, where many have been cruelly "done to death," I raise the cry "beware of gaming." It dishonors God, degrades man, wrecks honor, ruins business, destroys homes, breaks wifely hearts, steals babes' bread, brings mothers sorrowing to the grave, and at last, with reckless bravado launches the sinful soul into the path of God's descending wrath, to be overwhelmed forever."

The only argument offered by gamblers is that their business keeps money in circulation. It does, indeed, transferring it from the pocket of the fool to that of the knave, and thence to the pockets of the harlot or rumseller, but there is no gain in this transaction. Better the money had remained where it was or been put to other uses.

Young men will read these words who know not one card from another; who have no personal knowledge of lotteries, raffles, dice or betting. Yours is blissful ignorance, honorable innocence.

How I love the youth who can say, when cards are brought out for play in a private house, " I do not know one card from another. I have no desire to learn their use." Young heart of oak, give me thy hand. Some will sneer, I charge you to keep your honor bright.

Though people of good character persuade and gloss this evil, stand firm as the hills. Should professing Christians (God pity them) make of the painted paste-boards a social snare, be the company never so charming, the stakes never so trifling, beware. Once you play the first game, you are on the slant; the descent is smooth and swift, and the end is terrible.

You will hear sophistries about the difference between playing and gambling, and the harmlessness of cards and other Devil's toggery. Playing is the egg out of which the cockatrice is hatched. Handle it not.

Climbing a slippery pass to the Alps, one comes to a narrow icy path with a great rock on the one hand, and a deep gorge on the other. It is called by the guides the " Hell Place," and you are asked to creep cautiously there, a slip is destruction. The green cloth of the gaming table is the moral hell place to many souls; to this, sorrowing relatives, weeping wives, heart-broken mothers can point and say, " There my boy slipped, there my husband fell, lost property, position, honor, all." At the foot of this slant is the prisoner's cell, the maniac's cage, the suicide's grave; at the top the smiling decoy, shod with adder skin, or the smooth-tongued gamester, waiting to lure men to the fatal hazard.

Some will read these words who are already acquainted with the beginnings of this honeyed vice. They have shuffled the satanic pack, booked the bet, and perhaps pinched themselves in purse to pay the lost wager, or have now in pocket the coins won at gambling. Take these coins out and look at them; they are unclean, polluted.

Once, when the plague ravished an English village, the wretched people resorted to the bank of the stream near by, to get bread left there for them. They tossed the coins for payment into the brook where they were found hours afterwards by those who sold the food. They thought the water had cleansed the pestilent catagion from the coins. Perhaps it had, but no brook, river or sea hath tide medicinal enough to cleanse the curse from money won at gaming. It is cankered. It is blood-stained and tear-rusted. It will curse him that wins and him that loses.

My friend, you are yet only a novice in this black art. Let me, by all rational appeal, abjure you to abstain. It is the father of falsehood, forgery and fraud, and the covetous human heart is the mother of this ill-gotten brood.

Can you specify *one* instance where the gains of gambling have brought comfort or contentment? What would your father think, your employer say, if they knew that you were a gamester, spending your evenings where these human swine whet their tusks? Who sinks so low in the mire of infamy as the man who is kicked out of business or society with the millstone of gambling hung to his neck? Bitter is the ban and black is the brand put on the wretch whose hardened forehead is set against the hissing of that word " gambler."

Who are the associates a man finds at races and the card table? Are they not the Pariahs, social lepers whose touch is pollution? Would a man take his sisters or his children among these white-fanged wolves; are they not nameless at the hearth, unknown where high-toned and virtuous people meet? Think of the vile talk, the impure jest, the unclean associations. You cannot stoop to this. What can money buy, though you won every wager, that will repay you for the loss of wifely love, childhood's trust, the father's proud faith in his boy.

Consider the malign vicissitudes of this sport, see the ruined, forsaken, nerveless gambler, wrecked and wretched at last; abandoned to the gibes of men, and the anger of God; crawling into a lazaretto to die. Mother, with dimpled hands upheld to you at evening, and fair head pillowed on your bosom, think not, " My bonnie boy is safe." This fiend spares none. He will seek this braw lad to destroy him. With devilish cunning he will even persuade you to aid in your son's downfall; to teach him in the social game, to use the leprous papers of the pit, on which is inscribed the voiceless litany of woe.

Hell's utmost anguish surely has no deeper depth than

that of the mother who sees her son a degraded, sodden gamester, and remembers that she taught him to handle the implements of his ruin. If a mother can front the judgment and say,
" I never countenanced the evil, I bitterly opposed it always,
to the utmost of my power," she may feel when her dear son
is lost, the most unspeakable regret, but she escapes the remorse which eats the heart of her who unwittingly fostered
the serpent which compassed her child's destruction. Let us
ring our children round with circles of flame across which none
of these man hawks can come. Let us make home the happiest
place on earth. With mirth, laughter, music, books, friends; a
safe refuge, a snug harbor, a shadow of a great rock, and a
citadel for defence of our dear ones from this pitiless foe.

Let me sketch the career of an upright, kindly village youth
who longs for a wider field of action. He has mastered the
elements of business as practised in the rural community; he
desires to try his talents in the busy world, and chooses a mighty
city as the field of his endeavor. A roaring center of commercial activity; its streets a ganglion of business nerves; its mart
the engorged plexus of traffic, where the best and the worst
have habitation.

As I see this young fellow, with face like an open book,
standing for the first time in the city's streets, I am reminded
of a scene I once witnessed in the country. I stood on the
edge of a wood looking across a beautiful meadow. It was a
perfect day in June, and all the world seemed at peace. Crickets
were chirping in the grass, the yellow-hammer was tapping on
a tree above, the cattle were grazing brisket-deep in the lush
grass, the birds were singing as if to breathe were music. All
nature looked lovely. Far away across the brook, on a dead
tree, I noticed a number of buzzards, waiting for the sight of
something on which they might gorge their unclean appetites.

I think of this as I watch him alone on the city's streets
at evening, gazing into a window where the light falls on
diamonds, opals, rubies; amid the din of the city, near the
theatres and saloons, where music throbs, lamps flare, cabs
rattle, and through these noises comes a voice in modulated
semi-tones from one standing at his side, who asks: " Did you
hear of the big winning last night? " " No, sir, where was it? "
" Up the street at old Brad's place, No. 197. A fellow won
$6,000 in two hours. I am going up to try my luck. Come

along, just for the fun of the thing." He goes. The front of the house is dark; a red light burns over the stairway door— danger signal over a bottomless abyss. He is void of under- standing; a private key, pass word, or patron of the game is needed to secure entrance. The panel of the door slips aside, a whisper, then a reply. The door opens, upstairs they go. Men seated and standing scarcely look up—wheels click—dice rattle—cards shuffle—glasses clink—sooty servants glide with trays and bottles—cheap stucco statuary appears through the smoke—muttered curses tell of losses. He is led to the faro table, where a mastiff-faced man deals cards, and after he has sipped a little liquor, which is freely offered, he tells his guide that he has never played. He is informed that a man always wins his first bet—fortune favors his first play. Men put chips in his hands, saying, " Play this bet for me." " But I don't know the cards," he replies. " Put the bet down on any card, it will surely win." Down it goes—it wins—and as they rake in the gains, he thinks, " I might have won a month's salary in a moment." Lightly as snowflakes fall the cards; deft the touch; swift the shuffle. It seems so simple. He carries money saved from a father's toil, a sister's earnings offered to help him secure his stock of goods to start business. Mother has helped him, saying, " David will help me when I need his help. I will have a strong son to lean on when my old feet dip down falter- ingly to the cold river of death."

As he hesitates there on the porch of Perdition, he is told to bid farewell to peace, farewell to prospects of success, fare- well to the promise of his young manhood, farewell to the prayers of his parents. Pray, mothers! with clasped hands kneeling at this very hour under the pictures in your boy's room. Pray, " God be gracious to my boy. Gird him round with mercy." Sing, sister, sing! Sitting alone where the moon- light falls on thy fingers as they wander over the keys, sing soft and low the very hymn you sang at parting, " God be with you till we meet again." Sing! maiden, till the tears falling fast tell the fears uprising in thy heart.

Look, old father, down the road where the peaceful world lies transfigured in the mellow beams of the moon; down the road where he went away so cheery, brave, tender, looking back- wards from the coach with many a wave of the hand and fond good-bye. Listen, father, to the whip-poor-will in the copse answering the katydid in the hedge, frogs shrilling from the swamp, an owl hooting from the woods; the air grows cold, a chilling sense of discomfort shakes thy frame.

Ah, if thou would'st see thy son now, thy hope, thy pride—among knaves. He stakes his means—he wins—he has doubled his fund. Good, good—his face glows, his pulses are rythmic to the music of success. Excited, confident, reckless, he looses—doubles his loss—forgets all prudence, unrolls the savings of years on the little farm—mother's needle, father's plow, sister's music lessons, earned that hoard. He piles it on the board with burning eyes set on the cards, watches them coming one by one. Oh, unpicturable horror! Money, honor, parental hopes—all earthly and eternal weal staked on that hazard. The Sphinx-faced scoundrel slips the card—the young man hears the word "Lost!"—sees the sharpers laugh as the dealer draws in his all. The room swims before his sight; madness seizes him as the sneering taunt, "Another sucker done up," smites him like a lash across his face.

Frenzied, he clears the table at a bound, his brown fingers close around the white throat of the lean-faced hellion who has robbed him. Like a tiger uncaged he hurls him to the floor, and fronts the crowd of desperados with blazing face. In vain are all his struggles; many leap on him, he is beaten, kicked, hustled down stairs, where, hatless and bruised, he madly pounds the heavy door till his hand is a mass of bleeding pain. All in vain. He turns helplessly at last to the street, and through the gray light of dawn finds his room. For hours he hangs on misery's brink; haggard remorse sits opposite and suggests suicide. Swift as a homing dove his thoughts fly to the farm.

He sees his father in the furrow, his mother in the doorway, her face as radiant as the morning. She gathers a few honeysuckles for his empty room, to her it is a sanctuary now, and he liked them so, and 'twill seem as though he was coming home soon.

An organ beneath his room strikes up an air heavy with old memories; the tune of "The Old Folks at Home," quavers through his window. With a shuddering cry—"A gambler! a gambler! Oh, God, be merciful; let me die," he falls by the bedside and burning tears are vain to staunch the hurt in his heart.

He is now in the whirlpool; return seems impossible. You have seen an apple tree in May, rosy in pink and white blossoms, murmurous with bees, glad with birds and glorious with sunshine. In one night the frost kills the bloom; next day the tree hangs with damp, blighted blossoms and blackened buds, an unlovely spectacle.

Few escape the bitter end who begin a gamester's career.

Next we find him in snuggeries, curtained from basement bar-rooms, studying the cards at midnight, robbing unwary verdants. Conscience is seared as with a hot iron. His heart is flint. He strives with drink to banish thoughts of home, heaven and God; grows morose, cunning, merciless; works a little, hurries again to the feverish excitement of the game, herds with greasy disreputables in foul dens, amid the reek of pipes and hideous blasphemy. Soiled, unkempt, rag-clad, he nears the bottom of the slant. One night, crazed with vile rum, he mingles in a fight with fellow outcasts; blood is shed; the alarm brings the clattering patrol wagon, and through the red of early dawn he rides to a cell in murderer's row. Convicted, condemned, he goes to prison for life—years pass—his sorrowing parents think him dead. He *is* dead. He died that night when he climbed the stairs to " Old Brad's den."

His post is to open and close a gate in the prison yard. Seven years in stripes, holding out a hand which he will not take, trying to stir hope within him. They talk to him of freedom and home. He makes no sign of pleasure; hopeless vacuity rests on his imbruted face. He stares at his gate, shuts it, and says, " Seven years dead, seven years dead." There he stands, and will stand, till carried to the little graveyard of the prison, touching at last the lowest level of the slant on which the gambler stands.

I charge you with a jealous affection, born of an unfeigned brotherhood, and based on many years' study of the effects of this vice. Beware of the beginning of gambling. Have no commerce with the monster iniquity.

First of all, because it *dethrones God*. Seek its victims in the ranks of bankrupt merchants, in the cells of criminals, in the cellars of shame, or garrets of poverty; talk with them, or with those who have suffered through them, and you will find that the sad sequence of misery began with this heinous affront to God, viz.: a practical denial of His very existence and setting up in His place a blind deity called Chance, before whom they bowed, and on whose favor they risked their all. Even if in their darkened mind the votaries of gaming allow God to exist, they deny His government of the affairs of men. They flee away from all works that can win the help of Jehovah, and ask only the help of fortune. This is heathenry of the worst sort. The farmer plows, plants, cultivates, and hopes that the God of nature will help him by sending sun, rain and dew, that together they may produce the harvest. The sailor, by the march of the constellations and the veracity of the magnetic needle which God offers for his guidance, comes at last to port. The mason builds his wall by the laws of God, and his plumb line and level bear eloquent witness that he wishes to base his work on the certain laws which steadfastly bind the worlds together. These men, however much they ignore God in their speech, keep faith with Him in their work, knowing full well that they can only succeed in any task by keeping in line with His laws. Thus they have yoked the elements to the car of progress. The gambler, however, mocks at God's laws and insolently banishes Him. He asks no help from fixed laws ordained by the Father to bless His children; he scorns the co-operation of Nature, sets up a fetish called Fortune, and grovelling, courts its smiles. I know of no form of paganism more base than this, and it is not surprising that in the worship of this block-eyed god, the most obscene rites and debasing superstitions are practiced. Dreams, charms, spells, incantations, black art, even the help of the powers of darkness have been used in wooing his favor. The most frightful depths of moral and mental depravity are touched in this shameful business. The negro who sells stolen articles to buy lottery tickets has some gruesome cabalistic secret which he fondly hopes will bring the favor of fortune; the lady who cons the dream-book in her room to learn which number to buy, and fancies her night vision of a gallows tree or a burning Bible will bring propitious fate, are alike far from reason and from God.

Not only does gambling dethrone God, but it *degrades man.* In this evil work it is the most certain and effectual of all vices. It commonly works in iniquitious league with other sins, but alone it eats out honesty, affection and virtue from the heart, and leaves it as empty as a dead man's hand.

When this vice has had free course through the moral nature for a few years, the man is a mere shell, a human husk, within all is punk and hollowness.

The law by which the force of gravitation acts is not more resistless or irrevocable than this law of gaming. Other vices give their devotees intervals of rest, intermissions growing briefer until the last stages bring woe upon the heels of woe to drive the victim to his doom. The gambling demon, once admitted to the mind, never leaves. He haunts his slaves every waking hour, and flits on filthy wings athwart his dreams, spectre-like he walks at his side, keeping pace with his prey. The swift result of his influence is complete moral atrophy.

Ask yourself this question: Where is the dearest spot to man in all the wide creation's bound? Search all the stars that God has spilled like jewels through the blue abyss. Roam from bloom to bloom of that one tree once enrapt in primeval night, which, at His word, burst into blossoms of worlds like this. Yea, visit heaven itself, explore the city which has foundations whose builder and maker is God; the city of the jewelled walls and gates of pearl. Stand where the healing trees trail their branches in the crystal river of life; or walk amidst the asphodel and amaranth that deck the fadeless green of the Paradise of the Saints, and you will not find one spot so dear, so precious to our race, as that Judean hill whereon hangs One whose holy hands were nailed for our salvation on the cross. There, where wondering heaven bends to look pityingly on the exalted One, where dumb nature strives with darkened skies to hide the shame, where man, mad with rage, curses the Christ, and woman, bowed with sorrow, bewails her Lord. There, on that most sacred spot in all the universe, in the holiest hour ever marked on the dial of time, when heaven, earth and hell are quick with interest, who is it sits unmoved, unobservant, unstirred, concerned only with the game? Ruthless gamblers sit beneath the lowering skies, and on the palsied earth they shake the dice to win the garments of the man of sorrows.

This infamy was needed to make Christ's death as ignominious as a demon could desire. Only Apollyon could suggest the shameful scene on which the dying eyes of the Son of man rested, as the crowning demonism of it all. A group of gamblers bending over the few robes which were all His possessions. O, Satan, that was a monster stroke to embitter His last hour! No other being but a gambler could have put a fit climax to that day's iniquity.

At the time that I was apprenticed to the bricklaying trade,

I knew a lad who began to herd with gamesters. He learned that trade, I learned mine. He earned money, so did I. I was proud of mine, and now I hold up my hands and say, " If my voice should fail, I have an honest trade in my fingers by which I can win my bread."

I take my little ones in this very city to the walls where I worked. I show them the courses of brick their father laid, and proudly tell the story of my toil. Can this other man do likewise? Can he hold up his hands before men and say, " I have an honest trade in my fingers?" No, no; his face crimsons when his trade is mentioned, and though he spent more years at it than I did at mine, he is ashamed of his work to-day.

Young men, learn an honest trade which tends toward manliness. Be content with simple life and frugal means until you can rise honorably to luxuries. Acquire no money by sinful methods. Do not begin gaming as a relaxation, for it will soon become a business. Avoid pool-rooms, race-courses, faro banks, cock-fights, policy shops, lotteries, raffles, betting of every form. All such things are perilous. Where one grows rich, one hundred grow poor, and the one who wins is poorest of all. No man is as pitiably poor as the man who has money won by gambling. This form of evil doing will tempt you everywhere, on rail train and steamboat, in hotels, clubs and barber shops; in the loft of the barn, or the carpeted parlor. On the race-track and fair grounds, week days and Sundays, day and night, winter and summer, at home or abroad, in public and private, it will meet you. The suave snob, the seedy scoundrel, will inveigle you, try to win your confidence, borrow or lend, lead or drive; coax or threaten, sometimes with words smooth as butter, then with words that smite like hail. Stand fast, my son. " When sinners entice thee, consent thou not." Money unearned is blessingless. God's law is this: If a man gets anything from Nature he must give labor. If he gets anything from his neighbor he must give a fair equivalent. Only money gotten in this way can bring a blessing.

It is on record that one lottery drawing in London was followed by the suicide of fifty persons who held blank tickets. What rapacious miscreants they must be who ply this trade of spoilation.

It is well to bind the passions and lusts with strong vows and good resolutions. It is best of all to have the soul bound by the heaven-born spell which fills the whole being with delight. This bliss ineffable makes earthly and carnal joys seem contemptible, and drowns every evil desire in the great cry from the heart's depths:

> "Nearer, my God, to Thee,
> Nearer to Thee."

The third count in this black indictment is that gaming not only dethrones God and degrades man, but *destroys the most blessed of all human institutions, the home.*

Gamblers flock together as naturally as lean-necked vultures; they hunt in packs like coyotes, and intermingle like a knot of clammy vipers that crawl in the dank gloom of a sunless canyon. They have no share in the sweet sanctities of the fireside, and desire vehemently to be elsewhere. Even when the gamester sits at his own table, or embraces his own children, his heart is in another place. Physical contact is not intimacy. He may kiss the wife of his bosom and be as far from her as the east is from the west. Judas kissed Christ, yet at that moment one was in heaven and the other in hell. He hurries away to boon companions, and to the familiar scenes his soul covets. In vain the little ones beseech him to abide at home, in vain the wife entreats him to continue at work, in vain the mother asks the comfort of his presence, the help of his strong arm. He hopes to make a great winning some day, to buy a fine house for his family, then to make amends, turn over a new leaf, and soberly take up the duties of manhood. Some lucky hazard, some windfall, wager or bet will lift him to the level of his dreams. Meanwhile he sinks deeper, debauches himself more and more, till home becomes a hateful place; he deserts his family, or in self-defense is forbidden to cross the sill of the house he has desecrated.

I have gone on missions of comfort to the homes of the drunkard, the bankrupt, the convict, but never have I seen on woman's face such unutterable grief and pitiable misery as in the home of the gambler. A cyclone cannot level, nor a fire consume a home so surely as gambling. The infatuated bondman to this vice will let the fire go out on the hearth where his helpless brood crouches in the cold. He will let them ask mother in the lampless twilight with tear-stained faces, why papa does not come. How can the wife tell the weans, what delays his steps?

Was ever woman's love insulted as he insults it? If some pure passion for art or high scientific research detained him, she would smile, and explain it to the little ones. If profound books or merciful work of benevolence kept him late; if some grave problem of social welfare held him from her arms for awhile, she would bide the time, but the indignity put on her is this, that a loving, virtuous wife with all womanly charms and gentle ministries, waits unheeded while he consorts with disreputable dicers, and the clinging kisses of sweet-lipped babes are forgotten that he may enjoy the company of a lot of heartless card mongers hanging on the frayed edges of society.

When a man will toss away the priceless jewel of wifely love to clutch a bubble like this, turn from a warm, throbbing, palpitant, gentle helpmeet to herd with jackals, he puts a shameful affront on her, one that he will have to answer for at the bar of God.

Beginning with the specious plea of amusement, the player soon finds the game grow tasteless as an egg without salt unless there is a stake—at first a small stake, a few dimes or a dollar. Then comes the race-track, the raffle, the lottery. Life's duties seem dull, hilarious comradeship cheers him on, the perverted mind loathes clean food.

Sunday is the chosen day for this transgression. If the man works at all he slights his job, longs for a rainy day or breakdown in the machinery to let him off; quarrels with his overseer, hastens to the card table to sit till late at night; look on the foxiest tricksters around him with deference, thinks it a fine thing to be called a " sport," smells of tobacco and brandy, is put by society in moral quarantine, barred out of desirable and helpful company, grows more reckless and with all his honor raveled to dirty shreds, becomes a hanger-on, a roper, a steerer, or double-faced decoy to lure others to the sacrifice.

These are the usual gradations. Now, he is an Ishmael, with only two motives of action, hatred of society, and fierce lust for gain. These burn in his breast till the suicide's draught, or the crack of some outraged victim's pistol puts an end to the man who could date his downfall to the day he took up cards for an amusement.

He who might have been the head of a happy household goes down to death, his highest hopes being that he may be permitted to creep back.

"To the vile dust from which he sprung,
Unwept, unhonored and unsung."

His brother gamesters buy a wreath of flowers for his cheap coffin, and the blossoms wither as the baneful breath of these men falls on them when they file by for a farewell look. Poor lilies, you are out of place. A bunch of nightshades twisted with thorns were fitter for that casket. The preacher tries hard to say something consolatory, gives it up and dismisses the group, his soul sick within him' as he thinks on the outcast's doom and the fate of his fellows, already hurrying away to their den for another game. Such is the end of a sinful life wasted in gambling and associate vices.

The fourth and last charge I bring against gambling is as heavy as any yet stated, and is the direct and final result of the other three.

It damns the victim's soul!

Can the transient delights of a few years of idleness and sensual gratification atone for an eternity of banishment from hope and heaven? Will the poor pleasures of the voluptuary, the theatre and the wine cup, the fast pace, the boughten smiles of wantons, the flashing pin, the showy clothes, the jingling fob, the curled mustache, and the whole empty round which the successful gamester treads, solace him for the loss of his immortal soul? Will the fleeting hours spent with unscrupulous men, adepts in trickery and confidence games, touts and tipsters, skilled in marked cards, bogus boxes, wheel of (mis)fortune and loaded dice, adroit in fascinating the unwary with hollow smiles and lying speeches, like honey mingled in the hemlock's poisoned draught—will these repay the willing serf of Satan for a life wasted and a soul passed into hell? Surely not all the pleasures of this high-domed, blossoming world heaped in the balance can outweigh the loss of heaven.

Is there anything in fallacious hopes, unstable judgment, despairing ventures or desperate ruin, attended by parental grief, rejected love, and never dying remorse, to make men seek the blandishments of iniquity?

Let not this seducer of youth corrupt your morals, pull down fortune and cloud your future by his false promises. Let the downward career of others prove effectual warning. Rouse not this ungovernable lust for gain by hazard in your breast. Let the lottery, faro bank, pool-room, race-course, all such

20

places be as pest houses to you, unless you are prepared to brave God's intolerable scorn.

Remember that the man who, through any device of chance or knavery, takes money without giving anything in return, belongs in the class with the swindler and the thief. Remember that on the track of this evil follow defalcations, embezzlements, breaches of trust, false entries, forgeries, misappropriation of trust funds and crimes innumerable.

Rebuke this insidious flattery with stern face and do not tamper with the lightest fringe of it.

The burglar and the pirate are respectable citizens compared to these vampires. Even the bookmaker, who controls not only the horse, but the jockey whose skill you fondly hope to get a fair chance to win, is honorable by comparison. I had despaired of finding a match for the lottery shark, until I saw the man who would juggle with corn and wheat, cornering the necessities of life, using the increase on the price of the poor man's loaf to line his pocket, and by combination of capital and shrewd manipulations of contingencies, making the sewing-woman's oil a little dearer that he might pile his own full board, and indulge in more luxurious or wasteful excess.

I fear these men are nursing a Carracas earthquake under the social system of their land.

Perchance these words may come under the eye of one whose brow bears already the stigma of this craft.

Brother, there must be hidden somewhere in your heart a remnant of your early purity. Drop the implements of your calling; let my hand slip into yours; come apart where we can sit and talk together. Pardon me if I press the question home to your conscience. What is to be the outcome of all this? Shake off the palsy of years, I pray you, and essay an answer. I wait to hear your own verdict on your case. You cannot always be blind to the havoc you are making; you cannot always be deaf to the piteous cries that go up to heaven's chancery from women and children, kenneled in extreme want by reason of your profession.

Rise up, shake off this dark enchantment—dash down the dice, shred the cards into the flames—pass out into the pure air, and while there yet is hope ask heavenly help to break your heavy chains.

WHAT THE PRESS SAYS:

Mr. Quinn is able to present to his audience a most effective experience and a telling portraiture of the evils of gambling.—*Christian Advocate, N. Y.*

Mr. Quinn deserves and should have, the recognition and encouragement of the Christian community.—*Christian at Work, N. Y.*

No more practical sermon was preached in New York yesterday than that delivered by John P. Quinn. Association Hall was packed to the doors by an audience which followed the words of the speaker with almost breathless interest.—*Morning Journal, N. Y.*

Mr. Quinn in his lecture, pictures in striking language the evil effects of gambling.—*Chicago Inter Ocean.*

The work of ex-gambler John P. Quinn, in Boston bears fruit. His converts are numerous.—*Boston Evening Record.*

John Philip Quinn's powerful and practical sermon against gambling is convincing. The impressive and pathetic story of his life and experiences as a professional gambler, thrilled and swayed the large assemblage present in a wonderful manner.—*Boston Herald.*

After witnessing Mr. Quinn's marvelous exploit, no one save a lunatic, would, we are convinced, dream of pitting himself against a professional gambler—*London Daily Telegraph.*

An exhibition with the moral purpose of showing the dangers they run who gamble for money with persons of superior skill.—*London Daily Mail.*

Messrs. Maskelyne and Devant are very enterprising caterers for popular entertainment; and it was a bright idea on their part to engage Mr. John Philip Quinn (for ten weeks).—*John Bull.*

Mr. Quinn demonstrates to the audience with absolute success. The exhibition is most curious and fascinating to watch, both for Mr. Quinn's personality and the unfailing ease and certainty with which he makes the cards and dice, and the several variations on the roulette board which he uses, do exactly what he wants.—*London Times.*

It is certain that Mr. Quinn has done his best to bring to the knowledge of the general public the method by which they are swindled by unscrupulous men.—*Sunday Circle.*

His performance is interesting and instructive.—*Irish Independent* (Dublin.)

Mr. Quinn has an act which doubtless should prove a great warning to men of all ages who patronize pasteboard.—*Montreal Herald.*

Mr. Quinn successfully exposes the so-called games of chance. —*Ottawa Free Press.*

J. P. Quinn made a distinct hit. His revelations of the gambling game were highly interesting and instructive.—*Buffalo Evening Times.*

And the demonstration is an interesting thing for the young man who thinks he knows " a thing or two " and thinks he is " fly " enough to checkmate any " sharp " who tries to take his money away from him.—*Cleveland Plain Dealer.*

WHAT OTHERS SAY:

This is to certify that John P. Quinn has permission to give his lecture and entertainment in New York City. The police and other officers, will kindly do all in their power to see that he is not interfered with.—*W. L. Strong,* Mayor of New York City.

John P. Quinn is not required to take out a license for his illustrated lectures on gambling in Philadelphia.—*Geo. Bradford Carr,* Special Attorney for Com. of Pennsylvania.

Mr. Quinn's illustrated lecture should be heard and seen by every young man in any land. The police officials will render to the public great good by having him give his illustrated lecture in their city.—*Ex-Gov. Charles P. Johnson,* of Missouri.

We had Mr. Quinn in our auditorium, before a delighted audience. We therefore endorse and recommend him to all our pastors with whom he may come in contact.—*Fathers P. M. and T. M. Cauly;* St. Patrick's Catholic Church, Erie, Pa.

Mr. Quinn lectured in Plymouth Church. I cordially commend him and his work to all.—*Rev. Lyman Abbott, D. D.*

Mr. Quinn spoke in Emmanuel Church very effectively. I recommend him heartily.—*Rev. O. P. Gifford.*

John P. Quinn was called to our city the second time. He closed every gambling den in our city. A number of men were converted. I advise every church in this country to send for him.— *Rev. R. V. Hunter,* President Civic Federation, Terre Haute, Ind.

LECTURES AND MOVING PICTURE FILMS

based on subject matter contained in this book are now available for Churches, Societies, Educational Institutions, and Entertainments under other auspices.

For information and terms apply,

JOHN P. QUINN CO.,
Canton, Ohio.